W9-CBQ-099

The Literature of Ancient Egypt

The Literature of Ancient Egypt

An Anthology of Stories, Instructions, and Poetry

edited, with an introduction by William Kelly Simpson
with translations by
R. O. Faulkner
Edward F. Wente, Jr.
William Kelly Simpson

New Haven and London, Yale University Press, 1972

Designed by Sally Sullivan
and set in Linotype Janson type.
Printed in the United States of America by
Vail-Ballou Press, Inc., Binghamton, N.Y.

Distributed in Great Britain, Europe, and Africa by
Yale University Press, Ltd., London; in Canada by
McGill-Queen's University Press, Montreal; in Mexico
by Centro Interamericano de Libros Académicos,
Mexico City; in Central and South America by Kaiman
& Polon, Inc., New York City; in Australasia by
Australia and New Zealand Book Co., Pty., Ltd.,
Artarmon, New South Wales; in India by UBS Publishers'
Distributors Pvt., Ltd., Delhi; in Japan by John
Weatherhill, Inc., Tokyo.

Contents

49061

v

List of Illustrations

Abbreviations

ANET   Translations by John A. Wilson, in James B. Pritch-ard, ed., *Ancient Near Eastern Texts Relating to the Old Testament* (Princeton: Princeton University Press, 1950 and later editions).

ASAE   Annales du Service des Antiquités de l'Egypte, Cairo.

BIFAO   Bulletin de l'Institut français d'archéologie orientale, Cairo.

BiOr   Bibliotheca Orientalis, Leiden.

BSFE   Bulletin de la Société française d'Egyptologie, Paris.

JARCE   Journal of the American Research Center in Egypt, Boston and Princeton.

JEA   Journal of Egyptian Archaeology, London.

JEOL   Jaarbericht van het Vooraziatisch-Egyptisch Genoot-schap (Gezelschap), "Ex Oriente Lux," Leiden.

JNES   Journal of Near Eastern Studies, Chicago.

MDIK   Mitteilungen des Deutschen Archäologischen Instituts, Abteilung Kairo, Wiesbaden.

MIO   Mitteilungen des Instituts für Orientforschung, Berlin.

RdE   Revue d'Egyptologie, Paris.

VDI   ВЕСТНИК ДРЕВНЕЙ ИСТОРИИ, Moscow-Len-ingrad.

ZÄS   Zeitschift für Ägyptische Sprache und Altertums-kunde, Berlin-Leipzig.

Introduction

As for those learned scribes from the time of the successors of the gods, those who foretold the future, it has come to pass that their names will endure forever, although they are gone, having completed their lives, and although their offspring are forgotten. . . . They did not know how to leave heirs who were children who could pronounce their names, but they made heirs for themselves of the writings and books of instruction which they made. . . . Their mortuary servants are gone, and their memorial tablets covered with dust, their chapels forgotten. But their names are pronounced because of these books of theirs which they made. . . . More profitable is a book than a graven tablet, than a chapel-wall [?] well built. . . . A man has perished, and his corpse has become dust. . . . But writings cause him to be remembered in the mouth of the story-teller.

Is there any here like Hardedef? Is there another like Iyemhotep? There have been none among our kindred like Neferti and Khety, that foremost among them. I recall to you the names of Ptahemdjehuty and Khakheperre-sonbe. Is there another like Ptahhotpe or Kaires?

Those sages who foretold the future, that which came forth from their mouths took place. . . . They are gone, their names are forgotten. But writings cause them to be remembered.

From *Papyrus Chester Beatty IV*, translated after A. H. Gardiner

We are reasonably familiar with the art and architecture of ancient Egypt, with the pyramids and sphinx, the great temples of Karnak, Luxor, Edfu, Dendereh, and the wall reliefs and paintings in the chapels of the mastabas of the Old Kingdom and in the tombs of the nobles of the New Kingdom at Thebes. The tomb equipment of Tutankhamun and the head of Queen Nefertiti are well known and can be appreciated through color photography. The visual aspects of Egypt of the pharaohs have now become part of our heritage.

Yet its no less remarkable literature is still relatively unknown except to specialists. The culture of Egypt was not expressed in epics or drama, nor did it produce authors to rival Homer or Virgil, Aeschylus, Sophocles, and Euripides, thinkers to match Plato and Aristotle, or lyric poets on a level with Sappho and Catullus. Yet the minute fraction of its literature which has survived deserves a wider audience, and the sages cited in the quotation above should not be entirely unfamiliar. The lack of easily available translations in English is partly responsible.[1]

When the Egyptian language was gradually deciphered in the first decades of the nineteenth century, the texts proved to be of an extremely heterogeneous nature. They included led-

1. For many years the standard anthology for English readers has been A. Erman, *The Literature of the Ancient Egyptians*, trans. A. M. Blackman (London: Methuen and Co., 1927), a translation of Erman's *Die Literatur der Aegypter* (1923). A paper back reprint has appeared under the title, A. Erman, *The Ancient Egyptians: A Sourcebook of Their Writings*, trans. A. M. Blackman, with new introduction by W. K. Simpson (New York: Harper Torchbooks, 1966). There is also Gaston Maspero, *Popular Stories of Ancient Egypt*, trans. A. S. Johns (New York: University Books, 1967; reprint of 1915 edition), and Joseph Kaster, *Wings of the Falcon* (New York: Holt, Rinehart and Winston, 1968). The most reliable translations are those selections translated by John A. Wilson in James B. Pritchard, ed., *Ancient Near Eastern Texts Relating to the Old Testament* (Princeton: Princeton University Press, 1950; and subsequent editions), hereafter cited as *ANET*. Other than these anthologies and, of course, monographs and journal articles on individual texts, the reader has had to rely on the anthologies in French, German, and Italian. In many ways the most useful is G. Lefebvre, *Romans et contes égyptiens de l'époque pharaonique* (Paris: Adrien-Maisonneuve, 1949). This includes the narratives but omits the instructions and poetry; Lefebvre's notes and introductions are extremely useful. Next there is E. Brunner-Traut, *Altägyptische Märchen* (Düsseldorf-Köln: Eugen Diederichs Verlag, 1963). This includes all the narratives, a reconstruction of myths and fables, and also the demotic and Christian narratives; it omits the instructions and poetry. Lastly, there is the new volume by E. Bresciani, *Letteratura e poesia dell'antico Egitto* (Turin: G. Einaudi, 1969).

gers, inventories, payrolls, distribution lists of foodstuffs and equipment, and letters—all the usual components of a busy economy. Not unexpectedly, many of the inscriptions belong to the category of religious texts: hymns, prayers, rituals, and guidebooks to the underworld and the hereafter. On the temple walls are illustrated manuals of temple service and illustrated chronicles of the kings: their battles, conquests, and lists of tribute. In the tomb chapels of the officials are formulas relating to the provisioning of the funerary cult, a sort of perpetual care, and texts of a biographical nature relating their careers and describing in often stereotyped phrases their ethical probity. The texts from ancient Egypt include matters as diverse as the accounts of lawsuits, trials of thieves, medical and veterinary manuals, and magical spells against scorpions and other creatures.

Within the mass of material studied by several generations of Egyptologists there has emerged a series of compositions which can unquestionably be regarded as literature in our sense. The closest parallels are to be found in other parts of the ancient Near East in the literatures of Mesopotamia and the people of the Old Testament.[2] These compositions are narratives and tales, teachings (instructions), and poetry. Their identification, study, and analysis is a scholarly endeavor in its early stages, yet progressing rapidly; scholars of many countries are constantly contributing the results of their studies.

For some of these texts a single, complete papyrus has survived.[3] For others a few poor copies can be eked out with the

---

2. See in particular the texts in Pritchard, *Ancient Near Eastern Texts;* and T. Eric Peet, *A Comparative Study of the Literatures of Egypt, Palestine, and Mesopotamia,* The Schweich Lectures for 1929 (London: H. Milford, 1931).

3. For example, The Shipwrecked Sailor, The Tale of Two Brothers, and The Contendings of Horus and Seth.

help of numerous fragmentary excerpts on potsherds and lime-stone flakes.[4] Still others lack the beginning or end, or both.[5] Not a few compositions are known by title or a few sentences only, and there remains the slim chance that luck or excavation will produce more of the text.

The compositions in the anthology at hand have been selected on the basis of literary merit or pretensions thereto, with a few additions. The selections from the pyramid texts, the hymns in honor of Sesostris III, and the great hymn to the sun of Akhenaten belong strictly speaking to the religious literature. Similarly, the poem of victory in the stela of Thutmose III has parallels in the historical texts and is not literary in itself. But the literary merit and interest of these selections warrant their inclusion. There are other literary texts which we would have wished to include and which may be added in a second edition, notably The Satire on the Trades, The Plaintiff of Memphis (the tale of King Neferkare and the General), The Instruction of Ani, and The Satirical Letter of Hori to Amenemope, as well as several fragmentary compositions of various periods, and the Late Egyptian Miscellanies, the often copied exercise pieces assigned to apprentice scribes. Yet R. O. Faulkner, one of the collaborators in this enterprise, has remarked that Erman in his anthology cast his net far too wide.

The compositions have been arranged mainly by type rather than by date. The first section, the narratives and tales of the Middle Kingdom, consists of King Cheops and the Magicians, The Tale of the Eloquent Peasant, The Shipwrecked Sailor, and

4. The Teaching of King Ammenemes I, The Teaching for Merikare, and The Prophecies of Neferti.
5. The beginning is missing for King Cheops and the Magicians, The Teaching for the Vizier Kagemni, and The Man Who Was Tired of Life. The end is missing for The Tale of the Doomed Prince and The Report of Wenamon.

The Story of Sinuhe. These were probably set down in Dynasty 12 (1991–1786 B.C.), although the first relates events of the Old Kingdom and the foundation of Dynasty 5 (2494–2345 B.C.), and The Eloquent Peasant is set in Dynasty 9 / 10. The second section comprises the narratives of the New Kingdom, Dynasties 18–20 (1554–1085 B.C.), which are known as the Late Egyptian Stories since they are written in Late Egyptian. This section is the work of Wente and incorporates many new ideas on his part. The tales included are The Quarrel of Apophis and Seknenre, The Capture of Joppa, The Tale of the Doomed Prince, The Tale of the Two Brothers, The Contendings of Horus and Seth, The Blinding of Truth by Falsehood, Astarte and the Insatiable Sea, A Ghost Story, and The Report of Wenamon. The last is a literary report relating events in the first years of Dynasty 21. The third section, comprising wisdom or instruction literature and the lamentations and dialogues, encompasses a wide chronological range. The Maxims of Ptahhotpe, The Teaching for Merikare, The Teaching of King Ammenemes I to His Son Sesostris, The Man Who Was Tired of Life, The Admonitions of an Egyptian Sage, and the Prophecies of Neferti are presented in translations with notes by Faulkner. The Teaching for Kagemni, The Lamentations of Khakheperre-sonbe, The Loyalist Instruction, and The Instruction of Amenemope are the work of Simpson. In the fourth section are included songs, poetry, and hymns. The Poetry from the Oldest Religious Literature (the Pyramid Texts) and The Victorious King (stela of Thutmose III) are translated by Faulkner. The Cycle of Songs in Honor of Sesostris III, The Hymn to the Aten, and The Love Songs and The Song of the Harper have been prepared by Simpson.

Of the genres included, the most comprehensive is *narrative*. The term includes a wide variety of elements, purposes, and aspects. The Sailor and Sinuhe are ostensibly straightforward tales. Both have been recently explained, however, as "lehrhafte Stücke," instructions or teachings in the guise of narratives, with the protagonists, the unnamed sailor and Sinuhe, as models for the man of the times, expressions of the cultural virtues of self-reliance, adaptation to new circumstances, love of home, and so forth.[6] It is perhaps significant that there is no Egyptian term for narrative or story as such. A term *mdt nfrt* is usually rendered as *belles lettres* or fine speech. Otherwise, the terms for writings or sayings are employed. King Cheops and the Magicians is cast in the form of a cycle of stories, the recitation before the king of the marvels performed by the great magicians of the past, yet it concludes with a politically oriented folk tale of the birth of the first three kings of Dynasty 5. The narrative of the Peasant is a framework for an exhibition of eloquent speech in which injustice is denounced. In the Late Egyptian Stories the protagonists are frequently the gods, and the worlds of myth, religion, and folk history mingle.

The one genre for which the Egyptians had a specific term, *sboyet*, is the *instruction* or *teaching*. In almost every case these compositions begin with the heading, "the instruction which X made for Y." The practicality and pragmaticism of the advice given by Ptahhotpe and the author of the Instruction for Kagemni are frequently contrasted with the piety expressed in the later Instruction of Amenemope. The two earlier instructions are set in the form of advice given to a son by the vizier. The two royal instructions, Merikare and Ammenemes I, are of a different nature; they are political pieces cast in instruction form.

A third genre is *lamentation* and *dialogue*, of which The Lamentations of Khakheperre-sonbe, The Admonitions, and

6. E. Otto, in *ZÄS* 93 (1966): 100–11.

The Man Tired of Life are the main compositions. Each is extant in a single manuscript. The Prophecies of Neferti, on the other hand, was a popular text, to judge by the frequent Ramesside copies. Of similar nature are the nine speeches of the Peasant, although we have classified it under narrative. As a last category one can isolate the *love poems* and *banquet songs*. The love songs have survived only from the New Kingdom, but it is likely that the lyric was represented in the classical literature also. There are traces of songs in the tomb reliefs of the Old Kingdom.

Recent study has singled out two not mutually exclusive aspects for special attention: a *literature of propaganda* and a *literature of pessimism*.[7] Under the former are grouped those compositions which have in common the theme of extolling the king or royal dynasty. The Loyalist Instruction is a prime example, and the theme is also developed in its most unadulterated form in the cycle of Hymns in Honor of Sesostris III. Three compositions relate to the beginning of Dynasty 12. The Prophecies of Neferti, although ostensibly set in Dynasty 4,

7. The pioneering and seminal work on literature as propaganda is Georges Posener, *Littérature et politique dans l'Egypte de la XIIe dynastie,* Bibliothèque de l'Ecole des Hautes Etudes, Fasc. 307 (Paris: Honoré Champion, 1956). Posener has also begun a systematic catalogue of Egyptian literary compositions, even the fragmentary pieces, in a series of articles in *Revue d'Egyptologie* 6 (1951): 27–48; 7 (1950): 71–84; 8 (1951): 171–89; 9 (1952): 109–20; 10 (1955): 61–72; 11 (1957): 119–37; and 12 (1960): 75–82. The best introduction to Egyptian literature (without translations) is Altenmüller, Brunner, Fecht, Grapow, Kees, Morenz, Otto, Schott, Spiegel, and Westendorf, *Literatur* (zweite, verbesserte und erweiterte Auflage), in the series *Handbuch der Orientalistik* (ed. B. Spuler), Erste Abteilung: *Der Nahe und Mittlere Osten* (ed. B. Spuler), Erster Band *Ägyptologie* (Leiden/Köln: E. J. Brill, 1970). This comprises sections on many types of text not included in the present volume of translations, for example, religious and ritual texts, magical texts, medical, mathematical, and astronomical literature, historical annals, biographies, etc. For the texts included in our volume it presents fuller discussions and references than we have attempted in our head notes.

foretell the dire straits of the land and the restoration of Egypt under a savior king, Ammenemes I. The same king's Instruction is an apologia for his life and a manifesto in favor of his son Sesostris I. The third composition is Sinuhe, a narrative beginning with the death of Ammenemes I and presenting a highly favorable view of his successor, Sesostris I. All three compositions were recopied extensively in Ramesside times. The *literature of pessimism* comprises those compositions in which the land is described in great disorder, such as the just cited Prophecies of Neferti, the Lamentations, and the Admonitions. Here the theme is associated with the ideas of social and religious change. On a personal, psychological level The Man Who Was Tired of Life belongs to this category; it expresses most poignantly the man's distress and his necessary reorientation of values:

> To whom can I speak today?
> Brothers are evil,
> And the friends of today unlovable.

> To whom can I speak today?
> Gentleness has perished,
> And the violent man has come down on everyone.

Portions of the royal instructions and The Tale of the Eloquent Peasant reflect elements of the same pessimistic background.

With a few exceptions the texts in this anthology are translated from manuscripts written in hieratic in ink on papyrus.[8] Hieratic is the cursive form of hieroglyphic and bears roughly the same relation to the latter as our handwriting does to the

8. A lucid, informative, and highly interesting account of the subject is provided by Jaroslav Černý, *Paper and Books in Ancient Egypt*, An Inaugural Lecture delivered at University College, London (London: H. K. Lewis, 1952).

type set in books or typewritten material. Texts are written horizontally from right to left or vertically, with the first column on the right. Papyrus is a vegetable precursor of paper which was rolled for safekeeping; over a period of years it becomes extremely brittle and is always subject to insect damage. Hence many of these texts have large sections missing as well as frequent damages within an otherwise well-preserved sheet. Use was also made of writing boards, wooden tablets coated with stucco to receive the ink. A very common writing material is the limestone flake or potsherd, and extensive texts written in ink have survived on these unlikely materials. Black ink and a reed pen were the scribe's mainstays; he also used red ink for contrast in headings, corrections, and account totals.

The problems of translation are considerable. The older stages of the language lack conjunctions and specific indications of tense. A sentence can be translated in several ways:

When the sun rises, the peasant ploughs his field.
The sun rises when the peasant ploughs his field.

The past, present, or future tense can be used in either part of this example, and the word "if" substituted for "when." Common sense indicates the first sentence of the pair is the correct translation. It is sometimes difficult to determine if a dependent clause between two main clauses belongs to the first or second main clause. Contrast:

When the sun rose, the peasant ploughed his field. He saw a man approach . . .
The sun rose. Now when the peasant ploughed his field, he saw a man approach. . . .

In poetry it is not always clear if a line belongs to the end of one stanza or the beginning of the next. The exact meaning of many words is still unknown and may remain so. Frequently, a translation is little more than an informed guess. In the Ramesside period certain texts were so carelessly copied that one has the distinct impression that the respective scribes did not understand them. In such cases it is hopeless for the modern scholar to be certain of the meaning or to make much sense out of the words and phrases garbled by the ancient copiest.

There is prose, poetry, and symmetrically structured speech, although the dividing line is not necessarily sharp. A few texts are written in short lines, as is modern poetry. Yet the same composition may be found written continuously. The latter is the usual practice. Only a few of the texts set as poetry in this volume were written in short lines in the manuscript. In New Kingdom texts large dots above the line serve as a sort of punctuation, and these help in ascertaining divisions. Red ink was used for headings, a device equivalent to our paragraphing. Some translators set these rubrics in small capitals. In our volume we have not used them except as a guide for paragraphing.

The three translators have agreed that the use of archaic diction (e.g. *thou, thee, ye, shouldst, saith*) is artificial and distracting. They are indebted to several generations of scholars who have studied and translated the texts into English, French, and German in monographs, journal articles, and brief communications on specific words, sentences, or passages. For each composition the reader is referred to sources for bibliographies; the most recent articles are usually cited.

The volume is addressed to the general reader, the student, and the specialist. The student and specialist are advised, however, that free translations are often used for passages which are difficult or offer the possibility of alternative translations. The translation does not always reflect the final judgment of the translator; he cannot have consistently chosen the right alternative. In journal articles or monographs it is not uncommon to find a sentence discussed at length, with an equal number of pages devoted to the same passage several years later by another scholar. The translator of a text of some length for the general reader cannot burden it with extensive notes and investigations.

The few conventions used require identification. Brackets are employed for text which has been restored when there is a gap in the manuscript, and half brackets when the word or phrase is uncertain or imperfectly understood; three dots are used when the gap cannot be filled with any degree of certainty and represent an omission of indeterminate length: "Then the [wife] of the man ⌈wept⌉, and she said, [. . .]." Parentheses are used for phrases not in the original added as an aid to the reader; angle brackets are used for words which the copiest erroneously omitted: "His henchmen returned (to the house), and he went ⟨into⟩ the room." For convenience in reference the line or column numbers for many of the texts are provided in the margin. When the passage is set in prose a slash is used to indicate the change of line: "I went down to the shore / in the vicinity of the ship." The tag, "may he live, prosper, and be in health," frequently follows a royal name; following the usual custom, it is rendered in our texts as "l.p.h."

A word should be said on the language of the translations. In many cases the translator attempts to render an Egyptian sentence in such a way that its characteristics are retained in English. This often makes for a rather artificial diction, a kind of language not represented in everyday speech. Through this device the translator can indicate that the passive voice is used instead of the active, and so forth: "He was ferried across the river" is not as smooth a translation as "They ferried him across the river," yet the former may render the original more closely.

Similarly, a passage is translated thus: "Now after many days had elapsed upon this and while they were (engaged) in their daily practice, presently the boy passed by them." The sentence is equivalent to "After some time, while they were busy with their daily affairs, the boy happened to come upon them." In the second version an attempt has been made to render the sense, in the first the Egyptian sequence of words. Another example is, "Is it while the son of the male is still living that the cattle are to be given to the stranger?" A smoother translation would be: "Is it customary to give the cattle to the stranger while the son of the man of the house is still alive?" The original, however, employs a verbal form which places emphasis on the clause, "while the son of the male is still living." The first of the two alternatives brings out this emphasis more closely. Our translations attempt to strike a compromise between these two poles. To opt consistently for the smoother translation results in a paraphrase and leads to an interpretative retelling. Yet to retain the artificiality of Egyptian phrasing in English makes for a clumsiness foreign to the Egyptian text itself.

A short bibliography is included for those whom we hope to have interested in the study and appreciation of Ancient Egypt.

w. k. s.

PART I

*Narratives and Tales of Middle
Egyptian Literature*

King Cheops and the Magicians

This cycle of stories about the marvels performed by the lector priests is cast in the form of a series of tales told at the court of Cheops by his sons. The name of the first son is missing together with most of the story. The second son, Khaefre, later became king and is known as the builder of the Second Pyramid at Giza. The third son, Bauefre, is known from other sources; a later text indicates that he may have also become king for a short time. The fourth son, Hardedef, is known as one of the sages of the past, and part of his instruction has survived.

The text derives from a single manuscript of which the beginning and conclusion are missing. The papyrus was inscribed in the Hyksos period before Dynasty 18, but the composition appears to belong to Dynasty 12; the events described are set in the Old Kingdom. The last story is a prophecy of the end of Cheops's line through the birth of the three kings who founded Dynasty 5. The story of their actual birth is presented as a sort of annex. Elements of the miraculous royal birth are represented in later Egyptian and Near Eastern literature and even are reflected in the biblical accounts. The device of providing stories for the diversion of the king is also represented in The Prophecies of Neferti, The Admonitions, and The Eloquent Peasant, as well as several later compositions. The real substance of the composition is certainly the prophecy of the birth of the kings, and the other tales merely lead up to it. For bibliography and commentary on King Cheops and the Magicians (Papyrus Westcar), see Lefebvre, Romans et contes, *pp. 70–90, and* Erman, The Ancient Egyptians, *pp. xxiv, lxviii–lxix, 36-49.*

W. K. S.

First Tale: End of the Marvel in
the Time of King Djoser

1,12   [. . . His Majesty] / the King of Upper and Lower
Egypt, Khufu (Cheops), the vindicated, [said: Let there
be given . . .], one hundred jugs of beer, an ox, [. . . to]
the King of Upper and Lower Egypt, Djoser, the vindicated, [and may there be given . . .], a haunch of beef,
[. . . to the lector priest . . .]. [For I] have seen an example of his skill. And [they] did according as [His
Majesty] commanded.[1]

Second Tale: The Marvel which happened
in the Time of King Nebka

The king's son Khaefre (Chephren) arose [to speak, and
he said: I should like to relate to Your Majesty] another
marvel, one which happened in the time of [your]
father, [the King of Upper and Lower Egypt] Nebka,
1,20   the vindicated, as he proceeded to the temple of [Ptah, /
Lord of] Ankh-towy.[2]
Now when his Majesty went to [. . .], His Majesty
made an [appeal? . . . to] the chief [lector] Webaoner
2,1   [. . .]. But the wife of Webaoner [. . . was enamored /
of a townsman. She caused to be brought(?)] to him a
chest filled with garments [. . .], and he returned with

1. This is the conclusion of a tale of which the entire narrative
section is missing. It concerns a marvel performed by a lector
priest in the reign of Djoser, the builder of the Step Pyramid.
Perhaps the lector was Iyemhotep himself. There is no way of
knowing how much of the composition was lost at the beginning.
2. Nebka of Dynasty 3 is a predecessor of Cheops. Ankh-towy is
a designation for Memphis or a part thereof.

[the] servant.[3] [Now several] days [passed by . . .]. There was a greenhouse [4] [on the estate] of Webaoner. The townsman [said to the wife of Weba]oner: Is there a greenhouse [. . .]? [Come], let us pass time in it. [Then said the wife of] Webaoner to the caretaker who [cared for the estate]: Let the greenhouse be prepared, [. . .]

2,10 and she spent the day there drinking / [with the townsman . . . and] ⌈resting⌉ [. . .]. Now after [evening came . . .] he [went to . . .] the caretaker, and [the] servant girl [. . .].

[When] day broke, and the second day [came, the caretaker informed Webaoner of] this matter [. . .]. He gave

2,20 it to his / [. . .] of the water. Then [he(?)] lit [a fire]. [He said to his caretaker]: Bring me [. . . my chest] of ebony and gold [and he made . . . and he opened . . . and made] a crocodile [of wax . . .] seven [fingers long . . .]. He read out his [magic words saying . . .]: [If anyone] comes [to] bathe [in] my lake [. . .] the towns-

3,1 man. / Then he gave it to [the caretaker], and he said to him: After the townsman goes down to the pool, as is his daily fashion, you shall cast [the] crocodile after him. The [caretaker] went forth and he took the crocodile of wax with him.

Now the [wife] of Webaoner sent to the caretaker who was in charge of the [garden] saying: Let the greenhouse be prepared for I have come to stay in it. The greenhouse was prepared [with] every good thing. They (the wife

3,10 and the maid servant?) went forth, and they (spent) / a pleasant day with the townsman. After night fell, the

3. Evidently the adulterous wife makes a present to the good-looking townsman and he returns to thank her.
4. A sort of garden pavilion.

townsman returned as was his daily fashion, and the care-taker threw the crocodile of wax behind him into the water. [At once it grew] into a crocodile of seven cubits,[5] and it took hold of the townsman.

Webaoner tarried with His Majesty the King of Upper and Lower Egypt, Nebka, the vindicated, for seven days, all the while the townsman was in the [lake without] breathing. After seven days had passed, His Majesty the King of Upper and Lower Egypt, Nebka, the vindicated [came forth], and the chief lector Webaoner placed him-self in ⟨his⟩ presence and [he] said [to him]: May Your

3,20 Majesty / come and see the marvel which has taken place in Your Majesty's time. [His Majesty went with] We-baoner. [He called out to the] crocodile and said: Bring back the townsman. [The crocodile] came [out of the water . . .]. Then the [chief] lector [Webaoner] said: [Open up]! And he [opened up]. Then he placed [. . .].

4,1 Said His Majesty the King of Upper and Lower Egypt, / Nebka, the vindicated: this crocodile is indeed ⌜fearful⌝! But Webaoner bent down, and he caught it and it became a crocodile of wax in his hand. The chief lector Webaoner told His Majesty the King of Upper and Lower Egypt, Nebka, the vindicated, about this affair which the towns-man had in his house with his wife. And his Majesty said to the crocodile: Take what belongs to you! The croc-odile then went down to the [depths] of the lake, and no one knew the place where he went with him.

His [Majesty the King of Upper] and Lower Egypt, Nebka, the vindicated, had the wife of Webaoner taken

4,10 to a plot north of the capital, and he set / fire to her [. . . in] the river.

5. The cubit measures 20.6 inches.

⌈Such⌉ is a marvel which happened [in] the time of your father, the King of Upper and Lower Egypt, Nebka, one which the chief lector Webaoner performed. His Majesty the King of Upper and Lower Egypt, Khufu, the vindicated, said: Let there be offered to the King of Upper and Lower Egypt, Nebka, the vindicated, one thousand loaves of bread, one hundred jugs of beer, an ox, and two cones of incense, and let there be offered to the chief lector Webaoner a large cake, a jug of beer, a joint of meat, and one cone of incense, for I have [seen] an example of his skill. And it was done according to all His Majesty commanded.

Third Tale: The Marvel Which Happened in the Reign of King Snefru

Bauefre arose to speak, and he said: Let me have [Your] Majesty hear a marvel which took place in the time of your (own) father King Snefru, the vindicated, [one] which the chief lector / Djadjaemonkh [made] and which had not taken place [before] . . . [Now His Majesty had searched out the chambers] of the palace, l.p.h., to seek for him [some diversion . . . and he said]: Hasten, bring me the chief lector and scribe, [. . . Djadjaem]onkh! He was brought to him immediately. [His] Majesty said to him: [I have looked through the chambers of the] palace, l.p.h., to seek for myself / some refreshing matter, but I cannot find any. Djadjaemonkh said to him: Let Your Majesty proceed to the lake of the palace, l.p.h., and equip for yourself a boat with all the beauties who are in your palace chamber. The heart of Your Majesty shall be refreshed at the sight of their rowing as they row up and down. You can see the beautiful fish pools of your lake, and you can see the beautiful fields around it. Your heart will be refreshed at this. ⟨His Majesty said⟩: I will indeed fit out my rowing excursion. Let there be brought to me twenty oars made of ebony, fitted with gold, with the butts of sandalwood(?) fitted with white gold. Let there be brought to me twenty women, / the most beautiful in form, with hair well braided, with ⌈firm⌉ breasts, not yet having opened up to give birth. Let there be brought to me twenty nets, and let these nets be given to these women when they have taken off their clothes. Then it was done according to all that His Majesty commanded, and they rowed up and down. The heart of His Majesty was happy at the sight of their rowing.[6]

Now one of the strokes combed her tresses, and a fish-shaped charm of new turquoise fell in the water. She became silent and did not row, and her side of the boat became silent and did not row. His Majesty said: Are you not rowing? And they said: Our stroke / is silent and does not row. Then [His] Majesty said to her: [Why] do [you] not row? She said: A fish-shaped charm of new [turquoise] fell into the water. And [His Majesty said to her]: Would you like one to replace [it]? But [she said]:

6. Philippe Derchain, in *RdE* 21 (1969): 19–25, calls attention to the parallel of the maidens rowing and the goddess Hathor as a rower. The sense of the outing in his view is that of a sort of parody, with the king taking the place of the sun god Re navigating the heavens with the Hathors. The author of our tale would then have stressed the importance of the rulers of Dynasty 5 as the real adherents of Re, in distinction to Snefru as a ruler who merely parodied the god. Snefru indeed had close relationships with Re and Hathor, as is known from the monuments, but it is the author of our tale, according to Derchain, who casts him as a parodist.

I [like] my pot [down to the end].[7] His Majesty said: [Let there be brought again] the chief lector [Djadjaemonkh, and he was brought at once]. His Majesty said: 6,1 Djadjaemonkh, my brother,[8] I have done as you have said, and the heart of His Majesty was refreshed at the sight of their rowing. But a fish-shaped charm of new turquoise, belonging to one of the leaders, fell into the water. She was silent and did not row. And it came to pass that she ruined her side. I said to her: Why have you stopped rowing? She said to me: It is a fish-shaped charm of new turquoise which has fallen into the water. I said to her: Row! I will replace it! She said to me: I like my pot down to the end. Then said the chief lector Djadjaemonkh his magic sayings. He placed one side of the water of the 6,10 lake upon the other, and lying upon a potsherd he found the fish-shaped charm. Then he brought it back and gave it to its owner. Now as for the water, it was twelve cubits deep, and it amounted to twenty-four cubits after it was folded back. He said his magic sayings, and he brought back the water of the lake to its position. His Majesty passed a holiday with the entire palace, l.p.h. When he came forth, he rewarded the chief lector Djadjaemonkh with all good things.

Such is a marvel which took place in the time of your father, the King of Upper and Lower Egypt, Snefru, the vindicated, something done by the chief lector, scribe of the document, Djadjaemonkh. And His Majesty the King of Upper and Lower Egypt, Khufu, the vindicated, said:

---

7. Evidently a proverb with the sense that she wants the full amount or the same thing.
8. This familiar form of address places Snefru in a good light.

Let there be an offering made to His Majesty the King of
6,20 Upper and Lower Egypt, Snefru, the vindicated, / consisting of one thousand loaves of bread, one hundred jugs of
beer, an ox, and two cones of incense, and let there be
given a large cake, a jug of beer, and one cone of incense
to the chief lector, scribe of the document, Djadjaemonkh.
For I have seen an example of his skill. It was done according to all His Majesty commanded.

The Fourth Tale: A Marvel in the Time of King Khufu Himself

The king's son Hardedef arose to speak, and he said:
[You have heard examples of] the skill of those who have
passed away, but there one cannot know truth [from
falsehood]. [But there is with] Your Majesty, in your own
time, one who is not known [to you . . .]. His Majesty said:
What is this, Har[dedef, my son? Then said Har]dedef:
7,1 There is a townsman / named Dedi. He lives in Ded-
Snefru, the vindicated. He is a villager of 110 years, and
he eats 500 loaves, a shoulder of beef as meat, and as drink
100 jugs up to this day.[9] He knows how to reattach a head
which has been cut off, and he knows how to make a lion
go behind him, its tether on the ground. He knows ⌜the
arrangement⌝ of the secret chambers of the enclosure of
Thot. Now His Majesty the King of Upper and Lower
Egypt, Khufu, the vindicated, had spent much time in
seeking for himself these secret chambers of the enclosure
of Thot to fashion for himself their likeness for his horizon. His Majesty said: You yourself, Hardedef, my son,
you shall bring him to me. Boats were prepared for the

9. The Egyptians often wished for 110 years as a life span.

7,10   king's son, Hardedef, / and he sailed south to Ded-Snefru, the vindicated. After these boats were moored at the river bank, he went by land. He sat in a carrying chair of ebony, its poles made of *sesnedjem*-wood and sheathed in gold leaf.[10] When he reached Dedi, the carrying chair was put down, and he proceeded to address him. It was lying down on a mat at the threshold of his house that he found him, a servant at his head massaging him and another wiping his feet. The king's son Hardedef said: Your condition is like that of a man before old age, although senility has come, the time of mooring, burial, and interment. (Yet you) sleep until dawn, free from ailments, and there is no
7,20   coughing in your throat. Greetings, / O honored one! It is to summon you on the business of my father, King Khufu, the vindicated, that I have come here, and that you may eat the delicacies of the king's giving, the food of those who are in his following, and that he may send you in good time to your fathers who are in the cemetery. And this Dedi said: In peace, in peace, Hardedef, king's son, beloved by his father! May your father King Khufu, the vindicated, favor you! May he advance your station among the venerables. May your Ka contend with your enemy, and may your Ba learn the way to the Portal of the One Who Clothes the Weary One.[11] Greetings to
8,1   you, / O king's son!

    The king's son Hardedef stretched out his hands to him

10. Nobles are sometimes shown in such carrying chairs in relief sculpture in the Old Kingdom. A carrying chair much like this one was found in the tomb of Snefru's daughter Hetepheres, the queen of Cheops. The chair is now in the Cairo Museum, with a replica in the Museum of Fine Arts in Boston.

11. Formal greetings are exchanged on both sides. The Ka and Ba are spirits of the dead man and manifestations of his personality. The One Who Clothes the Weary One is the embalmer.

and raised him up.[12] He went with him to the riverbank, giving him his arm. Dedi said. Let me have a *kakau*-boat that it may bring me (my) students and my writings. There were made to attend him two boats and their crews.

Dedi went northward in the barge in which the king's son Hardedef was. When he reached the capital, the king's son Hardedef entered to report to His Majesty the King of Upper and Lower Egypt, Khufu, the vindicated. The king's son Hardedef said: Sovereign, my lord, I have brought Dedi. His Majesty said: Hasten, bring him to me. 8,10 His Majesty proceeded to the pillared hall / of the palace, l.p.h., and Dedi was ushered in to him. His Majesty said: What is this, Dedi, my not having seen you (before)? And Dedi said: It is only the one who is summoned who comes, Sovereign, l.p.h. I have been summoned and see I have come. His Majesty said: Is it true, the saying that you know how to reattach a head which has been cut off? Dedi said: Yes, I do know how, Sovereign, l.p.h., my lord. His Majesty said: Let there be brought to me the prisoner who is in confinement, that his punishment may be inflicted. And Dedi said: But not indeed to a man, Sovereign, l.p.h., my lord. For the doing of the like is not commanded unto the august cattle. So there was brought to him a goose, and its head was severed. Then the goose was placed on the western side of the pillared court, and its head on 8,20 the / eastern side of the pillared court. Dedi said his say of magic words. The goose arose and waddled and so did its head. The one (part) reached the other, and the goose stood up and cackled. Next he caused a waterfowl to be brought, and the like was done with it. Then His Majesty

12. Again a signal favor in that a prince condescends to raise up a commoner.

caused that there be brought him an ox, and its head was
felled to the ground. Dedi said his say of magic words,
9,1   and the ox stood up behind him with its tether fallen / to
the ground. ⟨The scribe has obviously omitted a paragraph
here dealing with the lion.⟩

Then [His Majesty] King Khufu, the vindicated, said:
Now as for the rumor that you know the ⌈arrangement⌉ of
the secret chambers of the enclosure of [Thot]? Dedi said:
By your favor, I do not know their ⌈arrangement⌉, Sovereign, l.p.h., my lord, but I do know the place where they are.
His Majesty said: Where are they? And Dedi said: There
is a passage of flint in a chamber called the Inventory in
Heliopolis: in that passage.[13] [His Majesty said: Hasten,
Bring it to me!] Dedi said: Sovereign, l.p.h., my lord, it
is not I who can bring it to you. His Majesty said: Who
then can bring it to me? Dedi said: It is the eldest of the
three children who are in the womb of Reddedet; he will
bring it to you. His Majesty said: I ⌈desire this indeed⌉.
But [as for] what you say, who is this Reddedet? Dedi
said: She is the wife of a *wab*-priest of Re, Lord of
9,10 Sakhbu, / and will give birth to three children of Re, Lord
of Sakhbu, of whom it is said that they shall exercise this
magisterial office in the entire land. The eldest of them
will be chief seer in Heliopolis.[14]

As for His Majesty, his heart became very sad at this,

13. The sense of the arrangement or number of the secret chambers
is entirely unclear. Possibly they were the architectural plan for
a part of the pyramid complex of Cheops, as suggested by the text.
In any case, the question of the chambers serves to introduce the
matter of Reddedet and the future kings.
14. In Dynasty 5 a particular emphasis is placed on the sun god Re
as the dynastic god. His chief place of worship was On (Greek
Heliopolis); Re, Lord of Sakhbu, is a local variant. Sakhbu is in
Lower Egyptian Nome 2.

and Dedi said: What now is this mood, Sovereign, l.p.h., my lord? Is it because of the three children? I say: First your son, then his son, then one of them.[15] His Majesty said: When shall she give birth, Reddedet? She shall give birth in the month of Proyet on the fifteenth day. His Majesty said: Then the sandbanks of the Two Fishes Canal will be cut off, my servant, (otherwise) I myself could visit it and then I could see the temple of Re, Lord of Sakhbu. Dedi said: I shall cause there to be water four cubits deep on the sandbanks of the Two Fishes Canal. His Majesty proceeded to his palace, and His Majesty said: Let it be commanded to Dedi to (go to) the house of the king's 9,20 son Hardedef that he may live there / with him. Fix his rations at one thousand loaves of bread, one hundred jugs of beer, an ox, and one hundred bundles of greens. And one did according to all His Majesty had commanded.

The Birth of the Kings

One of these days it happened that Reddedet took sick and her travail was painful. The Majesty of Re, Lord of Sakhbu, said to Isis, Nephthys, Meskhenet, Heket, and Khnum: [16] May you proceed that you may deliver Reddedet of the three children who are in her womb; they who shall exercise this magisterial office in the entire land. For they shall build the shrines in your towns, they shall provision your altars, they shall renew your offering

15. Evidently an abbreviated version of history in which only the builders of the Giza pyramids, Chephren and Mycerinus, are considered as coming between Cheops and the first king of Dynasty 5, Weserkaf.

16. Four goddesses associated with childbirth and the ram god Khnum, regarded as the creator of man on a potter's wheel in one myth.

tables, and they shall increase your divine offerings.[17]
These goddesses proceeded, and they transformed them-
10,1 selves / into musicians, with Khnum accompanying them
carrying the birthing-stool. When they reached the house
of Rewosre, they found him standing with his apron untied.[18] They proffered to him their necklaces and (their)
rattles. But he said to them: My ladies, see, there is a
woman in labor, and her bearing is difficult. They said to
him: Let [us] see her, for we are knowledgeable about
childbirth. So he said to them: Proceed! And they entered
into the presence of Reddedet. Then they locked the room
on her and on themselves. Isis placed herself in front of
her, Nephthys behind her, and Heket hastened the childbirth. Isis then said: Do not be strong (*wsr*) in her womb
10,10 in this your name of Wosref (*wsr rf*).[19] / This child
slipped forth upon her hands as a child one cubit long,
whose bones were firm, the covering of whose limbs was
of gold, and whose headdress was of real [20] lapis lazuli.

17. A graphic list of the usefulness of the kings to the gods.

18. Lit. "upside down." E. Staehelin, in *ZÄS* 96 (1970): 125–39,
discusses this passage at length. In her view, Rewosre has his apron
untied (unknotted) and hanging down as a sort of sympathetic
parallel to the untied garments of his wife during childbirth; parallels in other cultures are cited.

19. As each child is born, Isis makes a pronouncement involving a
pun on the king's name. Weserkaf means "his Ka is strong";
Sahu-Re probably means "one whom Re has well endowed," but
there is a pun on *sahu*, "to kick." In Neuserre Kakai there is a pun
involving Kakai and Keku, "darkness." H. Altenmüller, in *Chronique d'Egypte* 45 (1970): 223–35, suggested that Reddedet is a
pseudonym for Khentkaus, a queen of the end of Dynasty 4, and
that she was the mother of the first three kings of Dynasty 5. He
further suggests that she may have been the daughter of the same
prince Hardedef who introduces the tale. Hence she and her sons
would have been descendants of Cheops through a junior branch of
the family.

20. As opposed to faience or glass with this color.

They washed him, his umbilical cord was cut, and he was placed upon a cushion on bricks. Then Meskhenet approached him, and she said: A king who will exercise the kingship in this entire land! Khnum caused his limbs to move.

Next Isis placed herself in front of her (Reddedet), Nephthys behind her, and Heket hastened the childbirth. Isis said: Do not kick (*sah*) in her womb in this your name of Sahure (*sāhu-Re*). And this child slipped out on her hands as a child one cubit long, whose bones were firm, the covering of whose limbs were <of gold>, and whose headdress was of real lapis lazuli. They washed him, his

10,20 umbilical cord was cut, and he was placed / on a cushion on bricks. Then Meskhenet approached him and she said: A king who will exercise the kingship in this entire land! Khnum caused his limbs to move.

Then Isis placed herself before her, Nephthys behind her, and Heket hastened the childbirth. Isis said: Do not be dark (*kkw*) in her womb in this your name of Keku. And this child slipped forth upon her hands as a child one cubit long, whose bones were firm, the covering of whose limbs was of gold, and whose headdress was of real lapis

11,1 lazuli. Then Meskhenet approached him, / and she said: A king who will exercise the kingship in this entire land! Khnum caused his limbs to move. They washed him, his umbilical cord was cut, and he was placed on a cushion on bricks.

Now these goddesses came forth after they had delivered this Reddedet of the three children, and they said: May you be pleased, Rewosre, for there have been born to you three children. And he said to them: My ladies, what can I do for you? Please give this corn to your birthing-stool bearer, and take it as a payment for ⌜making beer⌝. And

Khnum placed the sack on his back. So they proceeded to
11, the place / from which they came. But Isis said to these
10 goddesses: What is this, that we are returning without
performing a marvel for these children and can report to
their father who sent us? So they fashioned three royal
crowns, l.p.h., and they placed them in the corn. Then
they caused the heavens to turn into a storm and rain, and
they turned back to the house and said: Would you please
put the corn here in a locked room until we can come
back on our northward journey? So they placed the corn
in a locked room.[21]

Reddedet cleansed herself in a purification of fourteen
11, days, and she said to her maidservant: Is the house / pre-
20 pared? She replied: It is outfitted with everything except
for jars (for beer-making), for they have not been
brought. Reddedet said: Why haven't the jars been
brought? The servant replied: There is not anything here
for ⌜(beer-) making⌝, except for some corn of these
musicians, which is in the room with their seal. So Reddedet said: Go and bring some of it, for Rewosre will give
12,1 them its equivalent when he returns. The servant went /
and she opened the room. And she heard the sound of
singing, music, dancing, and exultations—everything which
is done for a king—in the room. She returned and she
repeated everything that she had heard to Reddedet. So
she (too) went around the room but could not find the
place in which it was being done. Then she put her forehead to the bin and discovered it was being done in it.
(Then she placed it) in a chest which was (in turn)
placed in another sealed box tied with leather thongs, and

21. The goddesses leave magical tokens of the kingship for the
children in the sack of grain. They invent the storm as an excuse to
return.

she put it in a room with her stores and she sealed it off. When Rewosre came back, returning from the fields, Reddedet related this business to him, and his heart was more pleased than anything. They sat down and celebrated.

After some days had passed, Reddedet had an argument with the maidservant, and she had her punished with a beating. So the / maidservant said to the people who were in the house: ⌜Shall this be tolerated?⌝ She has given birth to three kings, and I am going and I will tell it to His Majesty the King of Upper and Lower Egypt, Khufu, the vindicated! So she started out, and she came upon her eldest brother, on her mother's side, tying flax yarn on the threshing floor. He said to her: Where are you off to, little girl? And she told him about this business. Her brother said to her: Is this indeed something to be done, your coming to me thus? And am I to agree to [this] denunciation? Then he took a whip of flax to her, and he gave her a real beating. The maidservant ran to get herself a drink of water and a crocodile caught her. [Her brother] went to tell it to Reddedet, / and her brother found her sitting with her head on her knee,[22] her heart very sad. He said to her: My lady, why are you so sad? She said to him: That little girl who grew up in this house, see, she has gone away saying: I am going and I will denounce. Then he put his head down and said: My lady, she stopped by, in going away, to tell me [. . .] that she might go off with me. And I gave her a sound beating, and she went to get some water, and a crocodile caught her . . .

(Here the papyrus breaks off.)

22. An attitude of mourning or sorrow.

The Tale of the Eloquent Peasant

This work was popular during the Middle Kingdom. Although cast in the form of a tale, it was primarily intended for a conscious literary essay in what the Egyptians regarded as fine writing. The introductory narrative is straightforward, but the peasant's speeches are, to modern taste, unduly repetitive, with high-flown language and constant harping on a few metaphors. However, as a form of writing which appealed to the educated Egyptian, the work could not be excluded from any anthology of Egyptian literature. For translations, commentary, and bibliography, see Lefebvre, Romans et contes, pp. 41–69; Erman, The Ancient Egyptians, pp. xxx–xxxi, 116–31; and A. H. Gardiner, in JEA 9 (1923): 5–25.

R. O. F.

R1   There was once a man called Khunanup, who was a peasant of the Wadi Natrun, and he had a wife named [Maryet]. And this peasant said to this wife of his: See, I am going down to Egypt to [fetch] provisions thence for my children. Go now, measure for me the barley which is in the barn, being the remainder of [the harvest]. There-

R5   upon he measured out to her [six] measures of barley. / And the peasant said to his wife: See, [here are] twenty measures of barley for provision (for you) [1] and your children; you shall make for me the six measures of barley into bread and beer for every day on which [I shall be traveling].

     So the peasant went down to Egypt, and he loaded his

1. Omitted in the original.

R10   asses with [2] reeds, *redemet*-plants, / natron, salt, wood from the [Hes]-tiu country, wands of *awent*-wood from
R15   the Farafra Oasis, / panther skins, jackal hides, *nesha*-
R20   plants, *kheperur*-plants, / *sahut, saksut*-pellets, *misut*-plants,
R25   *senet*-stones, *aba*-stones, / *ibsa*-plants, *inbi*-plants, pigeons,
R30   *naru*-birds (ostriches?), *weges*-birds, / *weben*-plants, *tebes*-
R35   plants, *gengenet*-pellets, hair fruit, and *inset*-pellets, / being full measure of all the goodly products of the Wadi Natrun. And the peasant traveled southward to Ninsu,[3] and he arrived at the district of Per-Fefi to the north of Medinet. And he found a man standing upon the riverbank whose name was Djehutinakhte; he was the son of
R40   a man / named Isry, and he was a tenant of the High Steward [4] Rensi, son of Meru. Now this Djehutinakhte said, when he saw the asses of this peasant, which were pleasing to his heart: O that I had some potent idol, that I might steal this peasant's goods from him! Now Djehuti-
R45   nakhte's house was on the riverside path, / which was narrow, not broad, for it extended to the width of a loincloth; its one side was under water and the other under barley. And Djehutinakhte said to his henchman: Go and bring me a cloth from my house. And it was brought to him immediately. Thereupon he spread it over the river-
R50   side path; / its fringe rested on the water and its hem on
B1,1   the barley. The peasant came on the public road, / and Djehutinakhte said: Take care, peasant! Are you going to

2. Here follows an itemized list of the goods which the peasant hoped to trade for food, many of which are not yet identified; among recognizable items are salt, natron, and skins of panther and jackal. A few items are also listed in the medical papyri. See Lefebvre, *Romans et contes,* pp. 47–48, and E. Edel, in *ZÄS* 96 (1969): 7.
3. Herakleopolis in Middle Egypt.
4. An important office at court.

tread on my clothes? And the peasant said: I will do your pleasure, for my way is good.[5] And he went up higher.

B1,5 Then said Djehutinakhte: / Is my barley a road for you? The peasant said: My way is good; the bank is high and the (only other) way is under barley, and you are obstructing our road with your clothes. Will you not let us pass upon the road? Now when he had finished uttering

B1,10 [this] speech, one of these asses filled / his mouth with a wisp of barley, and Djehutinakhte said: Look, I shall take away your ass, peasant, because of its eating my barley; look, it shall ⌈toil⌉ because of its offense. And the peasant said: My way is good, and one (wisp only) has been damaged. It is for its (the wisp's) price that I will buy

B1,15 back my ass if you take possession of it / for a (mere) filling of its mouth with a wisp of barley.[6] Now I know the lord of this estate, it belongs to the High Steward Rensi, son of Meru, and it is he who restrains every robber in this entire land; shall I then be robbed on his estate?

And Djehutinakhte said: Is this the proverb which men

B1,20 say, / "The name of a poor man is pronounced (only) on account of his lord"? It is I who am speaking to you, and it is the High Steward whom you are calling to mind! Thereupon he took a rod of green tamarisk-wood to him and belabored all his limbs with it; he took away his asses and drove them to his estate. The peasant

B1,25 / wept very much at the pain of what had been done to him, and Djehutinakhte said: Do not raise your voice, peasant; look, you are on the way to the city of the Lord of Silence![7] And the peasant said: You beat me, you steal

5. I.e. I am ready to oblige you.
6. See E. F. Wente, in *JNES* 24 (1965): 105–09.
7. The god of death; Djehutinakhte threatens to murder the peasant if he does not stop wailing.

my goods, and now you take away the complaint from my
B1,30 mouth! O Lord of Silence, give me / my goods (again)!
Then will I cease to call out so that Thou ⌜art disturbed⌝.
And the peasant spent a period of ten days appealing to
Djehutinakhte, but he paid no attention to it.

So the peasant went to Ninsu to appeal to the High
Steward Rensi, son of Meru; he found him as he was
B1,35 coming out of the door / of his house to go aboard his
state barge, and the peasant said: O that I were allowed
to inform you about this affair! It is a case for causing
your chosen retainer to come to me, that I may send him
to you about it. So the High Steward Rensi, son of Meru,
B1,40 caused / his chosen retainer to go in front of him,[8] so that
the peasant might send to him regarding this matter in all
its aspects. Then the High Steward Rensi, son of Meru,
accused Djehutinakhte to the magistrates who were with
him, but they said to him: My lord, it is probably a peasant
B1,45 of his who has gone to someone else beside him;[9] / see,
that is what they are accustomed to do to peasants of
theirs who go to others beside themselves. Is it a case for
punishing Djehutinakhte on account of a trifle of natron
and a trifle of salt? If he be commanded to replace them,
B1,50 he will replace them. / But the High Steward Rensi, son
of Meru, was silent; he did not answer these magistrates,
nor did he answer the peasant.

Now the peasant came to appeal to the High Steward
Rensi, son of Meru, and he said: O High Steward my
lord, greatest of the great, guide of everything; if you go
B1,55 down to the Lake of / Truth, you shall sail on it with a
fair breeze; the ⌜bunt⌝ of your sail shall not strip away,

8. As an agent in advance of Rensi's progress.
9. I.e. an absconding serf.

your ship shall not lag, no mishap shall befall your mast, your ⌐yards⌐ shall not break, you shall not ⌐founder nor run aground⌐, the current shall not carry you off, you B1,60 shall not taste the evils / of the river, you shall not see the face of fear, the darting fish shall come to you, and you shall end with fat fowl,[10] because you are a father to the orphan, a husband to the widow, a brother to her who is divorced, a garment to the motherless; let me make your B1,65 name / in this land ⌐in accord with⌐ every good law—a leader devoid of rapacity, a magnate devoid of baseness, who destroys falsehood and fosters truth, and who comes at the voice of the caller. I speak that you may hear: Do justice, O praised one whom the praised ones praise; [11] B1,70 do away with / my needs, for see, I am heavy-laden; examine me, for see, I am in a loss.

Now the peasant spoke this speech in the reign of His late Majesty King Nebkaure.[12] And the High Steward Rensi, son of Meru, went before His Majesty and said: B1,75 My lord, / I have found one of these peasants who is really eloquent; his goods have been stolen, and see, he has come to appeal to me about it. And His Majesty said: As you wish me well, make him linger here, without replying to anything that he has said; for the sake of his B1,80 continuing / to speak, keep silence. And let his speech be brought to Us in writing, that We may hear it. But make provision for his wife and his children, for see, one of these peasants will come up to the land about the poverty of his

10. All this is a high-flown metaphorical way of telling Rensi that if he does justice he will prosper.
11. A typical play on words, a favorite literary device of the Egyptians.
12. A King Nebkaure Akhtoy reigned at Ninsu-Heracleopolis in Dynasties 9 / 10.

house.[13] Further, make provision for this peasant himself; you shall have provisions issued to him without letting him know that it is you who have given them to him. So they gave him ten loaves and two jugs of beer B1,85 / daily; the High Steward Rensi, son of Meru, used to give them; he gave them to a friend of his, and it was he who gave them to him. And the High Steward Rensi, son of Meru, sent to the governor of the Wadi Natrun about the supplying of provisions for the peasant's wife, three measures of barley daily.

The peasant came to appeal to him the second time, and he said: O High Steward my lord! O greatest of the great, richest of the rich, whose great ones have one B1,90 greater, / whose rich ones have one richer! Steering oar of heaven, beam of earth, plumbline which carries the weight! [14] O Steering oar, do not diverge; O Beam, do not tilt; O Plumbline, do not swing awry! A great lord takes possession (only) of that which has no owner, and plunders on account of that alone.[15] But your sustenance is in your house, a *hin* of beer and three loaves; [16] what B1,95 do you expend in satisfying / your clients? A mortal man dies along with his dependants; will you be a man of eternity? Is it not wrong, a balance which tilts, a plummet which deflects, a straightforward man who has become a cheater? Look, justice has fled from you, having been ousted from its place; the magistrates make trouble, the norm of speech becomes one-sided, the judges snatch

13. I.e. we will have someone else coming in with a complaint.
14. The plumb line of the balance.
15. I.e. he plunders only ownerless property.
16. I.e. you have all you need without looking for more; a *hin* of beer is about one-half litre. The ration named is so small that it is clear that the peasant is being sarcastic.

B1   what has been ⌜taken⌝.[17] It means that a twister of speech
100   from its exact sense / makes a travesty of it; he who
should give breath languishes on the ground, he who takes
his ease causes men to pant, the arbitrator is a despoiler, he
who should destroy need is one who commands its
making, the town is its flood,[18] and he who should redress
wrong makes trouble.

Then said the High Steward Rensi, son of Meru: Are
your possessions more important to you than that my retainer should arrest you? And the peasant said: [19] The
105   measurer of / corn-heaps cheats for himself; he who
should fill for someone else pilfers his belongings, he who
should rule according to the laws orders robbery, so who
then will redress wrong? He who should expel ⌜weakness⌝
acts perversely; one goes straight on because of crookedness, while another is talked about through harm.[20] Do you
find anything here for yourself? [21] Redress is short, harm
is long, and good repute comes to its place of yesterday.[22]
110   Such is the precept: Do to the doer / so as to cause him to
do.[23] It is thanking him for what he should do, it is parry-
ing a thing before casting, it is the order to a craftsman.
O for a moment of destruction, overturning in your vine-
yard, scarcity among your birds, destruction among your
wildfowl! He who should see is turned blind, he who

17. The reading of the last word is doubtful.
18. I.e. its own destruction.
19. The High Steward interrupts the peasant's harangue with a
threat which the peasant ignores.
20. Only the wrongdoer acquires wealth and fame.
21. Does this cap fit you?
22. I.e. is not forgotten.
23. I.e. do as you would be done by, another typical play on words.
In the following sentences the gist is that fair dealing to another
anticipates benefits to yourself; if you are just you will get your
reward.

B1   should hear is deaf, he who should lead is become a false
       guide.

115   / O . . . , have you ever . . . ? [24] What would you
       do [. . .]? See, you are strong and influential, (yet) your
       hand is active, your heart is rapacious, mercy has passed
       you by. How miserable is the poor man whom you de-
       stroy! You are like a messenger of the Crocodile-god; see,

120   you surpass / the Lady of Pestilence! [25] If you have
       nothing, then she has nothing; if there is nothing due to
       you, there is nothing due to her; if you have not done it,
       then she has not done it. The possessor of ⌈bread⌉ should
       be merciful, (even though) the criminal is hard; thefts are
       natural to him who has no possessions, and possessions are
       snatched by the criminal; a bad state of affairs, but ⌈in-
       evitable⌉. One should not be angry with him; he is but

125   seeking for himself.[26] But you are sated / with your bread
       and drunken with your beer; you are rich [. . .]. The
       face of the helmsman should look forward,[27] but the
       ship [28] diverges as it will; [29] the king is indoors and the
       steering oar is [in] your hand, (yet) trouble is caused in
       your vicinity. (The task of) the petitioner is long and
       parting is heavy: What is he who is yonder? men will

130   say.[30] Act as / a shelter, that your coast may be clear; see,
       your abode is infested with crocodiles. Be accurate with
       your tongue, that you may not err; the limb in him [31] is a
       man's perdition. Do not speak falsehood, watch over the

24. Two untranslatable words.
25. The lioness-goddess Sakhmet.
26. The peasant is excusing himself in advance if he should have
to take to theft because of the loss of his goods.
27. Lit. "be to the front."
28. The metaphorical "ship of State."
29. Owing to the helmsman's inattention to duty.
30. Wondering who it is arguing so long with the High Steward.
31. His tongue?

B I   magistrates; what ⌜fattens⌝ the judges is a basket,[32] the telling of lies is their herbs,[33] and it lies light on their hearts. Wisest of all men, are you ignorant of my circumstances? Destroyer of every water's ⌜need⌝, see, I have a course without a ship. Bringer to shore of all who are drowning, save one who is shipwrecked; rescue me from . . .[34]

    The peasant came to appeal to him the third time, and

140 he said: / O High Steward my lord! You are Re, lord of heaven, with your entourage, and the sustenance of all men is from you, even like the flood; you are Hapy, who makes green the meadows and furnishes the wasted tracts.[35]

145 Restrain the robber, take counsel for the poor man, / do not become an inundation against the petitioner. Beware of the approach of eternity; will to live long, according to the saying: "The doing of justice is breath to the nose." Deal punishment to him who ought to be punished, and none shall be like your rectitude. Will the balance deflect?

150 Will the stand-balance incline to one side? Will Thoth / be lenient? Then you may make trouble. You shall make yourself an equal of these three; if the three are lenient, then you may be lenient. Do not answer good with evil, do not set one thing in the place of another, for speech grows more than a rank weed, more than suits the smeller!

155 Do not answer it, but water / what is to come, so as to cause a covering to grow.[36] There have been three occa-

---

32. A basketful of good things as a bribe.
33. Is profitable.
34. Untranslatable.
35. Gross flattery; the peasant likens the High Steward to the sun-god and the Nile-god.
36. Perhaps meaning: if you do not reply to talk, you will be covering yourself against future trouble. But the following clauses are very obscure.

BI   sions to cause him to act.[37] Steer according to the bunt (of the sail); [38] ⌜stave off⌝ the inundation so as to do justice; beware lest you run aground because of the tiller rope.[39] The true balancing of the land is the doing of justice; do

160   not speak falsehood, for you are great; / do not be light,[40] for you are weighty; [41] do not speak falsehood, for you are the balance; do not swerve, for you are rectitude. See, you are on one level with the balance; if it tilt, then you may tilt. Do not diverge, but steer (aright), pull upon the

165   tiller rope. Do not take, but act against the thief, / for he is not really great, that great one who is rapacious. Your tongue is the plummet,[42] your heart is the weight, your lips are its arm. If you veil your face against the violent,[43] who then shall redress wrong?

    See, you are a wretch of a washerman, rapacious in in-

170   juring / a friend, ⌜forsaking his partner⌝ for his client; he who comes and brings (something) to him is his brother.[44]

    See, you are a ferryman who ferries over (only) the possessor of a fare, a straight-dealing man whose straight-dealing has been cut off.

    See, you are a head of the storehouse who does not permit the needy man to pass ⌜in default⌝.[45]

175   See, you are / a hawk to the plebs, one who lives on

---

37. Possibly an allusion to the fact that this is the peasant's third petition. In that case "him" will refer to Rensi.
38. I.e. steer so as to keep the sail full of wind, steer a true course.
39. I.e. through misusing it.
40. Light-minded, frivolous.
41. A man of importance.
42. Of the balance.
43. I.e. look the other way.
44. He who comes with a bribe, and he only, ranks as a brother. This paragraph is the first of a series all beginning with the same word, a regular Egyptian literary device.
45. Apparently meaning: who allows no credit to the poverty-stricken.

B 1   (even) the meanest of the birds.

See, you are a purveyor whose joy is to slaughter and the mutilation thereof is not on him.[46]

See, you are a herdsman . . .[47] you do not pay. You should show less of the ravening crocodile, for shelter is absent from the abode of the entire land.

180   / O Hearer, you do not hear; why, pray, do you not hear?[48] Today I have driven off the savage one and the crocodile retires.[49] What profit is it to you that the secret of truth be found and that falsehood's back be put to the ground? Do not prepare for the morrow before it has come, for none know the trouble in it.

185   Now the peasant uttered / this speech to the High Steward Rensi, son of Meru, at the entrance of the judgment hall. And he[50] caused two apparitors to attend to him with whips, and they belabored all his limbs therewith. And this peasant said: The son of Meru goes on erring, and his face is blind to what he should see and deaf to what he should hear, one who is misguided con-

190   cerning what is told to him. See, you are a town / which has no governor, like an assembly which has no chief, like a ship in which there is no captain, a confederacy which has no leader. See, you are a sheriff who steals, a town governor who accepts (bribes), a district overseer who should repress plundering (but) who has become a pattern for the wrongdoer.

The peasant came to appeal to him the fourth time; he

195   found him / coming out of the door of the temple of

46. I.e. escapes the consequences.
47. Untranslatable and probably corrupt.
48. A play on the verb *hear*.
49. The peasant claims to have got the better of Rensi, to whom he refers in an insulting manner.
50. Rensi.

BI   Arsaphes,[51] and he said: O favored one, may Arsaphes, from whose temple you have come, favor you! Good is perished, and there is no cleaving to it; (perished also is) the flinging of falsehood's back to the ground. Is the ferryboat brought to land? How then can one cross? The deed must be effected, even though unwillingly. Crossing

200 / the river upon sandals, is (that) a good (way of) crossing? No! Who now can sleep until dawn? Perished is walking by night, traveling by day, and letting a man attend to his own right cause. See, there is no profit for him who says it to you! Mercy has passed you by; how

205 miserable is the poor man / whom you have destroyed! See, you are a hunter who slakes his ardor, one bent on doing what he desires, who harpoons hippopotamuses, shoots wild bulls, spears fish, and snares birds. There is no one quick of speech who is free from hasty talk, there is no one light-minded who is weighty of thought; be

210 / patient, that you may learn justice; curb your ⌈choice⌉, so that he who enters silently [52] may be happy. There is no one impetuous who practices excellence, there is none hasty-tempered whose aid is sought.[53] Let the eyes observe, that the heart may be informed; so do not be harsh in proportion to your power, that evil may not draw near

215 you. / Pass over a case, and it will become two.[54] It is the eater who tastes, and he who is questioned answers; it is

51. The patron deity of Heracleopolis, at the period of this tale the capital of the northern kingdom, the south being ruled by a Theban family.
52. The servant or client who must not be noisy in the presence of his lord.
53. Lit. "[whose] arm is brought" or "used."
54. I.e. a problem shelved becomes doubly difficult.

B1   the sleeper who sees the dream. As for the judge who ought to be punished, he is a pattern for the wrongdoer.

220 Fool, see, you are hit! Dunce, see, / you are questioned! Baler-out of water,[55] see, you are entered! [56] Helmsman, do not steer your ship awry; Lifegiver, do not let men die; Destroyer, do not let men be destroyed; Shade, do not act as the sun-heat; Shelter, do not let the crocodile take. The

225 fourth time of appealing to you, / am I to spend all day at it?

The peasant came to appeal to him the fifth time, and he said: O High Steward my lord! [. . .] The ⌈angler⌉ [. . .] kills the chance-come fish, the fish-spearer stabs the

230 . . . -fish, [57] the / . . . ,[58] and the fish-netter ravages the river; see, you are in like case. Do not despoil a poor man of his possessions, a feeble man whom you know, for his possessions are (the very) breath to a poor man, and to take them away is to stop up his nose. You were ap-

235 pointed to hear pleas, / to judge between suitors and to repress the robber, but see, what you do is to support the thief! Men trust in you, and you have become a transgressor. You were appointed to be a dam for the poor man; beware lest he drown, for see, you are a swift current to him.

240 / The peasant came to appeal to him the sixth time, and he said: O High Steward my lord! . . .[59] that he may lighten (the weight of) falsehood, foster truth, foster all good and destroy evil, even as satiety comes and ends

55. I.e. one who should dispose of troubles.
56. Obscure; perhaps meaning: You are involved in (i.e. responsible for) the troubles you should redress.
57. Unidentified kind of fish.
58. Untranslatable and probably corrupt.
59. A considerable omission by the copyist.

BI
245
hunger; (as) clothing (comes) and ends nakedness; even as the sky becomes serene after / a high wind and warms all who are cold; like a fire which cooks what is raw and like water which quenches thirst. See with your own eyes; the arbitrator is a despoiler; he who should make peace is
250 a maker of sorrow; / he who should put things right is a maker of suffering. The purloiner diminishes justice, so render good and full account; then justice will be neither filched from nor excessive. If you bring anything away, then give to your fellow. You talker [60] devoid of straight-
255 forwardness, my sorrow leads to / separation, my accusation brings about departure, for none know what is in the heart. Do not be sluggish, but deal with the charge. If you sever, who will join? The sounding pole is in your hand like a ⌈free⌉ pole when ⌈deep water has been found.⌉ [61] If a boat run aground, it is salvaged, but its
260 cargo for the land / perishes on every shore.[62] You are instructed, you are clever, you are complete, but not because of despoiling, (yet now) you assume the likeness of all mankind.[63] Your affairs are all awry; the cheater of the entire land goes straight onward, the cultivator of evil waters his garden with wrongdoing so as to make his
265 garden grow / with falsehood and to water trouble forever.

The peasant came to appeal to him the seventh time, and he said: O High Steward my lord! You are the steering oar of the entire land, and the land sails in accordance

60. Lit. "jaw."
61. Lit. "like an open stick, an occasion of water having happened"; the metaphor seems to be that Rensi is in safe waters because his pole cannot touch bottom.
62. I.e. the cargo is jettisoned to save the vessel and rots where it lies, washed up on shore and sandbank.
63. I.e. you have every wordly advantage, yet are no better than the common herd.

B1 with your command; you are the companion of Thoth,
who judges without showing partiality. My lord, be
270 patient, so that a man may invoke you / concerning his
own right cause. Do not be angry, for it does not become you. The farsighted man becomes apprehensive; do
not brood on what has not yet come and do not rejoice
over what has not yet happened. Forbearance prolongs
friendship and disposes of a past matter, for no one knows
what is in the heart. (As for) the subverter of law and
275 the destroyer of rectitude, there is no poor man / who can
live when he pillages, for justice has not addressed him.
Indeed, my belly was full,[64] my heart was heavy-laden,
and (my misery) issued from my belly because of its
condition. It was a breach in the dam, and its water
flowed; my mouth opened to speak. (So then) I plied my
sounding pole, I baled out my water,[65] I emptied out what
280 was in my belly, I washed my dirty linen. / (Now) my
utterance is achieved, my (tale of) misery is concluded
in your presence; what more do you want? Your sluggishness will lead you astray, your rapacity will make a fool
of you, your voracity will make you enemies. Will you
ever find another peasant like me? A sluggard—will a
285 petitioner stand at the door of his house? / There are
none silent whom you have caused to speak, there are
none sleeping whom you have caused to wake, there are
none downcast whom you have enlivened, there are none
with shut mouths whom you have opened, there are none
ignorant whom you have caused to learn, there are none
foolish whom you have taught.[66] (Yet) magistrates should

64. Of misery.
65. I.e. I unburdened myself of my grievances.
66. The repetition of "there are none . . ." is another example of
the literary device referred to in n. 44, above.

B1   be expellers of evil, lords of good, craftsmen in creating
      that which is, and joiners up of the head which is cut off.

290   / The peasant came to appeal to him the eighth time,
      and he said: O High Steward, my lord! Men fall far
      through greed; the rapacious man is devoid of success, his
      success is (only) in failure. You are rapacious, and it does
      not become you; you steal, but it does not benefit you,
      you who should allow a man to attend to his own right
      cause. *Your* portion is in your house, your belly is full, the
295   cornmeasure overflows, and when it runs over, / its sur-
      plus is lost on the ground. You who should arrest the
      robber are one who takes away the magistrates who were
      appointed to contend against trouble, for they are a
      shelter from the aggressive, (namely) the magistrates who
      were appointed to contend against falsehood. No fear of
      you makes me appeal to you, for you do not perceive my
      heart, (even of me) the silent one, turning back to make
      complaint to you, one who is not afraid of him to whom
300   he makes his claim, / and his brother cannot be brought
      for you from within the street.[67] You have your field-
      plot in the country; your reward is in the estate; your
      provisions are in the storehouse; the magistrates give to
      you; and (yet) you go on taking! Are you a robber? Do
      troops have to accompany you at the division of the field-
      plots? [68] Do justice for the Lord of Justice, the justice of
305   whose justice exists.[69] / You pen, papyrus, and palette of
      Thoth, beware of making trouble; when what is well is
      well, indeed it is well.[70] But justice is for eternity, and it

67. I.e. you can search the streets and not find anyone equal to me.
68. Lit. "are men ushered in to you, troops being with you, at the
division of the field-plots?
69. A play upon the word for *justice*; see n. 11, above.
70. Another play on words.

B1
310 goes down with him who does it into the realm of the dead; he is buried and the earth envelops him, / but his name is not obliterated on earth and he is remembered for goodness; such is the standard of the word of God. Is he a balance? It does not tilt. Is he a stand-balance? It does not incline to one side. Whether I shall come or
315 whether another shall come, answer! / Do not answer as one who addresses a silent man or as one who attacks someone who does not attack. You show no mercy, you do not trouble, you do not destroy,[71] you give me no reward for this goodly speech which comes forth from the
320 mouth of Re himself! / Speak justice and do justice, for it is mighty, it is great, it is long-enduring, its trustworthiness is discovered, and it leads to the blessed state. Does a
325 balance tilt? It is its scalepans which weigh things, / but no excess is possible to the norm. A mean act cannot attain to the city, but the ⌐hindermost¬ will reach land.

B2,91 / The peasant came to appeal to him the ninth time, and he said: O High Steward my lord! Their tongue is men's stand-balance, and it is the balance which searches out deficiencies. Deal punishment to him who ought to be
95 punished, and none shall resemble your rectitude. / ⌐Evil has gone astray¬, and as for falsehood, ⌐its business is settled¬,[72] for Truth has turned herself about to confront it. ⌐Truth comes out of falsehood¬,[73] and it is ⌐caused to flourish¬, it will not be . . .[74] If falsehood walk abroad, it

71. I.e. you take no action whatsoever, good or bad; you show complete indifference.
72. Perhaps as one might say: "its goose is cooked."
73. Lit. "truth is the property of falsehood," meaning probably "truth will out."
74. An unknown word.

B2 goes astray; it does not cross in the ferryboat, [it] makes
100 no progress. / As for him who is rich through it, he has
no children, he has no heirs upon earth; as for him who
sails with it, he does not reach land and his ship does not
moor at her city. Do not be heavy, for you are not light;
do not lag, for you do not hurry; do not be one-sided, do
105 not listen to / your heart, do not veil your face from one
whom you know, do not blind your eyes to one whom
you have seen, do not reject him who has a claim on you.
Forsake this sluggishness, that your maxim, "Help him
who helps you," may be repeated in the hearing of all
men, and that a man may invoke (you) concerning his
110 own right cause. A sluggard has no yesterday; / one deaf
to truth has no friend; the rapacious man has no holiday.
He who delated becomes a poor man, and the poor man
will be a petitioner, and the enemy becomes a slayer. See,
I appeal to you, but you do not hear it; I will go, that I
115 may appeal / about you to Anubis!

Then the High Steward Rensi, son of Meru, sent two
apparitors to bring him back, and the peasant was afraid,
for he thought that punishment would be dealt to him
because of the speech which he had spoken. Then the
peasant said: The approach of a thirsty man to water, the
120 reaching of / a suckling's mouth after milk, such is a
[death] that has been prayed for when he sees it coming,
when his death comes tardily for him. And the High
Steward Rensi, son of Meru, said: Do not be afraid, peasant; see, you shall arrange to act with me. Then the
125 peasant said: / Am I to live saying, "I will eat of your
bread and drink [of] your [beer] for ever"? And the
High Steward Rensi, son of Meru, said: Well, stay here
that you may hear your petitions. And he had [them]

B2   read out from a new papyrus-roll, each petition according
130 to [its] content. / Then the High Steward Rensi, son of
     Meru, sent it in to His late Majesty King Nebkaure, and
     it pleased him more than anything which was in this
     entire land. And [His Majesty] said: You yourself give
     judgment, son of Meru. Then [the High Steward] Rensi,
     son of Meru, caused two apparitors to go to [fetch Djehu-
135 tinakhte], / and he was brought in. An inventory was
     made of [all his goods . . .], his [servants], six persons,
     apart from [. . .] his barley, his emmer, [his] asses, his
     pigs, and [his flocks,] and Djehutinakhte's [house was
140 given to the] peasant, / [together with] all his [goods].
     [Then . . .] said [. . .] to Djehutinakhte [. . .] which is
     in [. . .] (*Last word or words of story lost.*)

It has come to an end.

The Shipwrecked Sailor

*The tale of the sailor is preserved in a single manuscript of the early
Middle Kingdom, and it has been suggested that it was written in
Dynasty 11. Unlike so many other compositions extant through
only one text, it seems to be complete from beginning to end, although the real beginning may be cut off. It begins abruptly with an
expedition commander's aide addressing him to console him on an
unsuccessful expedition to the south. In trying to cheer him up, the
aide relates a set of similar experiences which he had. In the course
of these a serpent relates a story. There is a story within a story
within a story. The nature and location of the Island of the Ka, the
enchanted island reached by the sailor, are still subjects for discussion. Some view the entire tale as a sort of psychological journey.
At the end of the story the commander speaks his only words; they
suggest that he is downcast at the thought of reporting on his unsuccessful mission. The tale represents one of the earliest examples
of a narrative of the unreal. The beginning is couched in terms of
a standard quarrying report such as might be found in the Ham-
mamat Valley or the Sinai. The real import of the tale perhaps
escapes us. It has recently been suggested that the sailor serves as a
model for the man of the times in the same way as does Sinuhe.
For bibliographical references and commentary, consult Lefebvre,*
Romans et contes, *pp. 29–40, and Erman,* The Ancient Egyptians,
pp. xxiii–xxiv, 29–35.

w. k. s.

The astute lieutenant spoke: May your wish be satisfied, commander. See, we have reached home. The mallet
has been taken, the mooring post driven in, and the prow
rope set upon the ground. Praise has been rendered, God

50

has been thanked, and every man embraces his companion. Our crew is returned safe without loss to our troops. Now that we have reached the limits of Wawat and we have
10 passed by / Senmut, we have returned in peace, and we have attained our land.[1]

Listen to me, commander. I am devoid of exaggeration. Wash yourself; place water on your fingers. Then you can reply when you are interrogated and speak to the king with self-assurance. You will answer without ⌐stammer-ing.⌐ For the speech of a man saves him, and his words
20 gain him indulgence. / Act according to your judgment. Yet speaking to you (in this fashion) is wearisome.

Let me tell you of a similar thing which happened to me myself.[2] I went to the mining country for the sovereign. I went down to the sea[3] in a boat 120 cubits long and 40 cubits wide.[4] One hundred twenty sailors from among the best of Egypt were in it. Whether they looked at the sky
30 or whether they looked at the land, / their hearts were ⌐fiercer⌐ than those of lions. They could foretell a storm-

1. A quarrying, mining, or military expedition has returned by Nile from the south, and its commander appears to be downcast at the prospect of facing the king after an unsuccessful mission. His chief aide tries to cheer him up. Wawat is northern Nubia, and Senmut is the island of Biggeh, just south of Aswan in the First Cataract region. The mission took place in the eastern desert or on the Red Sea. The expression, "our land," is not otherwise attested in Egyptian literature and may in fact have a patriotic nuance.

2. Here begins the story within the story.

3. The word for sea is literally, "the great green," and is used of the Mediterranean as well as the Red Sea. Since the mining country is either the Sinai peninsula or the eastern desert, since the serpent speaks of the land of Punt (a southern region in Africa or on the Red Sea), and since the produce is African (giraffe tails, etc.), the sea in our story is clearly the Red Sea.

4. The cubit is the Egyptian measurement of length, about 20.6 inches or .523 meters. The ship is about 206 by 70 feet.

wind before it came and a downpour before it happened.

A stormwind broke out while we were at sea, before we had touched land. The wind was lifted up,[5] but it repeated with a wave of eight cubits in it. There was a plank which struck it (the wave) for me.[6] Then the boat died. And of those who were in it not a single one survived.

40 Next I was set upon / an island by the surf of the sea, and I spent three days alone, my heart as my companion. I slept inside of a cabin of wood; [7] I embraced the shade. I stretched forth my two legs to learn what I might put in my mouth. There I found figs and dates, and all excellent kinds of vegetables. Sycamore figs were there and notched 50 sycamore figs. / And cucumbers as if they were cultivated. Fish were there and birds. There was not anything which was not within it. Then I ate to satisfaction, and I put (some aside) on the ground because of the overabundance in my hands. I cut a fire drill, lit a fire, and I made a burnt offering for the gods.

Then I heard the sound of a thunderclap, but I thought 60 it was the surf of the sea. The trees were shaking / and the ground was quaking. When I uncovered my face, I discovered that it was a serpent coming along. He was thirty cubits. His ⌐hood¬ was more than two cubits, and his body was plated with gold. His two ⌐markings¬ were of real lapis lazuli, and he was coiled up in front.[8]

He opened his mouth to me while I was on my belly in his presence, and he said to me: Who is it who has

5. Perhaps an idiom with the sense, "we traveled onward."
6. This passage difficult in the original.
7. Possibly the cabin of the boat, but conceivably a natural or man-made shelter.
8. The terms *hood* and *markings* have been interpreted in various ways by different scholars. The first is the usual word for beard.

brought you, who is it who has brought you, little one, 70 / who is it who has brought you? If you delay in telling me who it is who has brought you to this island, I shall see that you find yourself as ashes, transformed into one who is not seen.

Although he was speaking to me, I did not hear it; when I was in his presence, I did not know myself. He placed me in his mouth, and he took me off to his rest house. 80 He set me down without touching me, / and I was intact, without anything being taken away from me.

He opened his mouth to me while I was on my belly in his presence, and he said to me: Who is it who has brought you, who is it who has brought you, little one, who is it who has brought you to this island of the sea, the two sides of which are in waves? And I answered him, my arms bent in his presence, and I said to him: It is I (my- 90 self) who have gone down / to the mines on a mission of the sovereign in a boat 120 cubits long and 40 cubits wide.[9] One hundred twenty sailors from among the best of Egypt were in it. Whether they looked at the sky or whether they looked at the land, their hearts were ⌈fiercer⌉ than those of lions. They could foretell a stormwind before it came and a downpour before it happened. Each one of 100 them, his heart was ⌈fiercer⌉ / and his arm more valorous than his fellow's, without a fool among them. A storm-wind came forth while we were at sea, before we could make land. The wind was lifted up, but it repeated with a wave of eight cubits in it. There was a plank which struck it (the wave) for me. Then the boat died. And of those that were in it not a single one remained except for

9. This kind of repetition of an entire section is frequent in all ancient literature.

110 me. Behold me at your side. Then I was brought to this island / by the surf of the sea.

He said to me: Do not fear, do not fear, little one, do not turn white. You have reached me. Indeed, God has allowed you to live. He has brought you to this Island of the Ka [10] within which there is not anything which does not exist. It is full of all good things. See, you shall spend month after month until you complete four months within 120 this island. / A boat shall come back from home with sailors in it whom you know. You shall go home with them, and you shall die in your village. [11]

How joyful is the one who relates what he has tasted after painful affairs are past. Let me relate to you something similar which took place in this island when I was on it with my brothers and sisters and the children among them. [12] We were seventy-five serpents, my children and my brothers and sisters. And I will not call to mind to you a little daughter who was brought to me through ⌐prayer.⌐ [13]

130 Then a star / fell, and because of it these went up in fire. [14] It happened completely. Yet I did not burn, for I was not among them. But I died for them when I found them in a single heap of corpses. [15]

If you would be brave, regulate your desire. Then you will fill your embrace with your children, you will kiss

10. An island of the spirit or enchanted island.
11. Burial in a foreign land was abhorrent to the Egyptians, a theme developed in Sinuhe as well.
12. Here begins the story within the story within the story.
13. This curious phrase has not yet been satisfactorily explained.
14. A meteor? In the historical text of Thutmose III from Gebel Barkal there is a description of a falling star.
15. Here the serpent's story ends. Like the sailor, he was a sole survivor.

your wife, and you will see your house (again); for it is better than anything. You will reach the home in which you (once) were in the midst of your brothers and sisters.

As I was stretched out on my belly and touching the ground in his presence, I said to him: I shall relate your
140 prowess to the sovereign, and I shall inform him / of your greatness. I shall have brought to you ladanum, *heknu*-oil, *iudeneb,* cassia, and incense for the temples with which to satisfy every god. I shall indeed relate what has happened to me through what I have seen of your prowess. You will be thanked in (my) town in the presence of the magistrates of the entire land. I shall sacrifice to you oxen as a burnt offering, and I shall wring the necks of birds for you. I shall have brought to you transport ships loaded with all the specialties of Egypt, as should be done for a god who loves the Egyptians in a distant land which the Egyptians do not know.

Then he laughed at me because of these things which I
150 had said, out of the ⌜craftiness⌝ of his heart. / And he said to me: Myrrh is not abundant with you, although you have become a possessor of incense. Indeed, I am the Prince of Punt; myrrh belongs to me. That *heknu*-oil, of which you spoke about bringing me, why it is the main product of this island! Now it will come to pass that you will separate yourself from this place, and you will never see this island, since it will have turned into waves.

Then that boat came, as he had foretold before. I went and I set myself on a high tree, and I recognized those who were in it. I went to report it, but I found that he knew it. And he said to me: Farewell, farewell, little one, to your home! You will see your children. Place my good
160 repute in your town: this is all I ask / from you.

I placed myself on my belly, my arms bent in his presence. And he gave me a cargo consisting of myrrh, *heknu-*oil, *iudeneb*, cassia, *tishepses*, *shasekh*, black eye-paint, giraffe tails, large cakes of incense, elephant tusks, hounds, apes, baboons, and every kind of precious thing. I then loaded them onto this boat. It then came to pass that I placed myself upon my belly to thank him, and he said to me: You will arrive home within two months. You will fill your embrace with your children. You will become young again at home, and you will be (properly) buried.

170   I went down to the shore / in the vicinity of this ship, and I called out to the troops who were in this ship. I gave praise upon the shore to the lord of this island, and those who were in it (the ship) did likewise.

We sailed northward to the Residence city of the sovereign, and we arrived at the Residence in two months, according to everything he had said. Then I entered before the sovereign, and I presented to him this produce which I had brought back from within this island. He thanked me before the magistrates of the entire land. I was appointed lieutenant, and I was assigned two hundred

180 people. Look at me, / now that I have touched land, after I have seen what I have experienced. Listen to my speech. It is good for men to hearken.

He said to me: [16] Do not act the part of the astute man, friend. Who gives water to the goose at daybreak when it is to be slaughtered in the morning?

It has come, from its beginning to its end, as it has been found in writing, in the writing of the scribe excellent of

189 fingers, / Ameny's son Amen-aa, l.p.h.

16. These are the commander's only words in the story.

The Story of Sinuhe

The Story of Sinuhe is regarded by many as a more or less factual account of the adventures of an Egyptian courtier copied from the inscription in his tomb. No trace of the real Sinuhe, however, has yet been found through tomb reliefs, statuary, or stelae. In its present form the story is a narrative of interest—given its development, the psychology of the protagonist, the use of language, and the picture of the times in Syria and Palestine—and of considerable literary merit. Sinuhe is a resourceful man of his times, a prototype of the proper official at a time of rising prosperity in Egypt and its relations abroad. Impelled by some inner force he cannot explain to flee from the court, he makes his own way and recognizes later both the necessity to return to his king and the advantage of a traditional burial and funerary rites. The story begins with the death of the founder of Dynasty 12, Ammenemes I, in 1961 B.C. and the report of his death made to the army headed by his son, coregent, and successor, Sesostris I. The treatment of the latter in the story is excellent propaganda.

With the exception of religious texts and various standard formulas, no other composition is represented in as many copies or partial copies. Two papyri of Dynasties 12 and 13 provide a fairly complete text. In the Ramesside period in Dynasties 19 and 20 master scribes and their students copied the text in school on limestone flakes (ostraca). One of these has virtually the whole text inscribed on both sides of a large flake: J. W. B. Barns, The Ashmolean Ostracon of Sinuhe *(Oxford: Oxford University Press, 1952). For bibliographical details and commentary, see Lefebvre,* Romans et contes, *pp. 1–28; and Erman,* The Ancient Egyptians, *pp. xxiii, 14–29. The chapter headings are not in the original text; they have been added as an aid to understanding the main divisions of the narrative and for reference.*

W. K. S.

Introduction

R,1   The hereditary prince and commander, warden and
district officer of the estates of the sovereign in the lands
of the Asiatics,[1] this truly beloved royal agent, the follower Sinuhe, said:

I was a follower who followed his lord, a servant of the
king's harem and of the hereditary princess, greatest of
praise, wife of King Sesostris in Khnumet-sut and daughter
of King Ammenemes in Ka-nofru, Nofru, the possessor of
an honored state.[2]

Death of Ammenemes I and Sinuhe's Flight

Year 30, month 3 of Akhet, day 7. The God ascended
to his horizon, the King of Upper and Lower Egypt,
Sehetepibre. He flew up to the heavens, being joined to
the sun disk, the God's body being mixed with that of
him who made him.[3]

The capital was silent, desires were weak, the Great
10   Double Gate was locked, / the court was with head upon
knee,[4] and the nobles were wailing. Now His Majesty had
dispatched an expeditionary force to the land of the
Tjemehi with his eldest son as its leader, the good God,

1. The inhabitants of Palestine and Syria are designated in this
text as the Amu, the Setyu, and the Pedjtyu (bowmen); the first
two are rendered as "Asiatics."
2. Sinuhe identifies himself here as an official of Queen Nofru,
daughter of Ammenemes I, and wife of his son and successor,
Sesostris I. Ka-nofru and Khnumet-sut are respectively the pyramid
residence towns of these two first rulers of Dynasty 12.
3. A terse announcement of the death of Ammenemes I in the
year 1961 B.C.
4. The position of mourners.

Sesostris. He had been sent to strike the foreign lands and to smite those who were among the Tjehenu people.[5] And now he was returning, having brought back captives of the Tjehenu people and all kinds of cattle without number. The Companions of the Palace sent to the Western Half to inform the king's son of the affairs which had taken place in the council chamber. When the mes-
20 sengers found him upon the road / and reached him at dusk, he did not delay for a moment. The Falcon flew off with his followers without letting his expeditionary force know it.

Now [they had] written to the sons of the king who were in his following in this expeditionary force. When it
B,1 was being read out / to one of them, I was standing by and I heard his voice, as he spoke, being in the vicinity not far away. My senses were disturbed, my arms spread out, and trembling came over every part (of me). I took myself off by stealth (?) to find for myself a place of concealment. I placed myself between two shrubs in order to separate the road from its traveler. I went south. I did not plan to reach the capital, for I thought riots might occur, and I would not be able to say "life" after him (the king). I crossed the (place called) The Two Truths in the vicinity of The Sycamore, and I landed at The Island
10 of Snefru. I spent the day on the edge of / the cultivation. At dawn I came upon a man standing in the middle of the road. He greeted me respectfully, for he was frightened. When the time of evening meal came, I reached the wharf of Negau. It was in a boat without a rudder that I crossed over with the help of the west wind. I passed by to the

5. The Tjemehu and Tjehenu, people living to the west of Egypt, are Libyan tribes.

east of the Quarry, above the Mistress of the Red Mountain (that is, the opposite side of the river, beyond the cultivation, in the desert), and I gave a path to my feet northward (until) I touched the Walls of the Prince, which had been made to check the Asiatics and to crush the sand-travelers. I took a crouched position in the brush out of fear that the guard on duty on the walls might see. I went / by night, and when day came, I had reached Peten. I alighted at the Island of Kem-wer. Thirst overcame me; I was parched, my throat dry. And I said: This is the taste of Death. But I raised up my heart and gathered together my limbs. I heard the sound of the lowing of cattle, and I looked upon Asiatics. Their bedouin chief perceived me, a man who had been in Egypt. He gave me water and boiled milk for me, and I went with him to his tribe, and what they did for me was good.[6]

One land gave me to (another) land. I set out for Byblos (near Beirut), and I returned to Kedem. I spent / half a year there. It was Amusinenshi[7] who brought me back: he was the chief of Upper Retenu.[8] He said to me: You will be well with me, for you will hear the speech of Egypt. He said this for he knew my reputation. He had heard of my intelligence, for the people of Egypt who were there with him bore witness to me. And he said to me: Why have you come here? Has anything happened at the capital? I said to him: The King of Upper and Lower Egypt, Sehetepibre, has proceeded to the horizon,

6. In this description of Sinuhe's precipitous flight he indicates that he intended to flee to the south but was set on a northern course through the drifting downstream of the rudderless boat. The places designated as The Two Truths, The Sycamore, and The Island of Snefru may lie in the pyramid area of Memphis. See H. Goedicke, in *JEA* 43 (1957): 77–85.

7. An Egyptianized version of an Amorite (West Semitic) name.

8. A designation for part of Palestine and Syria.

and no one knows what may happen because of this. I then
spoke equivocally.[9] When I returned from an expedition
in the land of the Tjemehu, one announced (that) to me.
My mind vacillated. My heart was not in my body, and it
40 brought / me to the ways of flight. (But) no one accused
me, no one spat in my face. No reproach was heard, and
my name was not heard in the mouth of the town crier. I
do not know what brought me to this land. It was like
the plan of a God.

Praise of Sesostris I

He said to me: How shall that land fare without him,
that efficient God the awe of whom is throughout the
foreign lands like Sakhmet in a year of pestilence? [10] I said
to him so that I might answer him: To be certain, his son
has entered the palace and has assumed the inheritance of
his father. He is a God, indeed, without peer. No other
came into being before him.[11] He is a master of knowledge, excellent in planning and efficient in commanding,
one by whose command one comes forth and goes down.
50 / It was he who controlled the foreign lands while his
father was in the palace. He reported to him what he (the
father) decreed had come to happen. He is a champion
who acts with his own arms, a fighter without anyone like
him when he is seen attacking the bowmen and engaging
the fray. He is one who bends back the horn and renders
hands powerless, so that his enemies cannot muster their

9. The equivocal statement seems to lie in the fact that the announcement was made to the king's son, not to Sinuhe himself.
10. Sakhmet is the lioness-headed goddess responsible for pestilence.
11. The following amounts to a hymn in praise of Sesostris I and
should be regarded as one of the propagandistic elements of the
text.

ranks. He is vengeful when he cracks skulls, and no one stands up near him. He steps wide when he annihilates the fugitive. There is no chance for the one who shows his back to him. He is upright of heart at the moment of contact. He comes again and does not show his back. He is stalwart of heart when he sees a crowd, and he does not

60 allow cowardice around him. / He is eager when he falls upon the easterners, and he is joyful when he plunders the bow-people. As soon as he takes up his shield, he strikes down. He need not repeat the act of killing, for there is no one who can deflect his arrow nor one who can draw his bow. The bowmen retreat before him as if before the might of a great goddess. He fights having forseen the outcome, and he takes no care for the remnants. But he is well-favored and very gentle; through love he takes. His city desires him more than herself, and his people rejoice because of him more than for their gods. Now that he is king, husbands and wives rejoice because of him. While still in the egg, he conquered, and his face was set to it from birth. Those who were born with him have become

70 enriched, / for he is one whom the gods have given. How joyful is this land now that he has reigned. He is one to extend borders. He shall vanquish the southlands, and he will not even have to think about the northlands, for he was made to smite the Asiatics and walk over the sand-crossers. Write to him, and let him know your name. Do not cast a spell against his Majesty, for he will not fail to do good to a foreign land which is loyal to him.

Sinuhe in Palestine

And he said to me: Indeed, Egypt is fortunate, now that she knows that he flourishes. You are here, and you shall

be with me, and what I shall do for you will be good. He placed me in front of his children, and he married me to (literally, moored me to) his eldest daughter. He allowed
80 me to pick from his country / the choicest part of what he owned on his border with another country.

It was a wonderful land called Yaa. There were cultivated figs in it and grapes, and more wine than water. Its honey was abundant, and its olive trees numerous. On its trees were all varieties of fruit. There were emmer corn and barley, and there was no end to all varieties of cattle. That which fell to my lot from what came through love of me was great. He set me up as chief of a tribe of the finest in his land. I obtained rations as daily disbursements and wine as a daily requirement, cooked meat and roasted
90 birds, beside the desert game. / They hunted for me and they set (food) down before me, in addition to the catch of my hunting dogs. They made for me many sweet things and milk boiled in every fashion. I spent many years while my offspring became strong men, each man managing his tribe.

The messenger who came north and went south to the capital stayed with me, and I made all Egyptians stay. I gave water to the thirsty man, and I put the wanderer back on the road. I rescued the man who was robbed. When the Asiatics began to stir and to oppose the authority of the chiefs of the foreign lands, I counseled their
100 marches. This ruler /of Retenu had me spend many years as an officer of his troops. As to any land which I left, when I had made my attack it was driven off from its cultivation and wells. I had plundered its cattle and brought back its inhabitants, and their produce was taken. I killed the people in it by my strong arm, my bow, my maneuvers, and my efficient advice. It went well with me

in his favor, for he loved me and he recognized my bravery. He placed me at the head of his offspring when he saw my arms grow so strong.

The Combat

110   There came a strong man of Retenu to challenge me / at my tent.[12] He was a champion without equal, and he had defeated all of Retenu. He said that he would fight with me, for he thought to ruin me. He planned to take off my cattle, at the urging of his tribe. But that chief talked with me, and I said: I do not know him. I am not his friend that I could stride about in his camp. Had it ever happened that I opened his door, or have I scaled his walls? He is jealous, for he sees me carrying out your affairs. I am like a bull of a grazing herd in the midst of
120   another herd. The bull of the kine attacks him, / but the (Egyptian) bull prevails against him. Is a subject loved when he acts the master? There is no foreign bowman who is an ally of a Delta man. What is it that can join a papyrus plant to a rock? Does a bull wish to fight? Then a champion bull will wish to show his back through fear of one who might equal him. But if he wishes to fight, let him say so. Does God not know what is predicted for him, knowing how it is?

    I spent the night stretching my bow and I shot my arrows. I gave play to my dagger, and I fixed up my
130   weapons. When daybreak came, Retenu had come. / It had urged on its tribes, and it had collected the lands of

12. The following account of the fight with the champion of Retenu has frequently been compared to the David and Goliath duel, for which it may have served as a literary prototype. See G. Lanczkowski, in *MDIK* 16 (1958): 214–18.

both its halves. It had intended this combat. He (the strong man) came out to me where I was waiting, and I placed myself near him. Every heart burned for me, men and women yelled. Every heart was sick for me, saying: Is there another strong man who could fight him? He [took up] his shield, his axe, and his armful of javelins. But after I had come away from his weapons, I made his remaining arrows pass by me, as one was not close enough to the other. Then he let out a yell, for he thought to ruin me, and he approached me. I shot him, my arrow fixed in

140 his neck. He shouted and fell upon his nose. / I felled him with my axe. I yelled my war cry over his back. Every Asiatic yelped. I gave praise to Montu,[13] and his people mourned for him. This ruler, Amusinenshi, took me in his arms, and he kissed me in my clasp. I brought away his possessions, I seized his cattle. What he had thought to do to me I did to him. I took away what was in his tent. I uncovered his camp, and it was abundant for me therein. I became rich in treasure, a great proprietor of cattle.

Gods acts in such a way to be merciful to one whom he had blamed, one whom He causes to go astray to another

150 land. For today His heart is appeased. A fugitive fled / from his haunts, but my renown is in the capital. A wanderer wandered through hunger, but I give bread to my neighbor. Through nakedness a man departed from his land, but I have white clothes and fine linen. A man hurried for lack of something to send, but I have many servants. My house is fine, and my dwelling place is wide. The thought of me is in the palace.

13. The Egyptian god particularly associated with battle prowess.

Sinuhe wishes to return to Egypt

O God, whoever you are, who decreed this flight, may you be merciful and may you set me in the capital. Perhaps you will let me see the place where my desire lives. What can be more important than joining my dead body 160 to the land where / I was born? Come, help me! What has come to pass so far has been good. God has given me satisfaction. May He act similarly to better the end of one whom He had made miserable and be concerned about one whom He had shunted off to live in a foreign land. Today He is merciful, and He hearkens to the prayer of a man far off. May He change my region whence I roamed the earth for Him to the place from which He brought me.

The King of Egypt is merciful to me, and I live on his bounty. May I greet the mistress of the land who is in his palace, and may I attend to the errands of her children. My body will be youthful again. Old age has come down on me and feebleness has hurried upon me. My eyes are 170 heavy, and my arms are immobile. / My feet stumble, and my senses are exhausted. I am ready for passing on, when they shall send me to the cities of eternity. But may I still serve the Mistress-of-All that she may say something good for me to her children. May she pass eternity above me.[14]

Now this report was made to His Majesty, the King of Upper and Lower Egypt, Kheperkare,[15] who will be judged right, concerning this state in which I was. His Majesty sent to me with provisions of the royal bounty.

14. It seems that the queen is here identified with the sky goddess; her image, surrounded with stars, is generally placed on the underside of the coffin or sarcophagus lid above the body.
15. Sesostris I.

He rejoiced the heart of this servant as might be done for
a ruler of a foreign land. And the king's children who
were in his palace had me hear their messages.

The Royal Edict

Copy of the decree brought to this servant regarding
his being brought back to Egypt: The Horus Life of
Births, the Two Ladies Life of Births, the King of Upper
180 and Lower Egypt, Kheperkare, Son of Re / Sesostris,
living forever. The king orders Sinuhe: This decree of
the king is brought to you to tell you that you have
traversed the foreign countries and have come forth from
Kedem to Retenu. By your heart's counsel to you, land
has given you to land. What have you done that one
should act against you? You have not blasphemed that one
should reprove your words. You have not spoken in the
council of the elders that one should restrain your speech.
This idea, it took over your senses, although there was
nothing in my mind against you. This heaven of yours,
which is in the palace, she is well and she flourishes today
as in her former state in the kingship of the land, with her
children in the audience hall. You shall pile up the trea-
sures which they give you, and you shall live off their
bounty. When you have come to Egypt, you shall see the
capital in which you were born. You shall kiss the ground
at the Great Double Gate, and you shall associate with the
190 Companions. Today / old age has begun for you, and
potency has left you. You have thought about the day of
burial, the passing over to an honored state. The night
will be appointed for you with oils and poultices from the
arms of Tayet (goddess of weaving). A procession will be

made for you on the day of interment, the anthropoid sarcophagus (overlaid) with gold leaf, the head with lapis lazuli, and the sky above you as you are placed in the outer coffin and dragged by teams of oxen preceded by singers. The dance of the Muu will be performed at your tomb, and the necessary offerings will be invoked for you. They will slaughter at the entrance of your tomb chapel, its pillars to be set up in limestone as is done for the royal children. You shall not die in a foreign land, and Asiatics will not escort you. You shall not be placed in a ram's skin as they make your grave. All of this is too much for one who has roamed the earth. Take thought for your dead body and return.

Sinuhe's Reaction and his Reply

200   When this decree reached me, I was standing / among my tribe. As it was read out to me, I placed myself upon my belly and I touched the earth. I spread it out over my chest. Then I went about my encampment rejoicing and saying: How could such a thing be done for a servant whose senses led him astray to the land of the barbarians? Indeed, (your) benevolence is excellent, O you who have saved me from Death. Your Ka will allow me to spend the end of my life with my body in the capital.

Copy of the reply to this decree. The servant of the palace Sinuhe says: In peace, in peace. This flight which this servant did in his ignorance is well known by your Ka, O good God, Lord of the Two Lands, whom Re loves and whom Montu, Lord of Thebes, favors, as well as Amun, Lord of the Thrones of the Two Lands, Sobk-Re, Lord of Sumenu, Horus, Hathor, Atum and his Ennead,

Sopdu, Neferbau, Semseru, Horus the Easterner, the Mistress of Yemet, may she enfold your head, the council upon the flood waters, Min-Horus in the midst of the desert lands, Wereret, the Mistress of / Punt, Nut, Haoreis-Re, and the gods who are the Lords of the Beloved Land and the Islands of the Sea.[16] They give life and prosperity to your nostrils; they grant you their bounty. They give you eternity without end and everlastingness without limit. Fear of you is repeated in the lowlands and in the highlands, for you have conquered all that the sun disk encircles. Such is the prayer of this servant to his lord who has rescued him from the West.

Lord of perception, who perceives the people, may he perceive in the Majesty of the palace that this servant was afraid to speak. It is a heavy matter to repeat. The great God, equal of Re, knows the mind of one who has worked for him ˹of his own accord˺. For this servant is in the hands of someone who takes thought for him; I am set in his guidance. Your Majesty is the conquering Horus; your arms prevail over all lands. May now Your Majesty command that there be brought Meki from Kedem, / Khentiuwash from out of Keshu, and Menus, those who set your authority over the lands of the Fenkhu.[17] They are rulers whose names are worthy and who have been brought up in your love. Not to mention Retenu, for it belongs to you even as your dogs. This flight which your servant made, it was not premeditated. It was not in my mind. I did not prepare it. I cannot say what separated me from

16. The gods who make up this list are representative of the different parts of Egypt and the neighboring lands. See J. Yoyotte, in *Kêmi* 17 (1964): 69–73.
17. These three foreign rulers are thus commended by Sinuhe to the king.

my place. It was like a dream: as when a Delta man sees himself in Aswan or a man of the marshlands in Nubia. Yet I was not afraid. No one chased me. I did not hear a word of censure. No one heard my name in the mouth of the town crier. Except that my body cringed, my feet hastened, and my senses overwhelmed me, with the God

230 who decreed this flight / drawing me on. I am not stubborn ⌜in advance⌝. A man is modest when his homeland is known, for Re has placed the fear of you throughout the land and the dread of you in every foreign land. Whether I am in the capital or in this place, yours is everything which is covered by this horizon. The sun disk rises at your bidding, and the water of the river is drunk if you wish. The air of the heavens is breathed if you speak. Now that this servant has been sent for, this servant will hand over (his property) to his children, whom he has brought up in this place. May Your Majesty act as he wishes, for one lives by the air which you give. Re, Horus, and Hathor love your noble nostrils; Montu, Lord of Thebes, wishes that they live forever.

Sinuhe's Return

I was allowed to spend a day in Yaa to transfer my goods to my children. My eldest son was in charge of my

240 tribe. / My tribe and all my possessions were in his hands, as well as all my serfs, my cattle, my fruit, and all my productive trees. This servant proceeded south. I tarried at the Ways of Horus.[18] The commander in charge of the patrol there sent a message to the capital to give them notice. His Majesty had them send a capable overseer of

18. A frontier station on the border of Egypt.

field laborers of the royal estate and with him ships laden
with presents of the royal bounty for the Asiatics who had
come with me to lead me to the Ways of Horus. I called
each one of them by name. I started out and raised sail.
Each servant was at his task. (Dough) was kneaded and
strained (for beer) beside me until I reached the wharf of
Itjtowy.[19]

Sinuhe at the Palace

When dawn came and it was morning, I was summoned.
Ten men came and ten men went to usher me to the
palace. I touched my forehead to the ground between the
250 sphinxes. / The royal children waited in the gateway to
meet me. The Companions who showed me into the pillared court set me on the way to the reception hall. I
found His Majesty upon the Great Throne set in a recess
(paneled) with fine gold. As I was stretched out on my
belly, I lost consciousness in his presence. This God addressed me in a friendly way, and I was like a man caught
by nightfall. My soul fled and my body shook. My heart
was not in my body: I could not tell life from death.
His Majesty said to one of these Companions: Lift him
up and let him speak to me. And His Majesty said: See,
you have returned, now that you have roamed the foreign
lands. Exile has ravaged you; you have grown old. Old
age has caught up with you. The burial of your body is
no small matter, for now you will not be escorted by the
260 bowmen. Do not creep any more. You did not speak /
when your name was called out. I feared punishment, and
I answered with a timorous answer: What has my lord

19. The landing place of the capital, the residence city of the king.

said to me? If I try to answer, there is no shortcoming on my part toward God. Fear is in my body, like that which brought to pass the fated flight. I am in your presence. Life belongs to you. May Your Majesty do as he wishes.

The royal children were then brought in, and His Majesty said to the queen: Here is Sinuhe, who has returned as an Asiatic whom the bedouin have raised. She let out a cry, and the royal children shouted all together. They said before His Majesty: It is not really he, O Sovereign, my lord. His Majesty said: It is he indeed. Then they brought their *menyat*-necklaces, their rattles, and their *sistra* with them, and they offered them to His 270 Majesty. May your arms reach out / to something nice, O enduring king, to the ornaments of the Lady of Heaven. May the Golden One give life to your nostrils, and may the Lady of the Stars be joined to you. The crown of Upper Egypt will go northward, and the crown of Lower Egypt will go southward that they may unite and come together at the word of Your Majesty, and the cobra goddess Wadjet will be placed on your forehead. As you have kept your subjects from evil, so may Re, Lord of the Lands, be compassionate toward you. Hail to you. And also to the Lady of All. Turn aside your horn, set down your arrow. Give breath to the breathless. Give us this happy reward, this bedouin chief Simehyet,[20] the bowman born in Egypt. It was through fear of you that he took flight and through dread of you that he left the land. Yet there is no one whose face turns white at the sight of your face. The eye which looks at you will not be afraid. His 280 Majesty said: He shall not fear, / he shall not be afraid.

20. Si-mehyet, "son of the northwind," is a playful variant on Si-nuhe, "son of the sycamore."

He shall be a Companion among the nobles and he shall
be placed in the midst of the courtiers. Proceed to the
audience hall to wait upon him.

Sinuhe Reinstated

When I came from the audience hall, the royal children
gave me their hands, and we went to the Great Double
Gate. I was assigned to the house of a king's son. Fine
things were in it, a cooling room in it, and representations
of the horizon.[21] Valuables of the treasury were in it,
vestments of royal linen were in every apartment, and
first-grade myrrh of the king and the courtiers whom he
290 loves. / Every domestic servant was about his prescribed
task. Years were caused to pass from my body. I was dip-
ilated, and my hair was combed out. A load was given
to the desert, and clothes to the sand-dwellers. I was outfitted with fine linen and rubbed with the finest oil. I
passed the night on a bed. I gave the sand to those who
live on it and wood oil to those who rub themselves with
it. A house of a ⌜plantation owner⌝, which had belonged
to a Companion, was given to me. Many craftsmen had
built it, and all its trees were planted anew. Meals were
brought from the palace three and four times a day, in
addition to what the royal children gave. There was not
300 a moment of interruption. / A pyramid of stone was built
for me in the midst of the pyramids. The overseer of
stonecutters of the pyramids marked out its ground plan.
The master draftsman sketched in it, and the master sculp-
tors carved in it. The overseers of works who were in the
necropolis gave it their attention. Care was taken to supply

21. Perhaps wall frescoes.

all the equipment which is placed in a tomb chamber. Ka-servants were assigned to me, and an endowed estate was settled on me with fields attached, at my mooring place, as is done for a Companion of the first order. My statue was overlaid with gold leaf, its apron in electrum. His Majesty ordered it to be done. There was no commoner for whom the like had ever been done. So I

310 remained in / the favor of the king until the day of mooring came.

Its beginning has come to its end, as it has been found in writing.

(The traditional colophon marks the end of the story.)

PART 2

Late Egyptian Stories

The Quarrel of Apophis and Seknenre

For nearly a century Asiatic Hyksos rulers and their vassals had dominated Egypt, controlling the Delta and Middle Egypt. This Ramesside story of the origins of the conflict between Thebes in the south and the Hyksos King Apophis must be evaluated critically against documents contemporaneous with the war of the expulsion of the Hyksos. For in later times there was a tendency to exaggerate the harshness of Hyksos domination and their impiety toward the gods of the Egyptian pantheon other than Seth, whom the Hyksos may have identified with Baal. (See John Van Seters, The Hyksos *[New Haven: Yale University Press, 1966], chap. 12. This story may contain a propagandistic element designed to enhance the prestige of the Theban god Amon-Re; see Jürgen von Beckerath,* Untersuchungen zur politschen Geschichte der zweiten Zwischenzeit in Ägypten *[Glückstadt: J. J. Augustin, 1965], p. 110.) In the Ramesside historical romance King Apophis, seeking to agitate the Theban ruler Seknenre, presents him with a fantastic complaint. It is possible that the lost continuation of the story would have presented more substantive immediate causes for the war that ensued. Although King Seknenre's mummy shows that he met with a violent death, it is probable that he did not die in battle against the Hyksos, as is frequently maintained, for an inscription of Seknenre's son and successor Kamose indicates that the war of the expulsion was initiated by Kamose. This war, continued by Kamose's brother Ahmose, paved the way for the formation of the Egyptian empire in Dynasty 18.*

There are many lacunae in the text, and many of the restorations are conjectural. Bibliographical references will be found in Lefebvre, Romans et contes, *p. 133; Wilson, in* ANET, *p. 231; and Erman,* The Ancient Egyptians, *p. xxxiii. Donald B. Redford, in* Orientalia *39 (1970): 1–51, reconsiders the problem of the tradition of the Hyksos presence in Egypt and comments upon this story in his discussion.*

E. F. W.

1,1   It once happened that the land of Egypt was in misery, for there was no Lord, l.p.h., ⟨as⟩ (sole) king. A day came to pass[1] when King Seknenre, l.p.h., was (still only) Ruler, l.p.h., of the Southern City.[2] Misery was in the town of ⌈the Asiatics⌉,[3] for Prince Apophis, l.p.h., was in Avaris, and the entire land paid tribute to him, delivering their taxes, (and) even the north bringing every (sort of) good produce of the Delta.

    So King Apophis, l.p.h., adopted Seth for himself as lord, and he refused to serve any god that was in the entire land ex[cept] Seth. He built a temple of fine workmanship for eternity next to the House of [King Apo]phis, l.p.h., and he appeared [at break of] day in order to sacrifice . . . daily to Seth, while the officials [of the palace], l.p.h., carried garlands, ⌈exactly⌉ as is practiced ⟨in⟩ the temple of Pre-Harakhti.

1,5   Now as for / King A[pophis], l.p.h., it was his wish to s[end] an inflamatory message ⟨to⟩ King Seknenre, [l.p.h., the] Prince of the Southern City. And a[fter] many days following this, King [Apophis, l.p.h.], then had [the high official]s of his [⌈palace⌉] summoned, [and he proposed to them that a messenger should be] sent [to the Prince

---

1. See Wolfhart Westendorf, in *ZÄS* 79 (1954): 65–67. An alternative is to take *ḥrw* as a writing of *ḥꜣw* "time," and translate, "There was no Lord, l.p.h., ⟨as⟩ king of the time. It came to pass . . ."

2. I.e. Thebes.

3. The generally accepted emendation. The "town of the Asiatics" would thus be a designation of the Hyksos capital Avaris, whose location in the eastern Delta is still disputed. Von Beckerath, in *Untersuchungen*, pp. 151–57, argues for its location some distance east of Kantir; see also the discussion of Van Seters, *Hyksos*, chap. 9, where its location at Khatana-Kantir is suggested. However, the emendation to "town of the Asiatics" is by no means certain. Another possibility might be "town of Re-⟨At⟩um," referring to Heliopolis, the city of the sun-god, see Redford, in *Orientalia* 39:50.

of the Southern City with] a complaint . . . [concerning the] river, [but he was unable to compose it himself. Thereupon his] scribes and wise men . . . and ⌜high⌝ officials [said: O so]vereign, [our lord, demand that there be a withdrawal from the] canal of hippopotamuses [which lies at the east of the City⁴ because] they don't let [sleep come ⌜to us⌝ either in the daytime or at ni]ght, [for the noise of them is ⟨in⟩ our citizens' ear(s). And King Apophis, l.p.h., answered them saying: I shall send] to the Prince of the [Southern Ci]ty . . . ⌜command⌝

2,1 . . . [that we may assess the power of the god who is] / with him as protector. He does not rely upon any god that is in the [entire land] except Amon-Re, King of the Gods.

Now after many days following this, King Apophis, l.p.h., then sent to the Prince of the Southern City ⟨with⟩ the complaint that his scribes and wise men had concocted for him. And when the messenger of King [A]pophis, l.p.h., reached the Prince of the Southern City, he was then taken into the presence of the Prince of the Southern City. Then One⁵ said to the messenger of King Apophis, l.p.h.: Why have you been sent to the Southern City? Wherefore have you come journeying here?⁶ The mes-

2,5 senger then / told him: It is King Apophis, l.p.h., who has sent ⟨me⟩ to you in order to say, "Let there be a w[ith-drawa]l from⁷ the canal of hippopotamuses which lies at the east of the City, because they don't let sleep come

---

4. On *ḥnt*, "canal," see Hans Goedicke, in *ZÄS* 88 (1963): 88–97. Goedicke believes that this canal lay not to the east of Thebes but to the east of Avaris, yet an admittedly much restored passage in 2:8, does not appear to support Goedicke's view.

5. I.e. Seknenre.

6. See E. F. Wente, in *JNES* 28 (1969): 5. Sarah Groll, in *JNES* 28: 190, translates, "Why have you undertaken these journeys?"

7. Lit. "Let one withdraw from," possibly a means of expressing that activity at the canal should be terminated.

to me either in the daytime or at night," for the noise of them is ‹in› his citizens' ear(s).

Then the Prince of the Southern City became stupefied for so long a while that he became unable to render [a reply] to the messenger of King Apophis, l.p.h. Finally the Prince of the Southern City said to him: Is it ⌜through⌝ this (remark) that your Lord, l.p.h., would investigate matters regarding [8] [the canal of hippopotamuses which lies at t]he east of the Southern City? Then the messenger [said to him: Effectuate the m]atters for which he sent me. [Then the Prince of the Southern City caused] th[e messenger of King Apophis, l.p.h.], to be taken care of [with] good [thing]s: meat, cakes, . . . [The Prince of the Southern City said to him: Go and tell] your [lord], "As for whatever you will tell him, he [9] will do it," so you shall tell [him] . . . [Then the messenger of King] Apophis, l.p.h., hastened to journey to 3,1 where / his Lord, l.p.h., was.

So the Prince of the Southern City had his high officials summoned, as well as every ranking soldier of his, and he repeated to them every issue concerning which King Apophis, l.p.h., had sent to him. Then they were uniformly silent for a long while, without being able to answer him, be it good or bad.

Then King Apophis, l.p.h., sent to . . .

(The remainder of the story is lost.)

8. Or simply, "hear words concerning."
9. The text has "I," referring to Seknenre. The meaning of the passage is that whatever Apophis will tell his messenger or Seknenre, Seknenre will do it. Such confusion of pronouns is especially common in Late Egyptian.

The Capture of Joppa

The great pharaoh Menkheperre Thutmose III of Dynasty 18 had probably secured the vassalage of the Prince of Joppa during his initial campaign into Syro-Palestine. Subsequently Joppa, modern Jaffa, on the coast of southern Palestine, rebelled against Egyptian domination. The story The Capture of Joppa concerns the subjugation of the rebellious town by Djehuty, a prominent general and garrison commander under Thutmose III. Although the beginning of this fantastic story is lost, it can be surmised that the two contenders had met outside the town unarmed to discuss the situation. With the soldiers reduced to drunkenness, Djehuty offers to deliver himself and his family to the Prince of Joppa as part of his stratagem for recapturing Joppa. The introduction of baskets concealing soldiers into the town is reminiscent of the story of the Trojan horse and the tale of Ali Baba and his forty thieves. There is another fragmentary Ramesside story about Thutmose III's military activity published by Giuseppe Botti, "A Fragment of the Story of a Military Expedition of Tuthmosis III to Syria," JEA 41 (1955): 64–71.

For literature and bibliography pertaining to this story the reader may consult Lefebvre, Romans et contes, pp. 125–27; Erman, The Ancient Egyptians, p. xxxiii; Wilson, in ANET, p. 22; and the recent translation and discussion by Hans Goedicke, "The Capture of Joppa," Chronique d' Egypte, 43 (1968), pp. 219–33. Goedicke speculates that the episode involving the baton, or mace, of Thutmose III reflects a possible triple play of words on the root ʿwn.

E. F. W.

1,1   . . . 220 + Maryan-warriors[1] . . . them ⸢like⸣ baskets . . . [replied] to Djehuty: Let him be [given] 100 +

1. These, the elite Indo-Aryan chariot-warriors associated with the Hurrian movement into Syria-Palestine, apparently lent their sup-

[soldiers] [2] ⟨from⟩ the garrison of Pharaoh, l.p.h. . . .
. . . their faces.[3]

Now after an hour they were drunk, and Djehuty said
to [the Rebel of Joppa: I shall deliver] myself along with
(my) wife and children ⟨unto⟩ your town for yourself
1,5 personally.[4] Let the / gro[oms] [5] drive in [the chariot-
horses a]nd have fodder [giv]en to them; otherwise an
Apir may pass by [and steal one of] them.[6] So the
chariot-horses were secured and given fodder. And . . .
[ᵣthe great baton of¹] King Menkheperre, l.p.h., and
someone came and made report to Djehuty.

Now [when the Rebel of Jo]ppa said to Djehuty: It is
my wish to see the great baton of King Menkheperre,
l.p.h. [There is a woman here] by the name of Tiutnofre.[7]
By the Ka of King Menkheperre, l.p.h., she shall be yours
1,10 today / [if you will be so] kind as to bring it ⟨to⟩ me;
he acquiesced and brought the baton of King Menkheperre,
l.[p.h., concealed in] his apron.[8] And he stood straight up

port to the Prince of Joppa. On these warriors, see Van Seters,
The Hyksos, pp. 184–87, and Wolfgang Helck, *Die Beziehungen
Ägyptens zu Vorderasien im 3. und 2. Jahrtausend v. Chr.* (Wiesbaden: Otto Harrassowitz, 1962), pp. 522 ff.
2. Restoring *wʿw,* though *ʿ𝑘w,* "loaves," is also a possibility.
3. Perhaps restore [*r*]-*ḫrw.sn,* "before them."
4. On the nuance of *n ḥʿw.k,* see Goedicke, *Chronique d'Egypte,*
43 (1968), p. 221, and Ostracon Deir el Medineh 207, 3 and 4.
5. Reading *mrỉ,* cf. Goedicke.
6. Assuming that here the term Apir is used to describe a
marauding adventurer without specific ethnic or political ties.
Goedicke, p. 222, believes that this Apir was a foreign mercenary
in the Egyptian army and renders the passage "Or else one of the
mercenaries may surpass [them for] their [weariness]." On the
term see Helck, pp. 526 ff.
7. Meaning: The beautiful one is yours.
8. See Jac. J. Janssen, in *JEA* 52 (1966): 85, on *sḏy,* "apron." Presumably the king's baton accompanied the division of the army
under Djehuty's command and symbolized the king's presence in

and said: Look at me, O Rebel of [Joppa! Here is] King Menkheperre, l.p.h., the fierce lion, Sakhmet's son, to whom Amon has given his [strength. And he] lifted his hand and smote upon the Rebel of Joppa's temple so that

2,1 he fell / [sprawling] before him. And he put him in manacles . . . the leather. And he [said]: "⌐Let⌐ [there be brought to me] a clamp of copper. [We shall make a] ⌐restraint⌐ for this Rebel of Joppa. So the clamp of copper of four *nemset*-weight was attached to his feet.

And he caused the two hundred baskets, which he had had fabricated, to be brought and caused two hundred soldiers

2,5 to descend / into them. And their arms were filled ‹with› ropes and manacles, and they were sealed shut. And they were supplied with their sandals along with their carrying-poles ⌐and . . .⌐,[9] and every fine soldier was assigned to carry them, totaling five hundred men. They were told: As soon as you enter the town, you shall release your companions and seize hold of all persons who are in the

2,10 town and put them in rope-bonds / straightaway.

And someone came out to tell the charioteer of the Rebel of Joppa: Thus says your lord, "Go tell your mistress, 'Be of good cheer! It is ‹to› us that Seth has delivered[10] Djehuty along with his wife and his children. See, (here are) the first fruits of their servitude,' so ‹you› shall say to her regarding those two hundred baskets,"

---

military undertakings in which he did not actually take part. One might compare the presence of the standard of Amon, endowed with full divine force, that accompanied pharaoh on his campaigns.

9. The word *itll*, of undetermined meaning, may also have stood in a genitival relationship with *mꜣwḏ*, "carrying-poles."

10. Normally this second tense form is future, but for its use as a past tense, see Jac. J. Janssen, *Two Ancient Egyptian Ship's Logs* (Leiden: E. J. Brill, 1961), p. 29, n. 4, and also Charles F. Nims, in *JEA* 54 (1968): 162, n. 2.

which were (actually) filled with men and manacles and ropes.

Then he went in advance of them in order to impart the good news to his mistress saying: We have captured Djehuty! And the defenses of the town were opened up 3,1 for the arrival of the soldiers, / and they entered the town [and] released their companions. And they captured [the] townspeople, both young and old, and put them in rope-bonds and manacles straightaway. So the energetic arm of Pharaoh, l.p.h., captured the town.

At nightime Djehuty sent to Egypt to King Men-kheperre, l.p.h., his lord, saying: Be of good cheer! Amon, your good father, has delivered to you the Rebel of 3,10 [Jo]ppa and all his people as well as his / town. Send men to take them away captive that you may fill the Estate of your father Amon-Re, King of the Gods, with male and female slaves, who have fallen beneath your feet forever and ever.

Thus it concludes happily.

The Tale of the Doomed Prince

Although written in the simple and rather monotonous style characteristic of stories of the New Kingdom, this tale, as far as it is preserved, captures the reader's interest in its narration of the adventures of a young Egyptian crown prince. Like The Story of Sinuhe, the theme is that of the Egyptian abroad, but in this later story little attention is given to providing local color. Rather the emphasis is upon plot. The reader, who has initially been informed of the boy's true identity and the three possible fates that may ultimately prevail over him, seeks to learn how the youth will finally reveal his royal background to the foreigners among whom he lives and to see how Fate operates.

As J. Sainte Fare Garnot has pointed out (in Journal de Psychologie Normale et Pathologique 43 [Paris, 1950]: 230–38, and in "Colloque de Strasbourg, 17–19 mai 1962," Les Sagesses du Proche-Orient ancien [Paris, 1963], p. 120) this story is illustrative of a certain degree of flexibility in the Egyptian concept of predestination. Unfortunately, the conclusion of the tale is lost to us, so that the reader's whetted appetite remains unsatisfied. Drawing attention to a parallel in Diodorus Siculus, Georges Posener (in JEA 39 [1953]: 107) has suggested a happy ending to the story and indicated as well the mythological connotations of certain of the episodes. In addition to the bibliographical references in Lefebvre, Romans et contes, pp. 117–18, and Erman, The Ancient Egyptians, p. xxxii, the reader may wish to consult Jaroslav Černý, in ASAE 41 (1942): 336–38, and Girgis Mattha, in ASAE 51 (1951): 269–72.

E.F.W.

4,1   Once upon a time there was a king, so the story goes, to whom no son had ever been born. [But when His Majesty, l.p.h., re]quested a son for himself from the gods of his time, they ordered a birth to be granted him, and he went to bed with his wife in the night. Now when she [had become] pregnant and had completed the months of child-bearing, a son was thus born.

Presently the Hathors[1] came to determine a fate for him and said: He shall die through a crocodile, or a snake, or even a dog. Thus the people who were at the boy's side 4,5 heard and then reported it / to His Majesty, l.p.h. Thereupon His Majesty, l.p.h. became very much saddened. Then His Majesty, l.p.h., had [a house] of stone built [for him] upon the desert, supplied with personnel and with every good thing of the palace, l.p.h., so that the boy did not (need to) venture outside.

Now after the boy had grown older, he went up onto his roof and espied a greyhound following a grownup who was walking along the road. He said to his servant, who was beside him: What is it that is walking behind the grownup who is coming along [the] road? And he told him: It is a greyhound. And the boy told him: Have one like it obtained for me. Thereupon the servant went and 4,10 reported it / to His Majesty, l.p.h. Then His Majesty, l.p.h., said, "Let a young springer be taken to him [because of] his heart's ⌐disquiet⌐." And so someone ⟨caused⟩ the greyhound to be taken to him.

Now after days had elapsed upon this, the boy matured in all his body, and he sent to his father saying: What will the outcome be while I am dwelling here? For look, I am committed to Fate. Let me be released so that I may act according to my desire until God does what is his will.

1. According to popular religious belief in the New Kingdom, there were seven such Hathor goddesses, who determined the fate of a child at birth; see below, The Tale of the Two Brothers, 9, 8–9.

5,1 Then a chariot was yoked for him, equipped [with] / all sorts of weapons, and [a servant was put in] his following for an escort. He was ferried over to the eastern tract[2] and told: Now you may set out as you wish, [while] his greyhound was with him. He went northward over the desert, following his inclination and living on every sort of desert game.

Presently he reached the Prince of Nahrin.[3] Now none had been born to the Prince of Nahrin except a ⌐marriageable⌐ daughter. There had been built for her a house 5,5 whose window / was seventy cubits distant from the ground, and he sent for all the sons of all the princes of the land of Khor[4] and told them: As for the one who will reach the window of my daughter, she shall be a wife for him.

Now after many days had elapsed upon this and while they were (engaged) in their daily practice, presently the boy passed by them. They took the boy to their house, cleansed him, gave fodder to his team, did every sort of thing for the boy, salving him and bandaging his feet, 5,10 and / gave food to his escort. They said to him by way of conversation: Where have you come from, you handsome lad? He told them: I am the son of a chariot warrior of the land of Egypt. My mother died, and my father took for himself another wife, a ⌐stepmother⌐. She came to despise me, and [I] left her presence in flight. And they embraced him and kissed him over [all his] body.

[Now after many days had elapsed upon] this, he said

2. The desert edge forming the eastern margin of the Delta.
3. The land of the Mitannian kingdom, located east of the bend of the Euphrates river. Since this kingdom fell toward the end of Dynasty 18, the action of the story takes place at a time in this dynasty when Syrian princes owed their allegiance to Mitanni.
4. Here synonymous with Syria.

to the boys: What is this that you have become engaged in, [boys? And they told him: It has been three] full
6,1   [month]s till now that we have spent / time here [leaping up, for the one who] will reach [the] window of the daughter of the Prince of Nahrin, [he will] give her to him for [a wife. He] said to them: If I could but enchant my feet,[5] I would proceed to leap up in your company. They proceeded to leap up according to their daily practice, and the boy stood by afar off observing, while the eyes of the daughter of the Prince of Nahrin were upon him.

6,5   Now after (some while) had elapsed / upon this, the boy came in order to leap up along with the children of the princes. He leapt up and reached the window of the daughter of the Prince of Nahrin. And she kissed him and embraced him over all his body. Then someone went in order to impart the news to her father and told him: Somebody has reached the window of your daughter. Then the prince inquired about him saying: The son of which of the princes is he? And he was told: He is a chariot warrior's son. It was from his ⌜step⌝mother's presence that he came in flight from the land of Egypt.
6,10   Thereupon / the Prince of Nahrin became very much angered. He said: Is it to the Egyptian fugitive that I should give my daughter? Send him back home.

And someone came to tell him: Please set out for the place whence you came. But the daughter seized hold of him and swore by God, saying: By Pre-Harakhti, if he is taken away from me, I shall neither eat nor drink but shall

5. Other scholars have rendered the clause by: "If my feet were not paining me so," but neither the traces nor the length of the lacuna support the restoration of the negative *bn*. The determinative of the verb favors "enchant."

die right away. Then the messenger went and reported to
her father every <word> that she had said, and her <father>
6,15 sent men to slay him / while he was still where he was.
But the daughter said to <them>: By Pre, if he is slain, as
soon as the sun sets, I shall be dead. I will not stay alive an
hour longer than he.

7,1 Then [someone went] to tell it to her father. And /
[her father had] the [lad] and his daughter [brought
be]fore him. The lad [came before] him, and his worth
impressed the prince. He embraced him and kissed him
over all his body, and he said to him: Tell me your background. See, you are (now) a son in my eyes. And he
told him: I am the son of a chariot warrior of the land of
Egypt. My mother died, and my father took for himself
another wife. She came to despise me, and I left her
presence in flight. Then he gave him his daughter for a
7,5 wife and / gave him house and fields as well as cattle and
all sorts of good things.

Now after (some while) had elapsed upon this, the lad
told his wife: I am committed to three fates: crocodile,
snake, and dog. Then she told him: Have the dog which
follows you killed. And he told her: ⌜What a demand⌝! I
will not let my dog, which I reared when it was a puppy,
be killed. And she came to guard her husband very care-
fully, not letting him venture outside alone.

Now from the day that the boy had come from the
land of Egypt in order to travel about, the crocodile had
7,10 been / his fate. . . . It appeared [from the midst of] the
lake [6] opposite him in the town in which the lad was

6. The word used for "lake" is *ym*, "sea," used also to refer to
the lake of Apamea; see Alan H. Gardiner, *Ancient Egyptian
Onomastica*, 3 vols. (Oxford: Oxford University Press, 1947),
1:167*–68*, and Helck, *Beziehungen*, p. 307.

(living) with [his wife]. However, a water spirit was in it. Neither would the water spirit let the crocodile emerge nor would the crocodile let the water spirit emerge to stroll about. As soon as the sun rose, [they] both [would be] engaged ⌐there⌐ in fighting each and every day for a period of three full months.

Now after some days had elapsed upon this, the lad sat down and made holiday in his house. And after the end of the evening breeze the lad lay down upon his bed, and 8,1 slumber took possession of his body. Then / his wife filled one j[ar with wine and filled] another jar with beer. Persently a [snake] emerged [from its] hole to bite the lad, but his wife was sitting beside him without going to sleep. The [jars were thus standing] accessible to the snake, and it imbibed and became intoxicated. Then it reclined and turned upside down. Thereupon [his wife caused] it to be [split] into segments with her hand-axe. 8,5 She then awoke her husband . . . / him, and she told him: See, your god has delivered one of your fates into your hand. He will guard [you henceforth. Then he] made an offering to P[re], praising him and extoling his power daily.

Now af[ther some days had elapsed upon this], the lad went out to stroll about for relaxation on his property. [His wife] did not go out [with him], but his dog was following him. Then his dog took a bite,[7] [saying: I am your fate. Thereupon] he fled before it. Presently he reached the lake and descended into the [water in flight 8,10 before the] / dog. And so the crocodile [seized h]im and

7. See Hildegard von Deines and Wolfhart Westendorf, *Wörter-buch der medizinischen Texte*, 2 vols. (Berlin: Akademie Verlag, 1961–62), 2:947. Other translators have rendered: "Then his dog took on the (power) of speech."

carried him off to where the water spirit (usually) was, [but he was not there.

The] crocodile told the lad: I am your fate who has been fashioned so as to come in pursuit of you, but [it is three full months] now that I have been fighting with the water spirit. See, I shall let you go. If ⌈my⌉ [opponent returns to engage me] to fight, [come] and lend me your support ⟨in order to⟩ kill the water spirit.[8] But if you see the . . . see the crocodile.

Now after dawn and the next day had come about, the [water spirit] returned . . .

(The remainder of the tale is lost.)

8. Or possibly rather: "and boast of me in order that ⟨I⟩ might kill the water-spirit."

The Tale of the Two Brothers

This story is based upon a myth that concerned two gods of the Cynopolite or Seventeenth Nome of Middle Egypt (see J. Yoyotte, Revue d'Egyptologie 9 [1952]: 157–59; J. Vandier, Le Papyrus Jumilhac [Paris: Centre National de la Recherche Scientifique, n.d.] pp. 45–46, 105–06; Gardiner, Ancient Egyptian Onomastica, 2:103*-06*, and his The Wilbour Papyrus [Oxford: Oxford University Press, 1948], 2:50–51) and may reflect an ancient conflict between two neighboring towns that became unified just as the two divine protagonists are reconciled. The elder brother, Anubis, is well known to us, mainly through his role as god of the dead and embalming, but the hero of the tale, Bata or Bet, is less often encountered in the documentation surviving from ancient Egypt. Bata seems originally to have been a pastoral god, whose cult image was in the form of a mummiform ram (the Old Kingdom evidence is discussed by Peter Seibert in Die Charakteristik *[Wiesbaden: Otto Harrassowitz, 1967], Pt. 1, pp. 59–67), but sources later than the Old Kingdom indicate that Bata was primarily a bull, one of the forms he adopts in the story. In a number of Old Kingdom tomb chapels Bata appears as the subject of a peasant's song, while from the late period the* Papyrus Jumilhac *provides a version of the myth in which Bata is identified with Seth, and Anubis is the hero.*

Egyptian religious texts, such as the Pyramid Texts, contain many mythological allusions, but the absence of a running mythological account is striking. One form in which mythical concepts were transmitted as an expression of the Egyptian faith was the popular story which might be told by a raconteur in the marketplace. It is obvious that The Tale of the Two Brothers is not an "official" version of the myth as transmitted through the ages; its vernacular language and such a matter as Bata's appointment to be Viceroy of Kush betray the adaptation of the myth to a changing world. Through the mythically based short story, the commoner in ancient

Egypt was able to participate in a form of religious education. It would be wrong to view knowledge about the gods as the prerogative of a select class of priests; the public may have been far more knowledgeable in religious affairs than has often been maintained. For bibliographical references to this story, see Lefebvre, Romans et contes, *pp. 140–42;* Erman, The Ancient Egyptians, *p. xxxii; F. Jesi, in* Aegyptus *42 (1962): 276–96; as well as works cited in the footnotes.*

E. F. W.

1,1 Once upon a time there were two brothers, so the story goes, having the same mother and the same father. Anubis was the name of the elder, and Bata was the name of the younger. Now as for Anubis, he [possessed] a house and had a wife, [and] his younger brother was (associated) with him after the manner of a son, so that it was he (that is, the elder brother) who made clothes for him while he (that is, the younger brother) followed behind his cattle to the fields, since it was he who had to plow. It was he who reaped for him, and it was [he] who did for him every chore that was in the fields. Indeed, his younger brother [was] a perfect man: there was none like him in ⟨the⟩ entire land, for a god's virility was in him.

  After many days following this,[1] his younger brother
1,5 / [was tending] his cattle according to his daily habit, and he would [leave work] for his house every evening laden

 1. This and similar expressions marking the passage of time occur throughout the story as conventionalized formulas that are not always to be taken literally. See Westendorf, in *ZÄS* 79 (1954): 65–68. In fact, this paragraph and the following one are not really part of the narrative proper but serve to provide the necessary background for the action of the story that begins following the statement about the increase in the size of the herd. See E. F. Wente, in *JNES* 21 (1962): 308–09.

[with] every vegetable of the fields, [with] milk, with wood, and [with] every [good produce of] the field; he would place them before his [elder brother] while he was sitting with his wife, and he would drink and eat, and [he would leave to spend the night in] his stable among his cattle [daily].

After dawn and the next day had come about, [he prepared foods] which were cooked, and he would place them before his elder brother, [and he would] give him bread for the fields, and he would drive his cattle to let them graze in the fields while he followed behind his cattle. [And th]ey [would] tell him: The herbage of such and such a place is good. And he would listen to all that 2,1 they said and take them to the place / with good herbage which they were desiring. The cattle that were in his charge became so exceedingly fine that they multiplied their offspring exceedingly.

At plowing time his [elder] brother told him: Have a team [of oxen] made ready for us for plowing, for the soil has emerged so that it is just right for tilling. Also, you are to come to the field with seed because we shall begin to cultivate tomorrow.[2] So he said to him. Then 2,5 his / younger brother made all preparations that his elder brother had told him to [make]. And after dawn [and the next] day had come about, they went to the field carrying their [seed] and began [to] plow with [their hearts] exceedingly pleased about their project as [they] began to work.

2. In ancient Egypt the sowing of the seed for cereal crops was performed simultaneously with the plowing of the soil. Hence the word *sk3* can mean "plow," "till," or "cultivate." See T. G. H. James, *The Ḥeḳanakhte Papers and Other Early Middle Kingdom Documents* (New York: The Metropolitan Museum of Art, 1962), p. 18.

After many [days] following this, while they were in the field, they needed seed. He sent his younger brother, saying: You shall go and fetch us seed from town. His younger brother found the wife of his elder brother seated plaiting her (hair).[3] He told her: Get up and give me seed / so that ⟨I⟩ may hurry off to the field, because it is for me that my elder brother is waiting. Don't cause a delay. Then she told him: Go, open the magazine and fetch for yourself what you want. Don't make ⟨me⟩ leave my hairdressing unfinished.

Then the youth entered his stable and fetched a large vessel, since it was his desire to take out a lot of seed. He loaded himself with barley and emmer and came out carrying it. Then she said to him: How much is it that is on your shoulder? And he told her: It is / three sacks of emmer and two sacks of barley, totaling five, that are on my shoulder. So he said to her. Then she [spoke with] him, saying: There is [great] virility in you, for I have been observing your exertions daily. For it was her desire to know him through sexual intimacy. She got up, seized hold of him, and told him: Come, let's spend for ourselves an hour sleeping (together). Such will be to your advantage, for I will make you fine clothes.

Then the youth became like an Upper Egyptian panther in ⌜harsh⌝ rage [4] over the wicked proposition that she had made to him, and she became exceedingly fearful. He argued with her, saying: Now look, you are (associated) with me after the manner of a mother, and your husband

3,1

3,5

---

3. As the text stands, the translation should be, "His younger brother found the wife of his elder brother while one was sitting plaiting her (hair)." However, according to the statement of Anubis's wife in 5,1, she was engaged alone in fixing her hair at the time Bata came to her. If her words are to be trusted on this point, a probable emendation of the text is: iw.s ḥms.tw ḥr nbd.s.
4. Reading perhaps m ḳnd ḏri.

is (associated) with me after the manner of a father, for the one who is older than I it is who has brought me up.

4,1 What means / this great offense which ⟨you⟩ have said to me? Don't say it to me again. But I shall tell it to no one, for I will not let it escape my mouth to anybody. He picked up his load and went off to the field. Then he reached his elder brother, and they began to work ⟨at⟩ their project.

Afterward, at evening time, his elder brother left work for his house, while his younger brother was (still) tending his cattle and [would] load himself with all produce
4,5 of the field and bring back his cattle / before him to let them spend the night ⟨in⟩ their stable, which was in town.[5] The wife of his elder brother was fearful ⟨on account of⟩ the proposition which she had made. She then fetched grease and fat and feigningly became like one who has been assaulted[6] with the intention of telling her husband: It's your younger brother who has assaulted ⟨me⟩. Her husband left work in the evening according to his daily habit. He reached his house and found his wife lying (down), feigning (to be) sick, so that she did not pour water upon his hand(s) according to his custom, nor had she prepared lighting for his arrival, so that his house was in darkness as she lay vomiting. Her husband said to her: Who has quarreled with you? Said she to him: No one has quarreled with me
5,1 except your / younger brother. When he returned to take out seed for you, he found me sitting alone and said to

5. This sentence, which is also not part of the narrative proper, serves to explain how Anubis would customarily return home before Bata, thus setting the stage for the episode at the barn door; see Wente, *JNES* 21: 309–10.
6. Or, "and became like one who has been criminally assaulted."

me, "Come, let's spend an hour sleeping (together). You shall put on your braids." So he said to me, but I refused to obey him. "Isn't it so that I am your mother, and that your brother is (associated) with you after the manner of a father?" So I said to him. And he became afraid and assaulted <me> to prevent me from making a disclosure to you. Now if you let him live, I'll take my life. See, as soon as he returns, ⌜don't . . . him⌝, because I denounce this wicked proposition which he would have carried out yesterday.[7]

5,5 Then his elder brother became / like an Upper Egyptian panther, and he had his spear sharpened and placed it in his hand. His elder <brother> stood behind the door <of> his stable in order to kill his younger brother upon his return in the evening to let his cattle enter the stable. Now when the sun set, he loaded himself <with> all (sorts of) vegetables of the fields, according to his daily habit, and returned. The lead cow entered the stable and said to its herdsman: Look, your elder brother is standing in wait for you bearing his spear to kill you. You shall depart from his presence. He understood what his lead cow had

6,1 said, and / the next one entered and said it also. He looked under the door of his stable and observed his elder

7. A restoration that would permit the translation, "See, as soon as he returns, you are to kill him, for I am suffering from this wicked proposition which he would carry out yesterday," has been suggested by Klaus Baer, in *JEA* 51 (1965): 139 and 142, but his restoration of *mtw.k* is questionable on paleographic grounds. Although Horus and Seth, 3,10, may be cited in support of rendering *šn* by "suffer from," the determinative of the verb in Two Brothers is different and favors the verb *šni*, "curse." The term *yesterday* is used because day was over at sunset, even though the Egyptian day began at dawn; see Siegfried Schott, *Altägyptische Festdaten* (Mainz: Akademie der Wissenschaften und der Literatur, 1950), p. 20.

brother's feet as he was standing behind the door with his
spear in his hand. He set his load onto the ground and
hastened to run off ⟨in⟩ flight, and his elder brother went
in pursuit of him, carrying his spear.

Then his younger brother prayed to Pre-Harakhti,
6,5 / saying: My good lord, it is you who distinguishes wrong
from right.[8] Thereupon Pre heard all his petitions, and
Pre caused a great (gulf of) water to come between him
and his elder ⟨brother⟩, infested with crocodiles, so that
one of them came to be on one side and the other on the
other (side). His elder brother struck twice upon (the
back of) his hand because he had failed to kill him. Then
his younger brother called to him on the (other) side,
saying: Wait there until dawn. As soon as the sun rises,
7,1 I shall / be judged with you in his presence, and he shall
deliver the culprit to the just, for I will never ⌈again⌉ be
present in your company nor will I be present in a place
where you are. I shall go to the Valley of the Pine.

Now after dawn and the next day had come about,
Pre-Harakhti arose, and they observed each other. Then
the youth argued with his elder brother, saying: What's
the meaning of your coming in pursuit of me in order to
kill ⟨me⟩ unjustly [9] without having heard what I have to
7,5 say? For I am still your younger brother, and / you are
(associated) with me after the manner of a father, and
your wife is (associated) with me after the manner of a

8. See Rudolf Anthes, in *JNES* 16 (1957): 180, n. 17, and John A.
Wilson, in *JNES* 11 (1952): 78. P3 ꜥḏ3 can mean either "wrong"
or "the guilty one"; see Ricardo Caminos, *Late-Egyptian Miscellanies* (London: Oxford University Press, 1954), p. 237.

9. In the two occurrences of this expression, here and in 7,8, there
is disagreement in the determinatives. In the second occurrence
the writing suggests possibly, "in (all) readiness"; see Caminos,
p. 180.

mother, isn't it so? When you sent ⟨me⟩ to fetch us seed, your wife said to me, "Come, let's spend an hour sleeping (together)." But see, it has been distorted for you as something otherwise. Then he informed him about all that had transpired between him and his wife. He swore by Pre-Harakhti saying: As for your ⟨coming⟩ in order to kill me unjustly, carrying your spear, it was on account of a sexually exhausted slut. He fetched a reed knife, cut off his phallus, and threw it into the water. The catfish

8,1 swallowed ⟨it⟩,[10] and he / grew weak and became feeble. His elder brother became exceedingly grieved and stood weeping for him aloud. He could not cross over to where his younger brother was because of the crocodiles.

Then his younger brother called to him, saying: If you have recalled a grievance, can't you recall a kindness or something that I have done on your behalf? Please depart to your home and take care of your cattle, for I shall not stay in a place where you are. I shall go off to the Valley of the Pine. Now what you shall do on my behalf is to come and care for me if ⟨you⟩ find out that something has happened to me ⟨when⟩ I extract[11] my heart and put it on top of the flower of the pine tree. And if the

8,5 pine tree is cut down and falls to the ground, / you are to come to search for it. If you shall have spent seven years in searching for it, don't let your heart become discouraged, for if you do find it and put it into a bowl of cool water, then I will become alive in order that ⟨I⟩ may avenge the wrong done to me. Now you shall ascertain whether something ⟨has happened⟩ to me if a beaker of

10. For the god Bata's association with the catfish, see Seibert, *Die Charakteristik*, p. 63.
11. Supplying *m* before *p₃y.ỉ šd*.

beer is delivered to you in your hand and produces froth. Don't delay upon seeing that this comes to pass with you.

Then he went off to the Valley of the Pine, and his elder brother went off to his home with his hand(s) placed upon his head and his (body) smeared with dirt. Presently he reached his home, and he killed his wife, cast her ⟨to⟩ the dogs, and sat down in mourning over his younger brother.

After many days following this, his younger brother was in the Valley of the Pine with no one with him while he spent all day hunting desert game. He returned in the evening to spend the night under the pine tree on top 9,1 of whose flower his heart was. And after / many days following this, he built for himself a country villa with his (own) hands ⟨in⟩ the Valley of the Pine, filled with all (sorts of) good things, with the intention of establishing a home for himself.

Presently he went out from his country villa and encountered the Ennead[12] as they were walking (along) governing the entire land. The Ennead spoke in unison,[13] saying to him: Oh, Bata, Bull of the Ennead, are you alone here having abandoned your town before the face of the 9,5 wife of Anubis, your elder brother? / See, ⟨he⟩ has killed his wife, and thus you will be avenged upon him ⟨for⟩ every wrong done against you. For they were exceedingly sorry for him. Pre-Harakhti told Khnum:[14] Please fashion a marriageable woman for Bata so that he does not (have to) live alone. Thereupon Khnum made for him a house-

12. The company of the major gods.
13. Taking *n wꜥ ỉm.sn* for *m wꜥ ỉm.sn*, lit. "as one among themselves." But perhaps the passage is to be rendered, "spoke (first) among themselves and (then) said to him."
14. A creator god represented as shaping man on a potter's wheel.

companion who was more beautiful in her body than any woman in the entire land, for ‹the seed of› every god was in her. Then the seven Hathors [15] came ‹to› see her and said all together: It is by an execution knife that she shall die.

10,1 Then he proceeded to covet her exceedingly while she was dwelling in his house and while he spent all day / hunting desert game, bringing (it) back, and putting (it) down before her. He told her: Don't go outside lest the sea carry you away, for I will be unable to rescue you from it, because I am a female like you and my heart lies on top of the flower of the pine tree. But if another finds it, I will fight with him. Then he revealed to her all his inmost thoughts.[16]

10,5 After many days following this, while Bata went to hunt according to his daily habit, / the maiden [17] went out to stroll under the pine tree which was next to her house. Thereupon she beheld the sea surging up behind her, and she hastened to flee from it and entered her house. Then the sea called to the pine tree, saying: Seize hold of her for me. And the pine tree removed a braid from her hair. The sea brought it to Egypt and deposited it in the place of the launderers of Pharaoh, l.p.h. Then the scent of the braid of hair appeared in the clothes of Pharaoh, l.p.h., and the king wrangled with the launderers of Pharaoh, l.p.h., saying: Scent of ointment is in the clothes of Pharaoh, l.p.h. The king came to wrangling with them 11,1 daily, but / they didn't know what to do. The chief

15. The goddesses who determine an individual's fate; see The Doomed Prince, n. 1.
16. On the passage, see Hellmut Brunner, in *Archiv für Orientforschung* 17 (1954 / 55): 140–41.
17. Bata's wife is still a virgin.

launderer of Pharaoh, l.p.h., went to the bank with his mind exceedingly vexed as a consequence of the wranglings with him daily. Then ⟨he⟩ stopped still and stood by the seashore opposite the braid of hair that was in the water. He had someone go down, and it was brought to him. ⟨Its⟩ scent was found exceedingly fragrant, and he took it away to Pharaoh, l.p.h.

Then the learned scribes of Pharaoh, l.p.h., were brought. 11,5 They told Pharaoh, l.p.h.: As for this braid of hair, / it belongs to a daughter of Pre-Harakhti in whom there is the seed of every god. Now it is a tribute ⌜to you⌝ ⟨from⟩ another country. Send envoys forth to every foreign country in order to search for her. As for the envoy who will go to the Valley of the Pine, have many men go with ⟨him⟩ in order to fetch her. Then His Majesty, l.p.h., said: What you have said is very good, very good. And (they) were sent off.

After many days following this, the men who had gone to a foreign country returned to render report to His Majesty, l.p.h., whereas those who had gone to the Valley of the Pine failed to return, for Bata had killed them leaving (only) one of them to render report to His Majesty, l.p.h. Then His Majesty, l.p.h., again sent forth many soldiers as well as chariotry in order to fetch her, 12,1 there being / a woman among them through whom all (sorts of) beautiful feminine adornments were presented to her.[18]

The woman returned to Egypt with her, and there was jubilation for her in the entire land. Then His Majesty, l.p.h., proceeded to love her exceedingly, and the king

18. On the passage, see Hellmut Brunner, in *ZÄS* 80 (1955): 75, and Sergio Donadoni, *Rivista degli Studi Orientali* (Roma), 28 (1953): 143–48.

appointed her to be Chief Lady. The king spoke with her in order to have her describe the nature of her husband, and she said to His Majesty, l.p.h.: Have the pine tree cut 12,5 down and hacked up. The king sent / soldiers bearing their copper (implements) in order to cut down the pine tree, and they reached the pine tree. They cut off the flower upon which was Bata's heart, and he fell dead at the very same moment.

After dawn and the next day had come about and after the pine tree had been cut down, Anubis, the elder brother of Bata, entered his house and sat down and washed his hand(s). He was handed a beaker of beer, and it produced froth. Another of wine was handed him, and it turned 13,1 bad. Then he took his / staff and his sandals as well as his clothes and his weapons, and he hastened to journey to the Valley of the Pine. He entered the country villa of his younger brother and found his younger brother lying dead upon his bed. He wept when ⟨he⟩ saw ⟨his⟩ younger brother lying in a state of death, and he went to search for his younger brother's heart beneath the pine tree 13,5 under which his younger brother slept in the evening. / He spent three years in searching for it without finding it. Now when he had commenced the fourth year, his heart desired to return to Egypt, and he said: I shall depart tomorrow. So he said in his heart.

After dawn and the next day had come about, he began walking under the pine tree and spent all day searching for it. He gave up in the evening. Again he spent time in order to search for it, and he found a (pine) cone. He left for home with it. It was really his younger brother's heart. And he fetched a bowl of cool water, dropped it into it, and sat down according to his daily ⟨habit⟩.

14,1 After darkness had fallen, / his heart absorbed the water, and Bata shuddered over all his body and began looking at his elder brother while his heart was (still) in the bowl. Anubis, his elder brother, took the bowl of cool water in which was his younger brother's heart and ⟨had⟩ him drink it. His heart assumed its (proper) position so that he became as he used to be. Then each embraced the other, and they conversed with one another. Then Bata

14,5 said to his / elder brother: Look, I shall become a large bull that has every beautiful color and whose sort is unparalleled, and you shall sit upon ⟨my⟩ back. As soon as the sun rises, we shall be where my wife is that ⟨I⟩ may avenge myself, and you shall take me to where the king [19] is, for every sort of good thing shall be done for you and you shall be rewarded with silver and gold for taking me to Pharaoh, l.p.h., because I shall become a great marvel, and there shall be jubilation for me in the entire land, and (then) you shall depart to your (home) town.

15,1 After dawn / and the next day had come about, Bata changed into the form which he had mentioned to his elder brother. Then Anubis, his elder brother, sat down upon his back until dawn, and he reached the place where the king was, and His Majesty, l.p.h., was informed about him. He saw him and became exceedingly joyful over him. He served him a grand oblation, saying: It is a great marvel that has come to pass. And there was jubilation for

15,5 him in the entire land. Then / his weight was made up in silver and gold for his elder brother, who (again) took up his abode in his (home) town. The king gave him much personnel and a lot of goods, for Pharaoh, l.p.h., preferred him exceedingly over anybody (else) in the entire land.

19. Here and following, the Egyptian uses the term *One* in reference to the king.

Now after many days following this, he entered the kitchen and stood in the place where the Lady was. He began speaking with her, saying: See, I'm still alive! She said to him: Who are you, I ask? And he told her: I am Bata. I realize that when you caused the pine tree to be hacked up for Pharaoh, l.p.h., it was on account of me, 16,1 to keep me from staying alive. See, / I'm still alive, but as a bull.

The Lady became exceedingly fearful because of the revelation which her husband had made to her. Then he left the kitchen, and His Majesty, l.p.h., sat down and made holiday with her. She poured (drinks) for His Majesty, l.p.h., so that the king was exceedingly happy in her company. Then she said to His Majesty, l.p.h.: Swear to me by god as follows, "As for what ⟨the Lady⟩ will say, I shall grant it to her." And he heard all that she 16,5 said: Let me eat of the liver of this bull, / for he never will amount to anything. So she said speaking to him. The king became exceedingly vexed over what she had said, and Pharaoh, l.p.h., was exceedingly sorry for him.

After dawn and the next day had come about, the king proclaimed a grand oblation as an offering to the bull,[20] and the king sent a first royal cupbearer of His Majesty, l.p.h., to sacrifice the bull. And subsequently he was sacrificed. While he was upon the shoulders of the men, he trembled in his neck and caused two drops of blood to be shed beside the two doorposts of His Majesty, l.p.h., one landing on one side of the great portal of Pharaoh, l.p.h., 17,1 and the other on the other side. They grew into / two large Persea trees, each one of which was choice. Then someone went to tell His Majesty, l.p.h.: Two large

20. Or possibly, "as a sacrifice of the bull."

Persea trees have grown this night as a great marvel for His Majesty, l.p.h., beside the great portal of His Majesty, l.p.h. And there was jubilation for them in the entire land, and the king presented an offering to them.

After many days following this, His Majesty, l.p.h., appeared at the audience window of lapis lazuli with a wreath of every sort of flower on ⟨his⟩ neck, and he 17,5 ⟨mounted⟩ a chariot of electrum / and came out from the palace, l.p.h., in order to inspect the Persea trees. Then the Lady came out in a chariot following Pharaoh, l.p.h. His Majesty, l.p.h., sat down under one Persea tree, ⟨and the Lady under the other Persea tree. And Bata⟩ spoke with his wife: Ha, you liar! I am Bata. I'm alive ⌐in spite of⌐ you. I realize that as for your having had ⟨the pine tree⟩ cut down for Pharaoh, l.p.h., it was on account of me. And I became a bull, and you had me killed.

After many days following this, the Lady stood pouring (drinks) for His Majesty, l.p.h., so that the king was happy in her company. She told His Majesty, l.p.h.: Swear to me by god as follows, "As for what the Lady will tell me, I shall grant it to her." So you shall say. And he heard 18.1 / all that she said, and she said: Have these two Persea trees cut down and made into fine furniture. Then the king heard all that she had said, and after a brief moment His Majesty, l.p.h., sent skilled craftsmen, and the Persea trees were cut down for Pharaoh, l.p.h. The queen, the Lady, observed it (being done), and a splinter flew up 18,5 and entered the Lady's mouth. / She swallowed ⟨it⟩ and became pregnant in the space of a split second, and the king made out of them [21] whatever was her desire.

After many days following this, she bore a son, and

21. Referring to the Persea trees.

someone went in order to tell His Majesty, l.p.h.: A son has been born to you. Then he was brought, and nurse and maids were assigned to him. There was jubilation ‹for him› in the entire land, and the king sat down and made holiday and proceeded to hold him on his lap.[22] His Majesty, l.p.h., cherished him exceedingly immediately, 19,1 and the king appointed him / Viceroy of Kush.

After many days following this, His Majesty, l.p.h., made him crown prince of the entire land. And after many days following this, when he had completed many [years] as crown prince in ‹the› entire land, His Majesty, l.p.h., flew up to the sky.[23] Then the (new) king [24] said: Have my great officials of His Majesty, l.p.h., brought to me 19,5 that I may inform them regarding every situation / that I have been involved in. His wife [was] brought to him, and he was judged with her in their presence. A consensus was reached among them.[25] His elder brother was brought to him, and he appointed him crown prince in the entire land. He ‹spent› thirty years as King of Egypt. He departed from life, and his elder brother acceded to his throne on the day of death.

Thus it concludes happily and successfully.

22. Following the interpretation of Hellmut Brunner in *Die Geburt des Gottkönigs* (Wiesbaden: Otto Harrassowitz, 1964), pp. 205–06.
23. A common expression used to refer to the death of the king; see above, The Story of Sinuhe, R 6.
24. I.e. Bata. The relationship of this story to the Egyptian concept of royal succession has been discussed by Helmuth Jacobsohn, *Die dogmatische Stellung des Königs in der Theologie der alten Ägypter* (Glückstadt: J. J. Augustin, 1939), pp. 13–15; G. Posener, *De la divinité du pharaon* (Paris: Imprimerie Nationale, 1960), pp. 92–93, and Brunner, *Die Geburt*, pp. 205–06.
25. The implication is the condemnation of Bata's unfaithful wife, whose death by execution had been fated by the seven Hathors.

The Contendings of Horus and Seth

This, the longest of the New Kingdom stories, is perhaps the one with the least literary merit, for there is very little in the way of suspense that serves to carry the reader's interest throughout the narration of the story. It is the theme of Horus's superiority over his rival Seth that serves to bind together an episodically constructed tale, whose narrative style is especially monotonous. It has been suggested (see Joachim Spiegel, Die Ezrählung vom Streite des Horus und Seth in Pap. Beatty I als Literaturwerk *[Glückstadt: J. J. Augustin, 1937]) that the basic composition of The Contendings goes back to the early Middle Kingdom and that what is preserved to us is a rendition in the colloquial language of the New Kingdom. However, the early Middle Kingdom works of literature are considerably more sophisticated compositions, and even the religious literature from the First Intermediate Period may attain greater heights in utilizing the subtleties of the Egyptian language.*

The Contendings is best appreciated in terms of the function of the mythically oriented short story during the New Kingdom. This particular story is preserved to us on a papyrus that contains some other compositions of literary worth, so that it would seem that the papyrus may have been used by its owner for the purpose of entertaining himself and others. The behavior of some of the great gods is at points so shocking that it is hard to imagine that no humor was intended. Yet at the same time the story provides the reader with basic mythical concepts. Such a dichotomy between coarse humor, even about the gods, and seriousness in religion is an aspect of the Ramesside age, a period when men could both enjoy excesses in life and yet be extremely pietistic (see Alfred Hermann Altägyptische Liebesdichtung *[Wiesbaden: Otto Harrassowitz, 1959], pp. 156–66). In fact, the episode in which Isis harpoons the two rivals who had transformed themselves into hippopotamuses appears in two papyri that are calendars of lucky and unlucky days (Papyrus Sallier IV,*

"*Calendar of Lucky and Unlucky Days*," *recto 2, 6 ff., and Abd El-Mohsen Bakir*, The Cairo Calendar No. 86637 [*Cairo: Antiquities Department of Egypt, 1966*], *recto VII, 7 ff.). Thus in one context the passage might be enjoyed for its humor, while in the other it might be regarded in seriousness by people who were superstitious concerning each day's undertakings.*

Bibliographical references will be found in Lefebvre, Romans et contes, pp. 182–83, and discussion of the myth of Horus and Seth in J. Gwyn Griffiths, The Conflict of Horus and Seth from Egyptian and Classical Sources (Liverpool: University Press, 1960), and H. Te Velde, Seth, God of Confusion (Leiden: E. J. Brill, 1967).

E. F. W.

1,1 [There came to pass] the adjudication of Horus and Seth, mysterious in (their) forms and mightiest of the princes and magnates who (ever) came into existence. Now it was a young [god] that was seated [1] in the presence of the Universal Lord, claiming the office of his father Osiris, beautiful in (his) appearances, the [son of Pt]ah, who illumines [the west with] his [complex]ion, while Thoth was presenting the uninjured Eye to the great prince who is in Heliopolis. Then said Shu, the son of Re, in the presence of [Atum], the great [prince] who is in Heliopolis: Justice is a possessor of power. [Administer] it

1,5 by saying, "Award the office to [Horus]." / Said Thoth to the [Ennead]: It is correct a million times. Thereupon Isis [2] let out a loud [shri]ek rejoicing exce[edingly, and she came be]fore the Universal [Lord] and said: North wind, (go) to the west. Impart the good news to Onno-

1. Referring to Harpocrates, the child Horus, frequently represented in late bronzes as a squatting infant with his finger in his mouth.

2. Isis and Osiris are the parents of Horus.

phris,[3] l.p.h. Then said Shu, the son [of Re]: [The] one who presents the uninjured Eye [4] is loyal to the Ennead.

[State]ment by the Universal Lord: Indeed, what is the meaning of your exercising authority alone by yourselves? [Onuris] [5] said: He shall [assum]e the cartouche of Horus, and the White Crown shall be [placed] upon his head. The Universal Lord was silent a long [whi]le, [being] furious [at] this Ennead. Then Seth, the son of Nut, said: Have 1,10 him dismissed outside / with me that I may let you see my hand(s) prevail ‹over› his hand(s) [in the pre]sence of the Ennead, since there is not known [any] (other) method [of] dispossessing him. Said Thoth to him: Shouldn't we ascertain (who is) the impostor? Is it while Osiris's son Horus is still living that his office is to be awarded to Seth?

Pre-Harakhti became exceedingly furious, for Pre's wish 2,1 was / to give the office to Seth, great in virility, the son of Nut. Onuris let out a loud shriek before the face of the Ennead, saying: What shall we do? Then Atum, the great prince who is in Heliopolis, said: Have Banebdjede, the great living god, [summon]ed that he may judge between the youths. Banebdjede, the great god who resides in Sehêl,[6] and Ptah-Tatenen were brought before Atum, and he told them: Judge between the two youths and stop them from being engaged so in quarreling every day. 2,5 Thereupon / Banebdjede, the great living god, answered what he had said: Do not have us exercise (our) authority

3. A designation of Osiris meaning: He who is continually beneficent; see J. Gwyn Griffiths, *The Origins of Osiris* (Berlin; Verlag
Bruno Hessling, 1962), p. 57.
4. Referring to Thoth.
5. The restoration of this name is uncertain.
6. An island in the area of the First Cataract.

ignorantly. Let a letter be sent to Neith the Great, the God's Mother. As for what she will say, we shall do it.

The Ennead said to Banebdjede, the great living god: It is (already) a first time that they have been adjudged in the "One are the Truths" court. Then the Ennead said to Thoth in the presence of the Universal Lord: Please compose a letter to Neith the Great, the God's Mother, in the name of the Universal Lord, the Bull who resides in Heliopolis. Thoth said: I'll do so, surely; I'll do so, I'll do so. Then he sat down to compose the letter and wrote: The

2,10 King of Upper and Lower Egypt, / Re-Atum, beloved of Thoth, the Lord of the Two Lands, the Heliopolitan, the solar disk that illumines the Two Lands with its hue, the Nile mighty in flooding, Re-Harakhti (while Neith the Great, the God's Mother, who illumined the first face, is alive, in health, and rejuvenated), the living manifestation of the Universal Lord, the Bull in Heliopolis, being the good King of Egypt. To wit: (I), your humble servant, spend all night on Osiris's behalf consulting the Two Lands every day, while Sobek endures forever. What shall we do for these two individuals who for eighty years now

3,1 have been in the tribunal, but / neither of whom can be judged? Please write us what we should do.

Then Neith the Great, the God's Mother, sent a letter to the Ennead, saying: Award the office of Osiris to his son Horus. Don't commit such blatant acts of inequity which are illegal, or I shall become so furious that the sky will touch the ground. The Universal Lord, the Bull who resides in Heliopolis, ought to be told, Enrich Seth in his possessions. Give him Anath and Astarte, your two daugh-

3,5 ters, and / install Horus in the position of his father Osiris.

And so the letter of Neith the Great, the God's Mother,

reached this Ennead as they were sitting in the "Horus with the Projecting Horns" court, and the letter was delivered into Thoth's hand. Thereupon Thoth read it out in the presence of the Universal Lord and the entire Ennead, and they declared unanimously: This goddess is correct. Then the Universal Lord became furious at Horus and told him: You are despicable in your person, and this office is too much for you, you lad, the flavor of whose mouth is (still) bad.[7]

Onuris became furious to the nth degree and so did the entire Ennead constituting the Council of the Thirty, 3,10 l.p.h. Bebon,[8] the god, got right up and / told Pre-Harakhti: Your shrine is vacant. Pre-Harakhti took offense at the insult which was said to him and lay down on his back very much saddened. And so the Ennead went outside and let out a loud cry before the face of Bebon, the god. They told him: Get out; this offense that you have committed is exceedingly great. And they departed to their 4,1 huts. And so the great god spent a day / lying on his back in his pavilion very much saddened and alone by himself.

After a considerable while Hathor, Lady of the Southern Sycamore, came and stood before her father, the Universal Lord, and she exposed her vagina before his very eyes. Thereupon the great god laughed at her. Then he got right up and sat down with the Great Ennead. He said to Horus and Seth: Speak concerning yourselves. Seth, great in virility, the son of Nut, said: As for me, I am Seth, greatest in virility among ⟨the⟩ Ennead, for I slay

7. Perhaps referring to the bad breath of a young infant.
8. A god, in the form of a monkey or a dog, who is the opponent of Thoth; see Philippe Derchain, in *Revue d'Egyptologie* 9 (1952): 23–47.

4,5   the / opponent of Pre [9] daily while I am at the prow of
the Bark of the Millions, whereas not any (other) god is
able to do it. I should receive the office of Osiris. Then
they said: Seth, the son of Nut, is correct. Onuris and
Thoth let out a loud cry, saying: Is it while a bodily son
is still living that the office is to be awarded to a maternal
uncle? Then said Banebdjede, the living great god: Is it
while Seth, his elder brother,[10] is still living that the office
is to be awarded to the (mere) lad?

The Ennead let out a loud cry before the face of the
Universal Lord and said to him: What is the meaning of
the words that you have said which are unfit to be
heard? [11] Said Horus, son of Isis: It is no good, this cheat-
4,10   ing me in the presence of / the Ennead and depriving me
of the office of my father Osiris. Thereupon Isis became
furious at the Ennead and took an oath by (the) god in
the presence of the Ennead as follows: By my mother
Neith, the goddess, and by Ptah-Tatenen, with lofty
plumes, who curbs the horns of gods, these matters should
be submitted before Atum, the great prince who is in
Heliopolis, and also (before) Khepri, who resides in his
bark. And the Ennead said to her: Don't become angry.
The rights will be given to the one who is in the right.
All that you have said will be done.

5,1   Seth, the son / of Nut, became furious at the Ennead
when they had said these words to Isis the Great, the God's

9. The reference is to Seth's beneficial role as daily vanquisher
of Apophis, the snake-monster that embodied chaos.
10. Through fusion of myths Seth is both the brother of Horus
and his uncle.
11. The words of the Universal Lord have been omitted from the
story, possibly for the very reason that they were not fit to be
heard or written.

Mother. So Seth said to them: I shall take my scepter of 4,500 *nemset*-weight and kill one of you a day. And then Seth took an oath by the Universal Lord, saying: I shall not go to law in the tribunal while Isis is (still) in it. Said Pre-Harakhti to them: You shall ferry across to the Island in the Middle and decide between them there and tell

5,5 Nemty,[12] the ferryman, not to ferry / any woman across resembling Isis. And so the Ennead ferried across to the Island in the Middle and sat down and ate bread.

Then Isis came and approached Nemty, the ferryman, as he was sitting near his boat, after she had transformed herself into an old woman who walked with a hobble and (wore) a small golden signet-ring on her hand. She said to him: It is in order that you might ferry ⟨me⟩ across to the Island in the Middle that I have come to you, because it is for the young lad that I have come carrying this bowl-

5,10 ful of porridge, / since he has been tending some cattle [13] on the Island in the Middle for five days now and is hungry. He said to her: I have been told not to ferry any woman across. But she said to him: It is with reference to Isis that you have been told this which you have (just) mentioned. He said to her: What will you give me in order that you may be ferried across to the Island in the Middle? Said Isis to him: I will give you this cake. He said to her: What good is it to me, your cake? Is it in exchange for your cake that I should ferry you across to the Island in the Middle when I have been told not to ferry any

6,1 woman across? / Then she said to him: I will give you the

12. On the reading of the god's name, formerly read Anty, see O. D. Berlev, *VDI* 107 (Moscow, 1969): 3–30, a reference we owe to Prof. Klaus Baer.
13. Paronomasia here; the Egyptian word *ꜣꜣwt* can mean either "cattle" or "office."

golden signet-ring which is on ⟨my⟩ hand. And he said to her: Hand over the golden signet-ring. And she gave it to him. Then he ferried her across to the Island in the Middle.

Now as she was walking under the trees, she looked and saw the Ennead sitting eating bread in the presence of the Universal Lord in his pavilion. Seth looked and saw her when she had come closer from afar. Then she con-

6,5 jured by means of her magic, transforming herself / into a maiden whose body was beautiful and whose like did not exist in the entire land. Thereupon he desired her most lecherously.

Seth got right up from sitting eating bread with the Great Ennead and proceeded to overtake her, no one having seen her except himself. Then he stood behind a sycamore tree and called to her. He said to her: I am here with you, beautiful maiden. And she said to him: ⌜Reflect⌝, my great lord. As for me, I was a wife (living) with a cattleman to whom I bore a son. My husband died,

6,10 and the lad started tending his father's cattle. / But then a stranger came and settled in my stable. He said thus in speaking to my son, "I shall beat you and confiscate your father's cattle and evict you," said he in speaking to him. Now it is my desire to have you afford him protection.[14] Thereupon Seth said to her: Is it while the son of the male is still living that the cattle are to be given to the stranger?

And so Isis transformed herself into a kite and flew up and perched on top of an acacia tree. She called to Seth and said to him: Be ashamed of yourself. It is your own

7,1 mouth that has said it. It is your own cleverness / that has judged you. What comeback do you have now? And so

14. Or, "be a champion for him."

he became ashamed and went to where Pre-Harakhti was, (still) ashamed. Then Pre-Harakhti said to him: What's bothering you still? Said Seth to him: That wicked woman has come to me again. She has tricked me again, having transformed herself into a beautiful maiden before my eyes. She said to me, "As for me, I was a wife (living) with a cattleman. He died, and I bore him a son, who is tending 7,5 / some of his father's cattle. A stranger took lodging in my stable with my son, and I gave him meals. Now after many days following this, the visitor then said to my son, 'I shall beat you and confiscate your father's cattle, and they will become mine,' he said in speaking to my son." So she said to me.

Then Pre-Harakhti said to him: And what did you say to her? And Seth told him: I said to her, "Is it while the son of the male is still living that the cattle are to be 7,10 given to the stranger? So I said / to her. "The visitor's face should be smitten with a rod, and he should be evicted and your son put in his father's position." So I said to her. Thereupon Pre-Harakhti said to him: Now look here, it is you yourself that has judged your own self. What comeback do you have now? So Seth said to him: Have Nemty, the ferryman, brought and severe punishment inflicted upon him, saying, "Why did you let her be ferried across?" So it shall be said to him. Then Nemty, the ferryman, was brought before the Ennead, and the forepart of his feet 8,1 removed. So / Nemty abjured gold even to this day in the presence of the Great Ennead, saying: Gold shall be because of me an abomination unto my city.[15] Then the

---

15. Apparently gold was taboo in Nemty's town of Djufyet, located just north of Assiut; see Bakir, *The Cairo Calendar*, recto XIV, 2–3, and Gardiner, *Ancient Egyptian Onomastica*, 2:68*–71*.

Ennead ferried across to the western tract and sat down on the mountain.

Now ⟨afterward⟩ at evening time Pre-Harakhti and Atum,[16] Lord of the Two Lands, the Heliopolitan, wrote to the Ennead, saying: What are you doing still sitting here? As for the two youths, you will be having them finish out their lifetime in the tribunal! When my letter reaches you, you shall place the White Crown upon the head of Horus, son of Isis, and appoint him to the position

8,5 of his father / Osiris.

Thereupon Seth became terribly furious. And so the Ennead said to Seth: Why have you become so furious? Isn't it in accordance with what Atum, Lord of the Two Lands, the Heliopolitan, and Pre-Harakhti have said that (things) should be carried out? Then the White Crown was set upon the head of Horus, son of Isis. Seth, being very angry, let out a loud shriek before the face of this Ennead, saying: Is it while I am still living as his elder brother that the office is to be awarded to my younger brother? Then he took an oath as follows: The White Crown shall be removed from the head of Horus, son of Isis, and he shall be thrown into the water in order that I may contend with him for the office of Ruler. Pre-Harakhti acquiesced.

Thereupon Seth said to Horus: Come, let's both trans-
8,10 form ⟨ourselves⟩ into hippopotamuses and submerge in / the deep waters in the midst of the sea. Now as for the one

---

For another reference to an abomination of a town, see Jaroslav Černý and A. H. Gardiner, *Hieratic Ostraca I* (Oxford: Griffith Institute, 1957), pl. 46, 2, verso 7.
16. Pre-Harakhti and Atum were the morning and evening forms of the same god, as is evident in the lines following, where the first person singular pronoun is used.

who shall emerge within the span of three whole months, the office should not be awarded him. Then they both submerged. And so Isis sat down and wept, saying: Seth has killed Horus, my son. Then she fetched a skein of yarn. She fashioned a line, fetched a *deben*-weight's (worth) of copper, cast it in (the form of) a harpoon, tied the line to it, and hurled it into the water at the spot where Horus

9,1 and Seth had submerged. / But then the copper (barb) bit into the person of her son Horus. So Horus let out a loud shriek, saying: Help me, mother Isis, my mother. Appeal to your copper (barb) to let go of me. I am Horus, son of Isis. Thereupon Isis let out a loud shriek and told ⟨her⟩ copper (barb): Let go of him. See, it is my son Horus. He is my child. So her copper (barb) let go of him.

Then she again hurled it back into the water, and it bit into the person of Seth. So Seth let out a loud shriek, say-

9,5 ing: What have I done against you, my sister Isis? / Appeal to your copper (barb) to let go of me. I am your maternal brother, Isis. Then she felt exceedingly compassionate toward him. Thereupon Seth called to her, saying: Do you prefer the stranger to ⟨your⟩ maternal brother Seth? So Isis appealed to her copper (barb), saying: Let go of him. See, it is Isis's maternal brother whom you have bitten into. Then the copper (barb) let go of him.

Horus, son of Isis, became furious at his mother Isis and went out with his face as fierce as an Upper Egyptian panther's, having his cleaver of 16 *deben*-weight in his hand. He removed the head of his mother Isis, put it in

9,10 his arms, and ascended the mountain. Then Isis / transformed herself into a statue of flint which had no head. Said Pre-Harakhti to Thoth: What is that which has

arrived having no head? So Thoth told Pre-Harakhti:
My good lord, that is Isis the Great, the God's Mother,
10,1 after Horus, her son, removed her head. Thereupon /
Pre-Harakhti let out a loud cry and said to the Ennead:
Let us go and inflict severe punishment upon him. Then
the Ennead ascended those mountains in order to search
for Horus, son of Isis.

Now as for Horus, he was lying under a *shenusha*-tree
in the land of the oasis. Seth found him, seized hold of
him, threw him down upon his back on the mountain,
removed his two eyes from their sockets, and buried them
on the mountain so as to illumine the earth. The two
10,5 balls of his eyes became two bulbs / which grew into
lotuses. Seth came away and told Pre-Harakhti falsely:
I did not find Horus—although he had found him.

Then Hathor, Mistress of the Southern Sycamore, set
out, and she found Horus lying weeping in the desert.
She captured a gazelle and milked it. She said to Horus:
Open your eye(s) so that I may put this milk in them.
Then he opened his eye(s) and she put the milk in them,
putting some in the right one and putting some in the left
one. She told him: Open your eye(s). And he opened his
eye(s). ‹She› looked at them and found that they were
healed.

10,10 She / set out to tell Pre-Harakhti: (I) found Horus after
Seth had deprived him of his eye(s), but I have restored
him back (to health). See, he has returned. Said the
Ennead: Let Horus and Seth be summoned in order that
they may be judged. Then they were brought before the
Ennead. Said the Universal Lord before the Great Ennead
to Horus and Seth: Go and obey what I tell you. You
11,1 should eat and / drink so that we may have (some) peace.

Stop quarreling so every day on end. Then Seth told Horus: Come, let's make holiday in my house. Horus told him: "I'll do so, surely; I'll do so, I'll do so.

Now afterward, (at) evening time, bed was prepared for them, and they both lay down. But during the night Seth caused his phallus to become stiff and inserted it between Horus's thighs. Then Horus placed his hands be-
11,5 tween his thighs and received Seth's semen. Horus / went to tell his mother Isis: Help me, Isis, my mother, come and see what Seth has done to me. And he opened his hand(s) and let her see Seth's semen. She let out a loud shriek, seized her copper (knife), cut off his hand(s), threw them into the water, and restored for him hand(s) that were equivalent. Then she fetched some fragrant ointment and applied it to Horus's phallus. She caused it to become stiff and inserted it into a pot, and he caused his semen to flow down into it.

Isis at morning time went carrying the semen of Horus to the garden of Seth and said to Seth's gardener: What
11,10 sort of vegetable / is it that Seth eats here in your company? So the gardener told her: He doesn't eat any vegetable here in my company except lettuce.[17] And Isis added the semen of Horus onto it. Seth returned according to his daily habit and ate the lettuce, which he regularly ate. Thereupon he became pregnant with the semen of Horus.
12,1 So Seth went to tell / Horus: Come, let's go that I may contend with you in the tribunal. Horus told him: I'll do so, surely; I'll do so, I'll do so.

They both went to the tribunal and stood in the pres-

17. There is the possibility that lettuce was regarded as an aphrodisiac, for it is the plant associated with the ithyphallic god Min.

ence of the Great Ennead. They were told: Speak concerning yourselves. Said Seth: Let me be awarded the office of Ruler, l.p.h., for as to Horus, the one who is standing (trial), I have performed the labor of a male against him. The Ennead let out a loud cry. They spewed and spat at Horus's face. Horus laughed at them. Horus

12,5 then took / an oath by god as follows: All that Seth has said is false. Let Seth's semen be summoned that we may see from where it answers, and my own be summoned that we may see from where it answers.

Then Thoth, lord of script and scribe of truth for the Ennead, put his hand on Horus's shoulder and said: Come out, you semen of Seth. And it answered him from the water in the interior of the ⌈marsh⌉.[18] Thoth put his hand on Seth's shoulder and said: Come out, you semen of Horus. Then it said to him: Where shall I come from?

12,10 Thoth said to it: Come / out from his ear. Thereupon it said to him: Is it from his ear that I should issue forth, seeing that I am divine seed? Then Thoth said to it: Come out from the top of his head. And it emerged as a golden solar disk upon Seth's head. Seth became exceedingly furious and extended his hand(s) to seize the golden

13,1 solar disk. Thoth took it away / from him and placed it as a crown upon his (own) head. Then the Ennead said: Horus is right, and Seth is wrong.

Seth became exceedingly furious and let out a loud shriek when they said: Horus is right, and Seth is wrong.

18. Possibly for ⌜ n bndt, "bed of cucumbers"; see Gardiner, *Ancient Egyptian Onomastica*, 2:220*. Or *bnt* may be connected with the root *bn*, meaning "beget," "engender," or "phallus"; see William Ward, in *ZÄS* 95 (1968): 66–67, and Philippe Derchain, *Le Papyrus Salt 825* (Brussels: Académie Royale de Belgique, 1965), p. 175.

And so Seth took a great oath by (the) god as follows: He shall not be awarded the office until he has been dismissed outside with me and we build for ourselves some stone ships [19] and race each other. Now as for the one who 13,5 shall prevail over his rival, / he is to be awarded the office of Ruler, l.p.h. Then Horus built for himself a boat of pine, plastered it over with gypsum, and launched it into the water at evening time without anybody who was in the entire land having observed it. Seth saw Horus's boat and thought it was of stone. And he went to the mountain, cut off a mountain top, and built for himself a boat of stone of 138 cubits. They embarked upon their ships in the presence of the Ennead. Then Seth's boat sank in the water. So Seth transformed himself into a hippopotamus 13,10 / and scuttled Horus's boat. Horus took his copper (harpoon) and hurled it at the person of Seth. Then the Ennead told him: Don't hurl it at him.

He gathered the harpoons, put them in his boat, and sailed downstream to Saïs in order to tell Neith the Great, the God's Mother: Let judgment be passed on me and Seth, seeing that it is eighty years now that we have been 14,1 in the tribunal / and they have been unable to pass judgment on us, nor has he yet been vindicated against me; but it is a thousand times now that I have been in the right against him every day although he doesn't regard anything that the Ennead has said. I have contended with him in the "The Path of the Truths" court, and I have been vindicated against him. I have contended with him in the "Horus with the Projecting Horns" court, and (I) have

19. Seth is again deceived through his foolishness in this episode, for he misinterprets Horus's expression "stone ships" to mean ships made of stone rather than ships for transporting stone; see H. Goedicke, in *JEA* 47 (1961): 154.

been vindicated against him. I have contended with him in the "Field of Rushes" court, and I have been vindicated against him. I have contended with him in the "Pool of the Field" court, and I have been vindicated against him. And the Ennead said to Shu, son of Re: Horus, son of Isis, is correct in all that he has said.

14,5 / Statement which Thoth made to the Universal Lord: Have a letter sent to Osiris so that he may judge between the two youths. Then said Shu, son of Re: What Thoth has told the Ennead is correct a million times. Said the Universal Lord to Thoth: Sit down and compose a letter to Osiris that we may learn what he has to say. Thoth sat down to fill out a letter to Osiris with the words: Bull, the lion who hunts for himself; the Two Ladies, protecting the gods and subduing the Two Lands; Horus of Gold, who invented mankind in the primeval time; the King of Upper and Lower Egypt, Bull in the midst of Heliopolis, l.p.h.; son of Ptah, (most) glorious one of the Two Banks, appearing as father of his Ennead while he eats of gold and glaze, the possessor of sanctity, l.p.h. Please write us what we should do for Horus and Seth so that we do not exercise (our) authority ignorantly.

14,10 Now afterward, following this, the / letter reached the King, son of Re, Great in Bounty and Master of Sustenance. He let out a loud cry after the letter had ⟨been⟩ read out in his presence. Then he answered it very very quickly (writing) to the place where the Universal Lord was together with the Ennead, saying: Why should my son Horus be cheated when it was I that made you mighty and it was I (alone) who could create barley and emmer in order to sustain the gods as well as the cattle [20] following

20. Referring to mankind, see Papyrus Westcar 8,17.

the gods, whereas not any god or any goddess found himself (competent enough) to do it? So / Osiris's letter reached the place where Pre-Harakhti was, sitting together with the Ennead on the White Mound in Xois. It was read out in his and the Ennead's presence, and Pre-Harakhti said: Please answer for me the letter very quickly to Osiris and tell him in the letter, "If you had not come into being and if you had not been born, barley and emmer would exist anyway."

The letter of the Universal Lord reached Osiris, and it was read out in his presence. Then he again wrote to Pre-Harakhti as follows: It is exceedingly good, all that which you have done, O you who invented the Ennead as an accomplishment, although justice was allowed to sink down within the netherworld. Please look at the situation also on your part. As for / the land in which I am, it is filled with savage-faced messengers who do not fear any god or ⟨any⟩ goddess. I have but to let them go forth, and they will fetch the heart of whoever commits misdeeds and they will be here with me. Indeed, what is the meaning of my happening to be here resting in the west while you are all outside? Who among you[21] is there that is mightier than I? But see, you have invented injustice as an accomplishment. When Ptah the Great, South of his Wall, Lord of Ankh-tawi, created the sky, isn't it so that he told the stars that are in it, "It is in the west where King Osiris is that you shall set every night"? (And he told me), "Now after (the manner of) gods, so patricians and commoners also shall go to rest in the place where you are." So he said to me.

Now afterward, following this, Osiris's letter reached

21. The papyrus actually employs the third person plural pronoun.

the place where the Universal Lord was together with the Ennead. Thoth received the letter and read it out in the
15,10 presence of Pre-Harakhti / and the Ennead. They said: The Great in Bounty and Master of Sustenance, l.p.h., is doubly correct in all that he has said. Then Seth said: Let us be taken to the Island in the Middle so that (I) may contend with him. He went to the Island in the Middle, and Horus was vindicated against him. Then Atum, Lord of the Two Lands, the Heliopolitan, sent to Isis, saying: Bring Seth restrained with manacles. Isis brought Seth restrained with manacles, as a prisoner. Said Atum to him: Why do you not allow yourselves to be judged but (instead) usurp for yourself the office of Horus? Said Seth to him: On the contrary, my good lord. Let Horus, son of
16,1 Isis, be summoned and be awarded the office of / his father Osiris.

Horus, son of Isis, was brought, and the White Crown was set upon his head and he was installed in the position of his father Osiris. He was told: You are a good King of Egypt. You are the good lord, l.p.h., of every land unto all eternity. Thereupon Isis let out a loud shriek on behalf of her son Horus, saying: You are the good king. My heart is in joy. You have illumined earth with your complexion.

Then Ptah the Great, South of his Wall, Lord of Ankh-tawi, said: What shall be done for Seth? For see, Horus has been installed in the position of his father Osiris. Said Pre-Harakhti: Let Seth, son of Nut, be delivered to me so that he may dwell with me, being in my company as a son, and he shall thunder in the sky and be feared.

16,5 Someone / went to tell Pre-Harakhti: Horus, son of Isis, has arisen as Ruler, l.p.h. Thereupon Pre-Harakhti rejoiced exceedingly and said to the Ennead: You shall jubilate from one land to the next for Horus, son of Isis! Said Isis: Horus has arisen as Ruler, l.p.h. The Ennead is in festivity, and heaven is in joy. They donned wreaths when they saw Horus, son of Isis, arisen as great Ruler, l.p.h., of Egypt. As for the Ennead, their hearts were satisfied, and the entire land was in exultation when they saw Horus, son of Isis, assigned the office of his father Osiris, lord of Busiris.

Thus it concludes successfully in Thebes, the place of ⌈Truth.⌉

The Blinding of Truth by Falsehood

In Egyptian texts and iconography the concept of Truth is regularly personified as the goddess Maat, the daughter of Re. However, in this allegorical tale Truth is conceived of as a male who was blinded at his brother Falsehood's behest because of circumstances, not quite clear, involving Truth's treatment of a dagger that belonged to Falsehood. The theme of sibling rivalry is reminiscent of the Horus and Seth feud and The Tale of the Two Brothers. In none of these myths or stories is the antagonist totally annihilated, but rather a resolution is effected so that a harmonious situation is achieved with the elimination of further strife. Such a resolution of conflicting opposites is typically Egyptian and reflects the application of the principle of Maat, which embraces the concepts of balance and harmony as well as truth. One's appreciation of this short story would be enhanced if its beginning were preserved. For a discussion of the place of this tale in the history of literature and for bibliographical references, see Lefebvre, Romans et contes, *pp. 159–63. The conclusion of the story and juridical aspects of the dispute are discussed by A. Théodoridès in* Revue d'Egyptologie *21 (1969): 85–105.*

E. F. W.

1,5   . . . / [and] . . . went . . . [the Ennea]d . . . : . . . [a copper dagger of which the Moun]tain of E[l forms the blade, of which the ⌜woods⌝ of Coptos form the haft], of 2,1   which the / god's tomb forms the scabbard, and of which [the herds of] Kal form the belt.[1] Falsehood said to the

1. Falsehood had apparently lent a dagger, for which he gives fantastic dimensions, to Truth, who had either damaged or mislaid

Ennead: Let [Tru]th [be brought] and blinded ‹in› both his eyes and be assigned to be doorkeeper of my house. [The] Ennead then acquiesced to all that he said.

After many days following this, Falsehood raised his eyes
2,5 to have a look, and he observed / the exemplariness of Truth, his elder brother. Falsehood said to Truth's two servants: Please ab[duct] your lord and [cast] him [to] a dangerous lion that has many lionesses [as mate]s, and they shall [devour him. Then they] abducted him. Now as they were going up carrying him, Truth [told his ser-
3,1 vant]s: Don't abduct [me and] put / [an]other [in my place . . . One of you go to town] and find a bit of ⌐bread¬ for me . . . [So the servant] went that he might tell Falsehood: When [we] cast [him to the lion], . . . [And he] went out from the [house], and he called him in the . . .²

Now [after many days] following this, (the lady) N.³
3,5 / went out [from] her house [with her following], ⌐clad¬ . . . , [and they s]aw him [lying under the cover]t⁴ and

---

it. Although the location of the Mountain of El is unknown, Kal is well-known as an Egyptian province in the Sudan. A number of the terms used to describe the weapon are otherwise unattested. The word *š3tì*, rendered "haft," occurs also in Ostracon DM 319, recto 3; cf. W. Helck, *Materialien zur Wirtschaftsgeschichte des Neuen Reiches* (Mainz: Akademie der Wissenschaften und der Literatur, 1960–64), Pt. 5, p. 914. and *ìstn*, "belt," is recently discussed by W. K. Simpson in *Papyrus Reisner II* (Boston: Museum of Fine Arts, 1965), p. 37.

2. The restorations are uncertain.

3. The name of the lady is lost in all its occurrences.

4. On *bw3t*, "covert," see Caminos, *Late-Egyptian Miscellanies*, pp. 374–76, and I. E. S. Edwards, *Hieratic Papyri in the British Museum*, 4th ser., 2 vols. (London: The British Museum, 1960), 2:32, n. 17.

(saw) [that he was so handsome] that there was none like [him in the] entire land. Then [they] went [to where] (the lady) N. was and [said: Co]me [along with] us that

4,1 [you may s]ee / [the blind man] lying under the covert, and he shall be brought and assigned to be doorkeeper of our house.

(The lady) N. said ⟨to⟩ her: [5] You shall go to (fetch) him that I may see him. And she went and fetched him. [Then] (the lady) N. saw him, and [sh]e desired him exceedingly when she saw [how handsome] he was in all his ⌐body⌐. So he went to bed with her in the night, and

4,5 he had sexual intercourse with her. / So she became pregnant that night with a baby boy.

Now after many days following this, she gave birth to a son whose like did not exist in this entire land, [for he was] larger in . . . [than] a . . . being [in] the nature

5,1 [of] a young god. And he was sent to / school and mastered writing very well, and he practiced all the arts of war so that he (even) surpassed his older (school)mates who were at school with him. His (school)mates said to him: Whose son are you? You don't have a father. And they would revile him and mock him: [6] Truly, you don't have a father.

5,5 The / boy said to his mother: What is my father's name that ⟨I⟩ may tell it to my (school)mates? Truly, if they converse with me: "Where is your father?" they (always) say to me, and they mock me. His mother said to him: Do you see that blind man who is seated next to the door?

5. One of the lady's maidservants.
6. For the use of the conjunctive tense here, see Wente, *JNES* 21 (1962): 310.

6,1   That is your father. / So she said telling him. Then he said to her: The members of your family ought to be gathered together and be made to summon a crocodile.[7]

And so the boy brought his father and had him sit down with an armchair supporting him, and he put a footstool under his feet. And he placed food before him and let him 6,5   eat and / drink. The boy said to his father: Who is it that blinded you so that ⟨I⟩ may avenge you? And he told him: It was my younger brother who blinded me. And he told him all that had happened to him. So he set out ⟨to⟩ 7,1   avenge / his father, taking (along) ten loaves, a staff, a pair of sandals, a waterskin, and a sword. And he fetched an ox of very beautiful appearance and went ⟨to⟩ where Falsehood's herdsman was. He said to him: Please take for 7,5   yourself these ten loaves as well as this staff, this / waterskin, this sword, and this pair of sandals, and tend this ox for me until I return from town.

After many days following this, his ox had completed many months in the charge of Falsehood's herdsman. Then 8,1   Falsehood / went off to the fields to inspect his cattle, and he saw that that ox belonging to the boy was exceedingly beautiful in appearance. He said to his herdsman: Give me that ox that ⟨I⟩ may eat it. But the herdsman told him: It isn't mine, so I won't be able to give it to you. Falsehood said to him: See, all my cattle are at your disposition. Give one of them to its owner.

8,5   The boy learned / that Falsehood had appropriated his ox, and he came to where Falsehood's herdsman was and said to him: Where is my ox? I can't see it among your cattle. Said the herdsman to him: All the cattle are at

7. The boy is suggesting that his mother be condemned to death for her immoral conduct.

9,1   your disposition. Take /for yourself the one you want. Then the boy said to him: Is there an ox as large as my own ox? If it should stand on The Island of Amon, the tip of its tail would be lying <upon> the Papyrus Marshes, while one of its horns would be on the Western Mountain and the other on the Eastern Mountain, and the Great River would be its spot for lying down,[8] and sixty calves
9,5   would be born to it / daily.

     The herdsman said to him: Is there an ox as large as the one you have (just) mentioned? So the boy seized hold of him and took him off <to> where Falsehood was. And he
10,1   took / Falsehood to the tribunal before the Ennead. <They> said to the boy: [What you have said] is false.[9] We have [ne]ver seen an ox as large as the one you've mentioned. [Said] the boy [to the Ennea]d: Is there a copper dagger as large as the one you did mention, of which the Mountain of El forms the blade, of which the ⌜woods⌝ of Coptos form the haft, of which the god's tomb forms the scabbard, and of which the herds of Kal form the belt?
10,5   / [He] told the Ennead: Judge between Truth and Falsehood. I am his (i.e. Truth's) son. It is in order to avenge him that I have come. Then Falsehood took an oath by the Lord, l.p.h., saying: By [Amon] and by the Ruler, l.p.h., if Truth be found alive, I shall be blinded <in> both my eyes and be assigned [to be door]keeper in the [house

----

8. "The Island of Amon" is Diospolis Inferior in the far north-central Delta, and the Papyrus Marshes, the biblical Yam-sûph, "Sea of Reeds," is a swampy area near Lake Manzalah. The Great River is the main course of the Nile river.

9. For the restoration, compare Papyrus BM 10052, 3,18, and 14,7 (T. Eric Peet, *The Great Tomb-Robberies of the Twentieth Egyptian Dynasty*, 2 vols. [Oxford: Oxford University Press, 1930], vol. 2, pls. 27 and 34), and Horus and Seth 12,5.

11,1 of Truth]. Then / the boy [had his father brought to the tribunal before the Ennead], and it was verified that he was (still) alive. So [severe punishment] was inflicted [upon Falsehood]. He [was] smitten with a hundred blows and five open wounds, blinded ‹in› [both his eyes, and assigned to be doorkeepe]r [in] the house of Truth. And he . . .

[And so] the boy av[enged] h[is father] so that (the 11,5 dispute between) Truth and Falsehood was settled / . . . the . . .

[Thus it] concludes [happily and successfully].

(The concluding sentence is fragmentary.)

Astarte and the Insatiable Sea

This poorly preserved story is included in the collection because of its treatment of a theme found elsewhere in ancient Near Eastern literature. Some have proposed that the Egyptian version is directly dependent upon a Canaanite original (see Theodor H. Gaster, "The Egyptian 'Story of Astarte' and the Ugaritic Poem of Baal," BiOr 9 [1952]: 82–85 and 232), but Georges Posener ("La Légende égyptienne de la mer insatiable," Annuaire de l'Institut de Philologie et d'Histoire Orientales et Slaves 13 [1953]: 461–78) has argued that the roots of this legend of the conflict between the gods and the sea are to be found in indigenous Egyptian religious thought already as early as the First Intermediate Period, when The Instruction for Merikare was composed. The New Kingdom legend of the hostile and greedy sea is thus only superficially akin to West Semitic accounts through the inclusion of the Semitic goddess Astarte, the substitution of Seth, the equivalent of Baal, for Re, and the use of the Semitic word for sea to describe the liquid element. In this way an ancient myth was modernized for the more cosmopolitan Egyptian of the Empire period.

The bracketed portions of the following translation are conjectural and frequently follow restorations of John A. Wilson in ANET, pp. 17–18. For discussion and bibliography the reader is referred to Lefebvre, Romans et contes, pp. 106–10, and Erman, The Ancient Egyptians, p. xxxiii.

E. F. W.

1,x+1   . . . / his two oxen. I will adore you . . . -men. I will adore the . . . I will adore the Sky, ⌜her⌝ [dwelling] place . . . the Earth . . . the Sky.[1]

---

1. Reading *t₃ pt* rather than Gardiner's "Ptah."

Now when . . . the Earth, the Earth became satisfied
. . . in order that I might [un]cover its . . . [Then] they
1,x+5 bent down as if ⌜. . .⌝ .[2] / Thereupon [each] one embraced [the other. Now] after ⌜seven⌝ days the Sky . . .
ed . . . and descended upon . . . the Sea, and . . . the
Earth gave birth to . . . the four regions of the [Earth]
. . . in its midst as if ⌜suspended⌝ . . . [hi]s throne of
Ruler, l.p.h.,[3] and he . . . ed and delivered unto him tribute . . . in court. Thereupon Ernutet[4] delivered [the
1,   tribute to the Sea which was due him] / as Ruler, l.p.h.
x+10 [One of the gods said]: . . . [the] Sky. Now look, tribute
is brought to him . . . his . . . , otherwise he will take us
away cap[tive] . . . our own for . . . [Then] Ernutet
[delivered] his tribute consisting of silver, gold, lapis lazuli,
[and turquoise which filled] the boxes.

Thereupon they said to the Ennead: ⌜Let⌝ . . . the tribute for the Sea in order that he may investigate for us [all]
matters [pertaining to the Earth],[5] (for) protection is in
2,x+1 his charge. Is it that he will . . . ? . . . / since they are
fearful of . . . [the tribu]te for the Sea. Let . . . [th]e
tribute for the S[ea] . . . bad.

And Ernutet took a . . . Astarte. Thereupon [Ernutet]
said [to one of the] birds: Hear what I have to say. You
are not to depart . . . another. Hurry up and go to
2,x+5 Astarte . . . [and fly to] her house and cry out beneath
[the window of the room where] she is sleeping and tell
her, "If it should be that [you are awake, then hear my
voice; but] if it should be that you are asleep, I will

2. *Š₃ḳ* is a word of unknown meaning.
3. The Sea is the Ruler.
4. The harvest-goddess.
5. On *sḏm mdwt*, see H. Goedicke, in *JEA*, 48 (1962): 33. Or
render simply, "that he may hear for us [all] words [of the Earth]."

awa[ken you. The Ennead has to send tribute to the] Sea as Ruler over the [Earth and as Ruler over] the Sky. Please come before them right [away] . . . ⌐Asiatics¬. And

2, Asta[rte] /. . . the daughter of Ptah. Now . . . [tribute]

x+10 of the Sea, the . . . [Please] go yourself carrying the tribute for [the Sea] . . ."

Then Astarte wept . . . , [and] its Ruler, l.p.h., was

2, silent . . . : /. . . lift up your eyes . . . lift up your

x+15 eyes and you shall . . . [ou]tside. [Thus she] delivered [the tribute for] the Sea, and she . . . sang making sport of him. . . . [Then the Sea] saw Astarte as she was sitting on the shore of the sea. He said to her: Where have you come from, O daughter of Ptah, you furious and tempestuous goddess? Did you wear through your sandals that are ⟨on⟩ your feet and did ⟨you⟩ tear your garments that are on you when you were moving about between the sky and the earth?

3,1 Thereupon / [Astarte] said to him: . . . [Then the Sea said to Ptah]: . . . [the Enne]ad. If they give me your [daughter] . . . them. What shall I, on my part, do against them? And Astarte heard what the Sea had said to her, and she hastened to go before the Ennead to [the] place where they were gathered. And the great ones saw her and arose to meet her, and the lesser ones saw her and lay down on their bellies. And her throne was given to her, and she sat down. And the [⌐tribute for the Sea¬]

4,1 was presented to her [6] /. . . land . . . the beads . . . And the beads . . .

The messenger of Ptah went to tell these matters to Ptah and Nut. Then Nut untied the beads which were at her

6. Perhaps in turn to be presented to her future husband, the Sea, as a dowry.

5,1   throat. Lo, she put ⟨them⟩ upon the balance / . . . Astarte:
O my . . . It is [a dispu]te with the Ennead. Then he
shall send and request . . . the signet-ring of Geb . . .
[to fill] the balance with it.[7] Then . . . him together with

10,1   . . . s . . . [m]y basket of . . . ⌈her⌉. And he / . . . s of
the Sea . . . through the portals . . . portals. There came
forth . . . ⌈servants⌉ of the . . . If they come again
. . . , he . . . [the Se]a, and he shall ⌈go⌉ to cover the

15,1   ground and the mountains and / . . . his . . . [come] to
fight with him ⌈inasmuch as⌉ . . . sat himself down
calmly. He won't come to fight with us. Thus Seth sat
down . . .

    . . . ⌈You⌉ shall [protect] ⌈me⌉ together with your . . .
And the Sea ⌈left⌉ . . .
And . . . he . . .
The seven . . . him . . . together with the Sky and . . .

(The manuscript of the story is lost beyond this point.)

7. The individual gods of the Ennead seem to be divesting themselves of their jewelry to satisfy the Sea's appetite for more
tribute. The remainder of the tale is extremely fragmentary.

A Ghost Story

This Egyptian ghost story, incompletely preserved on a number of Ramesside ostraca, lacks the spooky quality that moderns associate with this genre of literature. Death for the deceased Egyptian who had undergone the rites of beatification was an extension of life, and as the practice of festal banqueting in tomb chapels indicates, rapport between the living and the dead was by no means always a gloomy affair. The living could communicate with the dead by means of letters, and in the Teaching of Ammenemes the dead king is conceived of as imparting advice to his son and successor. Egyptian ghosts were not so much eerie beings as personalities to whom the living reacted pragmatically.

Although the High Priest Khonsemhab was probably a fictitious character, the setting of the story in the Theban necropolis was familiar to its readers who lived and worked in western Thebes. We may assume that the story concluded with the successful completion of the spirit's tomb under Khonsemhab's direction.

Discussion and bibliography of the story will be found in Lefebvre, Romans et contes, pp. 169–72, whose translation, on pp. 173–77, makes use of certain unpublished ostraca. (Ostracon Gardiner 306, published in Černý and Gardiner, Hieratic Ostraca I, pl. 41, 4, is an important addition to the material utilized by Lefebvre.) Fragments of another ghost story have been published by Georges Posener in Revue d'Egyptologie 12 (1960): 75–82.

E. F. W.

T,1   . . . [according to] his habit . . . following the advice which . . . had given [to him] . . . [And he ferried] across and reached his home. He caused [there to be] made . . . [and] all sorts of good things.

Now while I was (looking) toward the west, he went
T,5 up onto the ro[of . . . , and he / invoked] the gods of the
sky and the gods of the earth, southern, northern, western
and eastern, and ⟨the⟩ gods of the ⌜underworld⌝, saying
to them: Send me that august spirit. And so he[1] came and
said to him: I am your . . . [who has come to sleep] during the night next to his tomb. Then the High Priest of
Amon Khonsemhab [said to him: Please tell me your
name], ⟨your⟩ father's [name], and your mother's name
that ⟨I⟩ may offer to them and do for them all that has to
be done [for one in their position]. Said [that] august
[spirit] to him: Nēbusemekh is my name, Ankhmen is my
T,10 father's [name], and Tamshas / is my mother's name.

Then the High Priest of Amon-Re, King of the Gods,
Khons[emhab said to] him: Tell me what you want that
I may have it done for you. / And I shall have a sepulcher
prepared [anew] for you and have a coffin of gold and
V,5 zizyphus-wood made for you, and you shall . . . , / and
I shall have done for you all that is done for one who is in
[your position. Said the spirit] to him: There is ⌜none
overheated[2] who is exposed⌝ ⟨to⟩ winds in winter, hungry without ⌜food⌝ . . . It is not my desire to flow on like
the inundation, nor . . . I would not occupy myself with
that (simply) to say . . .

Then the High Priest of Amon-Re, King of the Gods,
Khonsemhab, sat down and wept beside him, [and he said
V,10 to him: I will remain here] / without eating or drinking,
F,1 without g[rowing old / or becoming] young. [I] will not
see sunlight nor will I inhale northerly breezes, (but) darkness shall be in [my] sight every day. I will not get up
early to depart.

1. I.e. the spirit.
2. Or perhaps "passionate." This passage is extremely obscure.

Then the spirit said to him: When I was alive upon earth, I was overseer of the treasury of King Rahotpe,[3] l.p.h., and I was lieutenant of the army, for I used to be at the head of men and (just) to the rear of the gods. I went to rest[4] in Year 14, during the summer months, of the King of Upper and Lower Egypt, Men‹tu›hotpe,[5] l.p.h. F,5 / He gave me my four canopic jars and my sarcophagus of alabaster, and he had done for me all that is done for one in my position. He laid me to rest in my tomb, . . . See, the ground beneath has ⌐collapsed and dropped away¬ so that the wind blows (there) and ⌐seizes a tongue¬.[6] Now as for your having said to me, "I shall have a sepulcher prepared anew,"[7] I have it four times (already) that one will act in accordance with them.[8] But what am I to make of such things as you have said to me (once) again in order that all these promises may finally ⌐come to pass¬?[9]

Then the High Priest of Amon-Re, King of the Gods, F,10 Khonsemhab, / said to him: Please express to me a nice commission such as is fit to be done for you[10] in order that

3. The second king of Theban Dynasty 17 according to Von Beckerath in *Untersuchungen zur politischen Geschichte der zweiten Zwischenzeit,* pp. 179, 224, and 284. Von Beckerath prefers reading all royal names in this story as Rahotpe, but paleographic considerations do not tend to support this supposition.
4. I.e. died.
5. A possible reference to Mentuhotpe VI, the fifth king of Dynasty 17. However, since it is improbable that either this king or Rahotpe reigned for fourteen years, it is possible that the writer of the story, if he were really ignorant of the sequence of kings, intended the great Mentuhotpe of Dynasty 11.
6. An obscure passage, the last clause of which perhaps refers to the howling of the wind in the subterranean chambers of the tomb.
7. The variant has: "on new land."
8. "Them" perhaps refers to previous promises to have a new resting place prepared.
9. The emendation of *nn m mdwt* to *nn n mdwt* seems demanded because of the following *r-drw.*
10. Emending *n.i* here and following to *n.k.*

I may have it done for you. Otherwise, I shall (simply) have five men (servants) and five maidservants, totaling ten, devoted to you in order to pour libation water for you and (have) a sack of emmer delivered daily to be offered to you. ⌜Moreover⌝, the overseer of offerings shall pour libation water for you.

Then the spirit of Nēbusemekh said to him: Of what use are the things you do? Doesn't a tree grow through sunlight? Doesn't it sprout ⌜foliage⌝? [11] (But) stone will never proceed to age; it perishes (only) through . . .[12]

L,1   . . . [King] / <Neb>hep<et>re,[13] l.p.h., ⌜there⌝ . . . Amon-Re, King of the Gods, three men, each one . . . And he ferried across and ascended . . . next to the holy temple of King [Neb]hepetre, [Son of Re, Mentuhotpe],

L,5   l.p.h. And they [entered] . . . / in it. And they ⌜explored⌝ twenty-five cubits along the king's causeway ⌜at Deir el Bahri⌝.[14] Then they went back down <to> the riverbank, and they [returned to] the High [Priest] of Amon-Re, King of the Gods, Khonsemhab, and found him officiating in the temple of Amon-[Re, King of the Gods]. And he said to them: Hopefully you have returned having discovered [15] the excellent place for making the name [of

11. On the meaning of the verb in these two clauses, see Caminos, *Late-Egyptian Miscellanies*, pp. 342–43. A *srdd*, similarly written but with different meaning, occurs in Papyrus BM 10068, recto 2, 6 (Peet, *The Great Tomb-Robberies*, vol. 2, pl. 9).

12. The entire passage is obscure. Following it there is a lacuna of considerable length.

13. Assuming the king to be the famous Mentuhotpe of Dynasty 11, who possessed a large mortuary temple and tomb in the Deir el Bahri bay. This part of the narrative concerns the search for a new burial place in an especially sacred section of the Theban necropolis.

14. Reading *ḏsrt* for "Deir el Bahri"?

15. Emending *gm.i* to *gm.tn*.

that spirit] called [Nēbusemekh] endure unto eternity. Then the three of them said to ‹him› all together: We have discovered the excellent place to [make the name of that spirit endure]. And so they sat down before him and made holiday. His heart began to rejoice when they said:

L,10 . . . [when] / the sun came up from the horizon. Then he called the deputy of the estate of Amon Menkau, [and he informed him] about his project.

He returned at evening to spend the night in Nē,[16] and he . . . ed . . .

(The concluding words of the story are lost.)

16. I.e. the city of Thebes, located east of the Karnak temple of Amon.

The Report of Wenamon

The Report of Wenamon stands apart from the other New Kingdom stories in that it is an actual account of an Egyptian who traveled abroad at the end of the New Kingdom for the purpose of obtaining pine from Byblos in Phoenicia. The very format of the papyrus on which the report is written puts it into the category of official documents (see Černý, Paper and Books in Ancient Egypt). *Nonetheless, Wenamon's report is included in this volume because he did make a conscious effort to transform what may have originally been rough entries in a diary into a polished account that has literary merit.*

It has been customary to see in this report a vivid illustration of the decay of Egyptian prestige abroad at the end of the New Kingdom. Byblos, over the millennia, had had close commercial ties with Egypt, a land where good wood was scarce. There is the possibility that the difficult attitude adopted by the Prince of Byblos toward Wenamon arose not so much because of Egypt's overall decline in the eyes of the world but rather because Wenamon did not really represent the sovereign King of Egypt in his dealings. If it had been an envoy of the still reigning King Ramesses XI, the Prince of Byblos might have responded differently.

The papyrus has recently been published by M. A. Korostovtsev, The Voyage of Wenamon to Byblos *(in Russian)* (*Moscow: Akademia Nauk SSSR, 1960*), *and bibliographical references will be found in Lefebvre,* Romans et contes, *pp. 206–07, and Erman,* The Ancient Egyptians, *p. xxxiv. The reader is also referred to Jean Leclant, "Les Relations entre l'Egypte et la Phénicie du voyage d'Ounamon à l'expédition d'Alexandre," in William A. Ward, ed.,* The Role of the Phoenicians in the Interaction of Mediterranean Civilizations (*Beirut: 1968*), *pp. 9–11. Clarification of certain passages has been made recently by Charles F. Nims, "Second Tenses in Wenamūn,"* JEA *54* (*1968*): *161–64.*

E. F. W.

1,1   Year 5, fourth month of the third season, day 16,[1] day
on which the Elder of the Portal of the Temple of Amon,
[Lord of the Thrones] of the Two Lands, Wenamon,
departed in order to obtain lumber for the great and noble
riverine barge of Amon-Re, King of the Gods, [the name
of which is A]mon-Userhat.[2] On the day when I arrived
at Tanis at the place [where Smen]des and Tanetamon
are,[3] I gave them the dispatches from Amon-Re, King of

1,5   the Gods, and they / had them read out in their presence.
They said: Will do, will do according to what Amon-Re,
King of the Gods, our [lord], has said. I spent up to the
fourth month of the third season staying in Tanis. Smendes
and Tanetamon sent me off with the ship captain Men-
gebet, and I embarked on the great Syrian sea in the first
month of the third season, day 1.

         And I reached Dor, a Tjeker town,[4] and Beder, its prince,
1,10   had fifty loaves, one jug of wine, / and one ox-haunch

1. The date is in terms of the Renaissance era that was initiated
in the nineteenth year of Ramesses XI, at the time when the High
Priest of Amon, Herihor, apparently assumed a limited role as
king at Thebes, as illustrated in reliefs in the first court of the
Temple of Khonsu at Karnak. During this era Ramesses XI remained the official king of Egypt. The dates that follow in this
report are irreconcilable. Emendations have been suggested by
Lefebvre in *Chronique d'Egypte* 21 (1936), pp. 97–99, and in his
Romans et contes, p. 207.
2. The great barge of Amon, "Mighty of Prow," used in river
processions during major Theban feasts.
3. Tanis, located in the northeast portion of the Delta, was
governed by a couple who were probably of Theban origin. It has
been suggested that Smendes, who eventually became the first king
of the Tanite Dynasty 21, was the son of Herihor; see E. F. Wente,
in *JNES* 26 (1967): 174–75.
4. Dor, a port town on the north coast of Palestine, was controlled
by one of the Sea Peoples, who were related to the Philistines. The
Tjeker may be identical with the Teucrians; see Gardiner, *Ancient
Egyptian Onomastica*, 1:200*.

brought to me. A man belonging to my freighter absconded, stealing a golden [vessel worth] five *deben,* four silver jars worth twenty *deben,* and a bag of eleven *deben* of silver. [Total of what] he [stole]: five *deben* of gold and thirty-one *deben* of silver.[5]

I got up on that very morning and went to where the prince was, and I said to him: I have been robbed in your harbor. Now it is you who are the prince of this land, and it is you who are its investigator. Search for my money! 1,15 Indeed, as for this money, it belongs to Amon-Re, / King of the Gods, the lord of the lands; it belongs to Smendes; it belongs to Herihor, my lord, and the rest of the magnates of Egypt. It belongs to you; it belongs to Weret; it belongs to Mekmer; and it belongs to Tjekerbaal,[6] the Prince of Byblos.

And he said to me, "Are you serious, or are you ⌐fabricating⌐? Look here, I cannot comprehend this protestation that you have made to me. If it were a thief belonging to my land who boarded your freighter and stole your money, I would repay it to you from my own storehouse 1,20 until / your thief, whatever his name, has been found. Actually, as for the thief who has robbed you, he belongs to you and he belongs to your freighter. Spend a few days here visiting me that I may search for him.

So I spent nine days moored in his harbor, and I went unto him and said to him: See here, you haven't found my money. Please [send] me [off] with the ship captains and

5. The value of this money to pay for the lumber was equivalent to 1.2 lb. troy of gold and 7.5 lb. troy of silver.
6. The first two names are probably of the non-Semitic Sea Peoples type; see William F. Albright in George Mylonas, ed., *Studies Presented to David Moore Robinson,* 2 vols. (St. Louis: Washington University, 1951–53), 1:223–31. Tjekerbaal (Zakar-Baal) was the Phoenician Prince of Byblos.

those who go to sea. But he said to me: Quiet! [If you wish to] ⌜find⌝ [your money], hear [my words and do 1,25 what] I tell you, but don't / . . . the place where you will be. You shall take possession [of] their . . . and ⌜become compensated⌝ like . . . [until] they set out to search for their thief who [has robbed you] . . . the harbor. See, [you] . . . shall [proceed in this manner. And I reached] Tyre.[7]

I left Tyre at crack of dawn . . . Tjekerbaal, the Prince 1,30 of Byblos, . . . / a freighter. I found thirty *deben* of silver in it, and I seized possession of it. [I said to the ship owners:[8] I have seized possession of] your money. It shall remain in my possession [un]til you have found [my money or the thief] who stole it. I have not ⌜robbed you⌝, but am (only) going to ⌜confiscate⌝ it. But as for you, [you shall] . . . me to . . .

And so they went off, and I celebrated my triumph [in a] tent on the seashore in the harbor of Byblos. And [I found a hiding place for] Amon-of-the-Road[9] and placed his possessions within it. The Prince of Byblos sent to me, 1,35 saying: G[et out of / my] harbor! And I sent (back) to him, saying: Where should [I go]? . . . ⌜I⌝ go . . . If [you can find a ship] to transport me, let me be taken back to Egypt. And I spent twenty-nine days in his h[arbor while] he daily [spent] time sending to me, saying: Get out of my harbor!

Now when he offered to his gods, the god took posses-

7. The tenor of Beder's poorly preserved speech seems to be that Wenamon should exercise restraint in the hope that the money will be recovered, but apparently Wenamon impatiently left for Tyre.
8. The people whose money Wenamon confiscated may have been Tjeker.
9. The name of the idol that accompanied Wenamon on his trade mission.

sion of a page (from the circle of) his pages and caused him to be ecstatic. He[10] said to him: Bring [the] ⌐god⌐

1.40 up. Bring the envoy who is carrying him. / It is Amon who dispatched him. It is he who caused him to come. For it was after I had found a freighter headed for Egypt and after I had loaded all my (possessions) into it that the possessed one became ecstatic during that night, (this happening) while I was watching for darkness to descend in order that I might put the god on board so as to prevent another eye from seeing him.

The harbor master came to me, saying: Stay until tomorrow, so the prince says. And I said to him: Are you not[11] the one who daily spends time coming to me saying:

1.45 "Get out of my harbor!"? Isn't it / in order to allow the freighter which I have found to depart that you say: "Stay tonight," and (then) you will come back (only) to say, "Move on!"? And he went and told it to the prince, and the prince sent to the captain of the freighter, saying: Stay until tomorrow, so the prince says.

When morning came, he sent (for me) and took me up while the god was resting in the tent where he was on the seashore, and I found him sitting in his loft, having turned his back to a window so that it was to the rear of his head

10. I.e. the ecstatic page, on whom see G. Posener, in *Revue d'Egypologie* 21 (1969): 147.
11. Throughout the translation of this report *nn* has been interpreted as a negative. In those instances where *nn* is used as a single negative, we have either taken the clause as a negative statement or as a negative with an implied interrogative, as the context demands. On the use of *nn* in double negatives, see William F. Edgerton, in *American Journal of Semitic Languages* 48 (1931): 40–41, and Nims, in *JEA* 54 (1968): 162, n. 6. An alternative would be to regard *nn* in all its occurrences as a writing of the interrogative *in*, but in this case certain passages lose much of their force in dialogue.

1,50 that the waves of the great Syrian sea were breaking./I
said to him: "Amon be ⌜merciful⌝! And he said to me:
How long has it been until today since you came from
where Amon is? And I said to him: Five whole months
ago. He said to me: My, you're correct! Where is the
dispatch from Amon which is (supposed to be) in your
possession? Where is the letter from the High Priest of
Amon which is (supposed to be) in your possession? And
I said to him: I gave them to Smendes and Tanetamon.
And he became exceedingly annoyed and said to me: Now
look here, as for dispatches and letters, there is nothing (of
the sort) in your possession. Where is the ship for (transporting) pine wood [12] which Smendes gave you? Where
1,55 is / its Syrian crew? Wasn't it in order to let him murder
you and have them throw you into the sea that he entrusted
you to that barbarian ship captain? With whom (then)
would the god be sought, and you as well, with whom
would you also be sought? So he said to me.

And I said to him: Certainly it is an Egyptian ship and
an Egyptian crew that are sailing under Smendes. He has
no Syrian crews. And he said to me: Surely there are
twenty cargo ships here in my harbor which are in com-
2,1 merce with Smendes. As for that Sidon, / the other (port)
which you passed, surely there are another fifty freighters
there which are in commerce with Warkatara, for it is to
his (commercial) house that they haul.[13]

12. A "ship of pinewood" can designate not only a ship made of
pine but also a ship for transporting pine; see Goedicke, in *JEA*
47 (1961): 154.
13. Or: "It is at his (commercial) house that they tie up"; see
Coptic *ōth e*, "tie upon." in W. E. Crum, *A Coptic Dictionary*
(Oxford: Oxford University Press, 1939), p. 532*b*. Albright, in
Robinson, regards the name Warkatara as southwestern Anatolian,

I kept silent for such a long time that he responded, saying to me: On what sort of business have you come? And I told him: It is in quest of lumber for the great and noble barge of Amon-Re, King of the Gods, that I have

2,5 come. What your father did and / what your father's father did, you will also do. So I said to him. And he said to me: They did in fact supply it.[14] You have but to pay me for supplying it, and I will supply it. Actually, it was only after Pharaoh, l.p.h., had sent six freighters loaded with Egyptian products which were unloaded into their warehouses that my (people) carried out this commission. But you, what is it that you have brought me in my turn?

He had a journal roll belonging to his ancestors brought and had it read out in my presence. It was verified that a thousand *deben* of silver and miscellaneous items (had

2,10 been entered) in his journal roll. / And he said to me: As for the Ruler of Egypt, he has been the lord of what is mine, and I have been his servant as well.[15] It was not with the words, "Carry out the commission from Amon!" that

---

rather than Semitic Warkat-El, as Helck (*Beziehungen*, p. 372) still maintains. Helck (pp. 462 and 465) believes that Warkat-El was a Syrian merchant residing in Egypt.

14. Since in the following two clauses the pronoun *sw* must be for the feminine suffix pronoun *s*, referring back to *t3 tt*, "the lumber," it is probable that the *sw* in this clause also is for the feminine singular dependent pronoun in reference to the lumber.

15. Since *ir* as a conditional particle in Late Egyptian can only be followed by (circumstantial) *sdm.f* or by a circumstantial *iw*-clause, *ir* here must serve to introduce a frontal extraposition before a nominal sentence. It is perhaps significant that Tjekerbaal utilizes the term *Ruler*, referring to the Egyptian king in a generic sense rather than designating a specific king. It would seem that Tjekerbaal is not denying his allegiance to the Egyptian king but is seriously questioning Wenamon's authority to represent the sovereign power of Egypt.

he used to send silver and gold.[16] Was it not a delivery of royal gifts that used to be made unto my father? As for me in my turn, I am not your servant and neither am I a servant of the one who sent you. I have but to let out a cry unto the Lebanon so that as soon as the heavens open up, the logs are (already) lying here on the seashore.[17]

2,15 Give / me the sails that you have brought to take your freighters which are to carry your logs to ⟨Egypt⟩. Give me the ropes [that] you have brought [to lash the pine log]s which I am to fell in order to supply them to you . . . ⌈which⌉ I am to make for you (to be) [18] the sails for your freighters, or the yards may become too heavy and break and you may perish ⟨in⟩ the midst of the sea. Look here, it was only after he had placed Seth beside him that Amon could thunder in the sky. Now it is all the lands that

2,20 Amon / has founded. It was after he had initially founded the land of Egypt, where you have come from, that he founded them. Thus it was in order to reach the place where I am that technology issued from it, and it was in order to reach the place where I am that learning issued from it. What is (the purpose of) these foolish journeys that you have had to make? [19]

But I said to him: That's wrong! They are not foolish

16. If *nn* is here the negative, it must serve to negate the nexus between a positive verbal construction and its adverbial adjunct. For an example of *wn iir.f sḏm* used to express the imperfect of a second tense, see BM 10052, 4,21 (in Peet, *The Great Tomb-Robberies*, vol. 2, pl. 28, and Peet's note thereto in 1:161).
17. In other words, Tjekerbaal has the power to make it rain logs.
18. Or: "for."
19. Tjekerbaal audaciously claims that Amon's purpose in endowing Egypt was for the ultimate benefit of Byblos. Amon is efficacious only after Seth, equivalent to Semitic Baal, was installed beside him; see Nims, in *JEA* 54 (1968): 163–64.

journeys that I am on. There is not any ship upon the river [20] which doesn't belong to Amon. His is the sea, and his is the Lebanon, which you say belongs to you. It is for

2,25 Amon-Userhat, the lord of every ship, that he maintains / a growing-tract [21] (there). Indeed, he said, namely Amon-Re, King of the Gods, in speaking to Herihor, my lord, "Send him forth!" [22] and he had me come bringing this great god. Now look here, you have made this great god spend these twenty-nine days moored in your harbor while you surely knew that he was here. Certainly he is (still) what he used to be. You have been engaged to conduct trade over the Lebanon with Amon, its lord. As for your saying that former kings used to send silver and gold, if they had had life and health, they would not have sent

2,30 such products. / It was instead of life and health that they sent such products to your fathers. Now as for Amon-Re, King of the Gods, it is he who is the lord of Life and Health, and it is he who was the lord of your fathers. They spent their lifetimes offering to Amon. You too, you are a servant of Amon. If you say, "Will do, will do so for Amon," and accomplish his commission, you shall live and prosper, and be healthy and good for your entire land and your people. Do not covet for yourself anything belonging to Amon-Re, ⟨King⟩ of the Gods. Truly, a lion covets

2,35 his own possessions. Have your scribe brought to me / that I may send him to Smendes and Tanetamon, the foundation [23] that Amon has installed in the north of his land, and

---

20. Either specifically the Nile or a general reference to riverine ships.
21. Where the cedars of Lebanon grow.
22. Lit. "Send me forth."
23. See Jaroslav Černý, *The Cambridge Ancient History*, 2 vols. (Cambridge: Cambridge University Press, 1965), 2: 39, n. 4.

they will have whatever is (necessary) brought. I will send him to them with the words, "Have it brought until I shall go (back) to the south, and I shall (then) remit to you whatever debt is still due you," [24] so I said to him.

And he put my letter in his messenger's hand, and he loaded (on board) the keel, the bow-post, the sternpost, along with four other hewn timbers, totaling seven, and he sent them to Egypt. His messenger, who had gone to Egypt, returned to me in Syria in the first month of the second season, Smendes and Tanetamon having sent along 2,40 / four jars and one *kakmen*-vessel of gold, five jars of silver, ten articles of clothing of byssus, ten veils of thin cloth of good quality,[25] five hundred mats of smooth linen,[26] five hundred ox-hides, five hundred ropes, twenty sacks of lentils, and thirty baskets of fish, while she sent me (personally) five articles of clothing of thin cloth of good quality, five veils of thin cloth of good quality, one sack of lentils, and five baskets of fish. So the prince rejoiced, and he detailed three hundred men and three hundred oxen and assigned supervisors in charge of them to have them fell the timbers. So they felled them, and they spent the winter lying there.

Now in the third month of the third season they hauled them to the seashore, and the prince went out and attended 2,45 to them. He sent to me / saying: Come! And when I pre-

24. Wenamon is asking for an advance from the Tanite rulers which he promises to pay back as soon as he returns to Thebes.
25. *Ḥrd* is a garment, possibly a veil; see Jaroslav Černý, *Bulletin de l'Institut Français d'Archéologie Orientale* 57 (1958): 208; for *šmᶜ nfr*, see Černý, *Hieratic Inscriptions from the Tomb of Tutᶜankhamūn* (Oxford: Griffith Institute, 1965), p. 10, n. 3.
26. *Ḳn* is a word for mat, and the palette sign is to be read *nᶜᶜ*, "smooth linen"; see Janssen, *Two Ancient Egyptian Ship's Logs*, p. 74.

sented (myself) near him, the shadow of his lotus fan fell upon me, and Penamon, a cupbearer whom he had, shoved me aside, saying: The shadow of Pharaoh, l.p.h., your lord, has fallen upon you. But he [27] became angry at him, saying: Leave him alone! I presented (myself) near him, and he responded, saying to me: Observe that the commission which my fathers carried out previously, I (also) have carried it out, although you in turn have not done for me what your fathers used to do for mine.[28] See, the last of your lumber has arrived and is (already) stacked. Do according as I desire and go to load it on board, for surely 2,50 they are going to give it to you. / Do not go (simply) to observe the terror of the sea. If you observe the terror of the sea, you will have to face my own. Truly, I have not done to you what was done to Khaemwase's [29] envoys when they had spent seventeen years in this land, and it was at their jobs that they died. And he said to his cupbearer: Take him, let him see their tomb in which they lie.

But I said to him: Don't make me see it. As for Khaemwase, they were humans whom he sent to you as envoys, and he himself was a human. You don't have one of his envoys (now before you) that you should say, "You should go and see your fellow men." Can't you be so joyful 2,55 / as to have a stela [made] for yourself and say upon it, "Amon-Re, King of the Gods, sent to me Amon-of-the-Road, his envoy, l.p.h., and Wenamon, his human envoy,

27. I.e. Tjekerbaal.
28. The text has "for me," which may also make sense if Tjekerbaal had previously received payment from Ramesses XI.
29. Khaemwase is probably the pharaoh Ramesses XI, who in the first part of his reign may have sent envoys to Byblos. The fact that Wenamon subsequently refers to Khaemwase as a human would reflect Theban bias in favor of Herihor as against Ramesses XI.

in quest of lumber for the great and noble barge of Amon-Re, King of the Gods. I felled it; I loaded it on board. I provided it (with) my own freighters and my own crews. I let them arrive back home in Egypt in order to request for me fifty years of life from Amon in excess of my fate." [30] And it may chance after another day that an envoy comes from the land of Egypt, who is acquainted with writing, and he reads your name on the stela, and (then) you will receive water of the West like the gods who are
2,60 / there.

And he said to me: That is quite a wordy bit of testimony you have said to me. And I said to him: As for the many things that you have told me, if I arrive home to where the High Priest of Amon is and he sees your commission, it is your commission which will draw in profit to you.

So I went off to the seashore to where the timbers were stacked and watched eleven freighters coming in from the sea belonging to the Tjeker, (who were) saying: Imprison him. Do not release [31] a freighter of his to the land of Egypt. So I sat and wept. And the letter scribe of the
2,65 prince came out to me / and said to me: What now? And I said to him: Surely you can see the migratory birds who have already gone down twice to Egypt. Look at them setting out for the cool water district.[32] Until what occurs

30. An indication that a person's fate could be altered through prayer to a god; see the comment on predestination in the introduction to The Tale of the Doomed Prince.
31. Or possibly "send"; see E. F. Wente, *Late Ramesside Letters* (Chicago: The University of Chicago Press, 1967), p. 54, n. 1.
32. On this passage relating to the migration of birds, see Elmar Edel, *Zu den Inschriften auf den Jahreszeitenreliefs der "Weltkammer" aus dem Sonnenheiligtum des Niuserre*, 2 parts (Göttingen: Die Akademie der Wissenschaften, 1961–63), 2:107–08.

shall I be abandoned here? For surely you can see those who have come back to imprison me.

And he went and told it to the prince, and the prince started to weep because of the words which had been told him, for they were disagreeable. And he sent out to me his letter scribe bringing to me two jugs of wine and one sheep. He had Tanetnē, an Egyptian songstress whom he had, brought to me, saying: Sing for him! Don't let his mind be preoccupied with concern. And he sent to me, 2,70 / saying: Eat and drink, don't let your mind be preoccupied with concern. You will hear whatever I have to say tomorrow.

When morning came, he had his assembly summoned, and he stood in their midst and said to the Tjeker: What is (the purpose of) your journeys? And they said to him: It is in pursuit of those ⌜damnable⌝ freighters which you are sending to Egypt with our competitors that we have come. And he said to them: I won't be able to imprison the envoy of Amon within my land. Let me send him off, and (then) you may set out in pursuit of him in order to imprison him.

And he put me on board and sent me off from there at the harbor of the sea. The winds wafted me to the land of 2,75 / Alasiya,[33] and the townsmen came out against me to kill me. And so I picked my way[34] through them to the place where Hatiba, the princess of the town, was. I met her after she had left from one house of hers and as she was about to enter her other one. I saluted her and said to the people who were standing around her: Surely there is one among you who understands Egyptian. And one of them

33. I.e. Cyprus.
34. See Etienne Drioton, in *ASAE* 40 (1940): 59.

said: I understand. So I said to him: Tell my lady that I used to hear as far away as Nē,[35] where Amon is, that (although) it is in every town that injustice is practiced, it is in the land of Alasiya that justice is practiced. Is it here (too) that injustice is being practiced every day?

2,80 And she said: What is the meaning of / your speaking so? And I said to her: If the sea rages and the winds waft me to the land where you are, you should not let them take charge over me to kill me seeing that I am an envoy of Amon. Now look here, as for me, I shall be searched for until whatevery day (shall come). Regarding this crew of the Prince of Byblos whom they are seeking to kill, surely its lord will find ten crews belonging to you and kill them in return.

And so she had the people summoned, and they were arraigned. And she said to me: Spend the night . . .

(The remainder of the report is lost.)

35. Nē, meaning "The City," was the popular designation of Thebes.

PART 3

Instructions, Lamentations, and Dialogues

The Maxims of Ptahhotpe

This manual of good and polite conduct is one of the most difficult of Egyptian literary texts, but at the same time it is an excellent example of a genre *of great popularity in Ancient Egypt. The earliest manuscript of this work is the Prisse Papyrus, preserved in the Bibliothèque Nationale in Paris; it dates from the early Middle Kingdom and by good fortune is complete; another early manuscript, unfortunately fragmentary, is in the British Museum. It would appear that in later times the Egyptians themselves found this text difficult to understand, and in the New Kingdom a second edition was produced in which the original text underwent a good deal of emendation; this later version is represented most fully by British Museum Papyrus 10509. The following translation is based entirely on the Prisse Papyrus, as being the oldest and therefore most authentic; in view of the dfficulty of this composition, due acknowledgment must be paid to the work of Z. Žába,* Les Maximes de Ptahhotep *(Prague: Editions de l'Académie Tchécoslovaque des Sciences, 1956), of which the present writer has made full use, though at times differing materially from Žába's conclusions. For bibliography, see Erman,* The Ancient Egyptians, *pp. xxvi, 54–66.*

R. O. F.

4,1   The teaching of the City Governor and Vizier Ptahhotpe under His Majesty the King of Upper and Lower Egypt Izezi—may he live forever and ever! [1]

4,2   The City Governor and Vizier Ptahhotpe said: O Sover-

1. King Izezi reigned in Dynasty 5, ca. 2350 B.C. If the attribution to the vizier Ptahhotpe is correct, then the original composition is a good deal older than the earliest extant copies, which date from the Middle Kingdom.

eign my lord! Decrepitude has come into being, old age has befallen, woe has come, weakness is renewed, and he [2] has gone to rest ⌜in discomfort⌝ every day. The eyes are dim, the ears are deaf, strength is perishing because of my lassi-

5,1 tude, the mouth is silent and cannot speak, / the mind has come to an end and cannot remember yesterday, the bone(s) suffer all over, good is become evil, all taste has gone, the nose is stopped up and cannot breathe, standing and sitting are irksome, and what old age does to men is evil in every respect.[3] May it be permitted to your humble servant to appoint a staff of old age; [4] then will I tell him the words of the judges, the counsels of those who were aforetime, who in the past obeyed the gods. Then shall the like be done for you, troubles shall be driven away from the people, and the Two Banks shall serve you.

5,5 Then said the Majesty of this god: Teach him / what has been said in the past; then he will set a good example to the children of the magistrates, and judgment and all exactitude shall enter into him. Speak to him, for there is none born wise.

Here begin the maxims of good speech spoken by the hereditary noble and Count, God's father, beloved of the god,[5] eldest bodily son of the king,[6] the City Governor and Vizier Ptahhotpe, when instructing the ignorant to know

2. Ptahhotpe, who is complaining of the miseries of old age.
3. This clause, which sums up the evils of old age, is displaced in Prisse, presumably by a copyist's error; in the translation it has been restored to the natural position it occupies in the later version.
4. I.e. a pupil or disciple who would care for the sage in his declining years.
5. A religious and court title.
6. A titular rank; Ptahhotpe was an old man and could not be the physical son of King Izezi, but he may well have been of royal blood.

according to the standard of good speech, being weal to him who will hear and woe to him who will disobey it. Thus he said to his son:

1. Do not be arrogant because of your knowledge, but confer with the ignorant man as with the learned, for the limit of skill has not been attained, and there is no crafts-
5,10 man who has (fully) acquired his mastery. / Good speech is more hidden than malachite, yet it is found in the possession of women slaves at the millstones.

2. If you find a disputant arguing, one having authority and superior to you, bend down your arms and bow your back; if you disagree with him, he will not side with you. You should make little of the evil speaking by not opposing him in his argument; it means that he will be dubbed an ignoramus when your self-control has matched his prolixity.[7]

3. If you find a disputant arguing, your equal who is on your own level, let your virtue be manifest against him in silence when he is speaking ill; great will be the talk on the part of the hearers, and your name will be fair in the opinion of the magistrates.

6,1 4. / If you find a disputant arguing, a humble man who is not your equal, do not be aggressive against him in proportion as he is humble; let him alone, that he may confute himself. Do not question him in order to relieve your feelings, do not vent yourself against your opponent, for wretched is he who would destroy him who is poor of understanding; men will do what you wish, and you will defeat him by the disapproval of the magistrates.

7. In dealing with argumentative persons, keep quiet and let them talk themselves out; they will get muddled, and your self-control in remaining quiet will be much admired. The same theme crops up in the next two sections.

5. If you are a leader, controlling the destiny of the masses, seek out every good thing, until there is no fault in 6,5 your governance. / Truth is great and ⟨its⟩ ⌐effectiveness endures¹; it has not been confounded since the time of Osiris. Men punish him who trangresses the laws, and it is a transgression (even) in the eyes of the rapacious; it is baseness which takes away wealth, and wrongdoing has never brought its venture safe to port. He ⁸ says, "I acquire for myself," and does not say, "I acquire because of my occupation," ⁹ but when the end comes, rightdoing endures. That is what a man learns ¹⁰ from his father.

6. Do not inspire terror in men, for God also is repelled. A man expects to live by it ¹¹ and (consequently) is lacking bread to eat. A man expects to become wealthy ⟨through it⟩ and says, "I will acquire for myself what I perceive"; a man says, "I will plunder someone else," and he ends by giving it to someone whom he does not know. 6,10 No / terror of man has ever been effective; it is (only) the ordinance of God which is effective. Plan to live in peace, and what men give will come of its own accord.

7. If you are one of the guests at the the table of one who is greater than you, accept what he gives when it is set before you. Look at what is before you and do not 7,1 pierce him / with much staring, for to annoy him is an abomination of the spirit.¹² Do not speak to him until he calls, for no one knows what may be displeasing; speak when he addresses you, and what you say will (then) be pleasing. As for a magnate when he is at the distribution of

8. The wrongdoer.
9. I.e. "I acquire by hook or by crook and not by honest toil."
10. Lit. "relates."
11. By inspiring terror.
12. Something altogether wrong or unwise.

food,[13] his conduct is in accordance with the command of his will. He will give to whomsoever he favors, for it is the counsel of the night which comes to pass,[14] and it is the will which extends his hands; a magnate gives (only) to him who has attained to being a man (of position). The eating of bread is under the dispensation of God, and it is (only) the ignorant man who will complain about it.

8. If you are a trusted man whom one magnate sends to another, be utterly exact when he sends you. Do business for him exactly as he says; beware of calumny in speech which might ⌜embroil⌝ one magnate with another, to the distortion of truth; angry speech spoken by anyone, great 7,5 or small, should not be repeated, / for that is an abomination to the spirit

9. If you cultivate and there is growth in the field, and God puts it into your hand in quantity, do not sate your mouth [15] in the presence of your kindred, for great respect is given to the quiet man. If a virtuous man is an owner of property, in the tribunal (even) he seizes like a crocodile. Do not put a claim on him who has no children, do not speak ill or boast about it; there is many a father in trouble and (many) a mother who has borne, and another is more content than she. It is the lone man whom God fosters, and the lord of a tribe, it prays that he may follow.[16]

10. If you are lowly and serve a wealthy man, let all your conduct be good before God. When ⟨his⟩ former poverty is known to you, do not be arrogant against him because of what you know about his former state; respect

13. Lit. "is behind bread," i.e. standing behind a pile to hand it out.
14. I.e. the donor has slept on his decisions.
15. Perhaps "do not boast about it."
16. An obscure passage, meaning perhaps that the head of a large family is pestered by his offspring to follow *their* desires.

him in proportion to what has accrued to him, for property does not come of itself: such is its law for whoever desires it. If <it> becomes superabundant, men respect him on his own account, for it is God who made him wealthy, and he defends him when he is asleep.

11. Follow your desire as long as you live and do not perform more than is ordered;[17] do not lessen the time of following desire, for the wasting of time is an abomination to the spirit; do not use up / the daytime more than is (necessary) for the maintenance of your household. When riches are gained, follow desire, for riches will not profit if one is sluggish.

7,10

12. If you are a wealthy man, beget a son who will make God well-disposed. If he is straightforward and reverts to your character and takes care of your property in good order, do for him everything good, for he is your son who belongs to what your spirit begot. Do not separate your heart from him, for ⌜ill-will⌝ makes quarreling. If he errs and disobeys your counsel and defies all that is said and babbles evil words, ⌜punish⌝ him for all his speeches, show displeasure at them; / it will mean that an impediment is implanted in the body for him.[18] Their[19] guidance cannot err, and those whom they make boatless cannot cross (the river).

8,1

13. If you are in the portal,[20] carry on[21] according to your procedure which was commanded to you on the first day. Do not pass by,[22] or you will be detained. Be

17. Lit. "said."
18. I.e. he will come to grief.
19. The gods.
20. The gate of judgment, where pleas are heard.
21. Lit. "stand and sit."
22. I.e. play truant.

alert for him who enters and reports, with freedom of
8,5   movement for him who is summoned. The portal / is (to
be conducted) according to the normal standard, and all
conduct is according to rule; it is God who advances
position, and those who elbow in do not succeed.

14. If you are with people, make for yourself a partisan
of a trustworthy man, for a trustworthy man is one who
does not distort speech in his mind;[23] he himself will become a leader, an owner of property by reason of his own
conduct. Then your name will be fair without your having to speak; your body will be provided, your face will
be toward your kindred,[24] and men will make presentation
to you of what is unknown to you. As for him whose
8,10 heart obeys his belly, he puts dislike of himself / in the
place of love; his heart is sad and his body unanointed.
Joyous are the hearts of those whom God has given, but
he who obeys his belly has an enemy.

15. Report your business without dissembling; display
your conduct in your master's council. If one overflows[25]
to him when he speaks, it will not be bad for the messenger
who reports ⌐without expression,⌐[26] but who is he who
realizes it? Is the magnate against his[27] affair in error? If
he[28] plans to oppose him because of it, he[29] will keep
silence, saying: "I have (already) spoken."

9,1   16. If you are a leader, be far-reaching / of governance
in what is entrusted to you, and you shall do distinguished

23. Lit. "in his body."
24. I.e. you will look kindly on them.
25. I.e. reports fully.
26. The translation is not certain, but the meaning seems to be:
"who reports accurately and dispassionately."
27. The messenger's.
28. The magnate.
29. The messenger.

things. Remember [30] the days which are to come, that no (awkward) matter may come up in the midst of favors; (else) a crocodile will get in and hatred supervene.[31]

17. If you are a leader, be pleased when you hear the speech of a petitioner; do not rebuff him until his belly is 9,5 emptied of what he has planned / to tell you; the victim of wrong prefers the venting of his feelings to the performance of that for which he has come. As for him who rebuffs petitions, men say: "Why does he reject them?" Not everything about which he [32] has petitioned is what shall come to pass, but a kindly hearing is a soothing of the heart.

18. If you desire to preserve friendship in a home into which you enter, whether as lord or as brother or as friend, at any place into which you enter, beware of approaching 9,10 the women, / for no good comes to a place where this is done, nor is it clever to reveal them; [33] a thousand men are turned aside from what is good for them. A little moment, the semblance of a dream, and death reaches you because of knowing them. To shoot an enemy is a ⌜crime⌝; men go out [34] because of doing it, and the heart should thrust it away.[35] As for him who fails by reason of lusting after them no plan at all will succeed in his hand.

10,1 19. If you desire / your conduct to be good, refrain yourself from all kinds of evil. Beware of an act of avarice; it is a bad and incurable disease. Intimacy is made impossible by it; it alienates fathers and mothers and maternal

---

30. Emending *n.f* into the second person *n.k* after the imperative.
31. I.e. beware that nothing can be brought up against you when you are getting on; if it happens, ill-feeling will result.
32. The plaintiff.
33. Show them in their true colors?
34. Leave home?
35. I.e. the wise person refrains.

brothers, it drives wife and husband apart, it is a gathering of all that is evil and a bag of all that is hateful. The man who is exact in right-doing and who walks according to its 10,5 procedure will long endure; / he will achieve a testament thereby,[36] but there is no tomb for the rapacious man.

20. Do not be rapacious over the division,[37] do not be covetous except as concerns your own property. Do not be rapacious toward your kindred, for greater is the claim of the gentle man than that of the strong. It is scarcity which comes forth from among his [38] kindred, and he is devoid of what speech can bring.[39] Even a little of what is coveted turns a quarrelsome man into an amicable one.

21. If you are well-to-do and can maintain your household, love your wife in your home ‹according to good› custom.[40] Fill her belly, clothe her back; oil is the panacea 10,10 for her body. / Make her happy while you are alive, for she is land profitable to her lord. Neither judge her nor raise her to a position of power . . .[41] her eye is a storm-wind when she sees ‹. . .› [42] Soothe her heart with what has accrued to you; it means that she will continue to dwell in your house. If you repulse her, it means ⌈tears⌉.[43] A vagina is what she gives for her condition; [44] what she asks about is who will make a canal for her.[45]

36. I.e. will have something to leave his family.
37. Of the estate of a testator.
38. The strong man's.
39. I.e. gets only a refusal when he asks.
40. The text is corrupt; read *mr·k ḥmt·k m ẖnw·k r tp-ḥsb*.
41. Corrupt and unintelligible.
42. A textual omission here; the following clause about soothing her heart is supplied from the badly damaged Middle Kingdom papyrus BM 10371/10435.
43. Lit. "water"; presumably the result of not making it up after a quarrel.
44. I.e. marital relations are the price she pays for being given a home.
45. I.e. her one anxiety is that she may be properly fed and clothed.

11,1   22. / Propitiate your friends with what has accrued to you, that being possible to one whom God favors; as for one who fails to propitiate his friends, men will say that he is a selfish character. No one knows what may happen when he perceives tomorrow, and the straightforward character who is content with it is a (real) character. If occasions of favor arise, it is friends who say "Welcome!" If one cannot bring peace to an abode, one has recourse to friends when there is trouble.

11,5   23. / Do not repeat slander; you should not hear it, for it is the result of hot temper. Repeat (only) a matter seen, not what is heard. It should be left alone; do not speak at all, and your vis-à-vis will know ⟨your⟩ virtue.[46] A theft is commanded to be done and is brought about in order to take it, being what is hateful according to law. See, it is the destruction of a dream, a covering of it over.

    24. If you are a trusted man who sits in the council of his lord, set your heart on excellence. If you are quiet,
11,10 / it will be more profitable than *tftf*-plants; speak (only) when you know you can clarify the issue. It is the expert who speaks in the council, for speech is more difficult than any craft, and it is he who can interpret it who gives it authority(?).[47]

    25. If you are powerful and inspire respect of yourself, whether by knowledge or by pleasantness of speech, do not give orders except as concerns business. The quar-
12,1 relsome man falls into wrongdoing; / do not be haughty, lest he is humiliated; do not keep silence, but beware lest you offend or answer a word with anger. Avert your

46. There is apparently a considerable textual omission here, for what follows seems to have no connection with what precedes. The other texts give no help.
47. Lit. "who puts it at the rod."

face, control yourself, and the flames of hot temper will sweep past [48] the pleasant man who is offended and whose path is contested. One who is serious all day will never have a good time, while one who is frivolous all day will never establish a household. He who shoots will be ⌈paid in full⌉ like one who works the steering-oar on an occasion
12,5 ⌈for landing⌉, and another ⌈is arrested⌉.[49] / He who obeys his heart will ⌈be well provided⌉.

26. Do not oppose the action of a magnate,[50] do not vex the heart of him who is overburdened, for his ill-will will arise against one who is hostile to him, but goodwill will be released through one who loves him, for he who dispenses goodwill is with God, and what he desires is what is done for him; ⌈make calm⌉ [51] after the storm. Content is due to his goodwill, but illwill is due to an enemy; it is goodwill which makes love grow.

12,10 27. Instruct a magnate in what is profitable to him; / bring about his reception into the company of men, that you may cause his wisdom to fall upon its owner, for your sustenance will depend on his goodwill. The body of love is more than contentment, and your back will be clothed by it. When he is accepted, you can attend to [52] the life of your house through your rank which you desire. It is

48. Lit. "sweep over" in the sense of "pass over and be gone."
49. A series of sentences of which the meaning is obscure.
50. Lit. "do not oppose yourself at the moment (of action) of a magnate."
51. Emending the corrupt reading into *sḥtp* as did Dévaud; lit. "pacify the face." Žába, reading the corrupt group as *sḳd* and translating as "(sa face) se retourne vers toi après la colère," misses the contrast between *sḥtp* and *nšny*, "storm"; further, *r·k* after the corruptly written verb, which has no suffix, seems to indicate an imperative. The person addressed is advised to pacify the angry magnate.
52. Lit. "your face will be toward."

he who will live by means of it, and he will make a good arm toward you;[53] quiet will last long, for the love of you is in the bodies of those who love you; see, it is good-will which desires to hear.

13,1   28. / If you act as a man of rank belonging to the tri-bunal, an envoy who pleases the masses, ⌜adopt impartial-ity of judgment⌝ [54] when you speak; do not be one-sided. Beware lest he tell his affair ⟨to⟩ the magistrates in order that he may cause the matter to be (decided) in his favor;[55] direct your actions to true judgment.

29. If you are lenient concerning a matter that is past
13,5 and favor[56] a man / because of his straight dealing, pass him by, do not remember him, since he was silent toward you on the first day.[57]

30. If you have become great after your poverty and have achieved property after former need in the city which you know, do not ⌜boast of⌝ what has accrued to you in the past, do not trust in your riches, which have accrued to you by the gift of God; you will not be subordinate to anyone else to whom the like has happened.

13,10   31. Bend your back to your superior, / your steward of the palace; so will your house endure because of its goods, and your payment will be at the proper time. Wretched is he who is in opposition against a superior, for men live only for the season of his leniency; the arm is
14,1 never bent[58] when he is despoiled. Do not rob / the house

53. I.e. He will give you a helping hand.
54. Corrupt; the translation depends on the context. So also Žába.
55. Lit. "that he may put speech on the side thereof."
56. Lit. "incline to."
57. I.e. if an erstwhile offender is running straight, do not rake up old scores.
58. I.e. no one shows him respect any longer.

of neighbors, do not steal the goods of one who is near you, lest he should make a complaint against you until you hear < ⌜about it⌝ >; it is a ⌜fault⌝ of a ⌜recalcitrant⌝ heart. If he knows it, he will ⌜litigate⌝, and wretched is he who is in opposition against his environment.[59]

14,5   32. Do not copulate with a woman-boy,[60] for you know that / what is (generally) opposed will be a ⌜necessity⌝ to his heart, and that which is in his body will not be calmed. Let him not spend the night doing what is opposed in order that he may be calm after he has ⌜quenched⌝ his desire.

33. If you would search out the nature of a friend, do not question one who is near him, but deal with him privately until you are no longer troubled about his condition. Argue with him after a while; prove his mind in an occasion of speech. If what he has seen escapes from him and 14,10 he deals so as to make you angry with him, either / <keep silence>[61] or be friendly with him; do not avert your face. Be wary when he has revealed a matter; do not answer with an act of hostility, do not remove yourself from him, do not ⌜humiliate⌝ him. Never has his time failed to come, for no one can escape from him who has predestined him.

34. Be cheerful while you are alive; as for what goes out from the storehouse, it cannot go in (again). It is bread 15,1 for sharing out / over which men are covetous; he whose belly is empty is the one who complains and he who is in opposition becomes a ⌜grumbler⌝. Do not let him be one

59. A difficult passage. What the writer is trying to convey seems to be that to rob one's neighbor is a stupid act which would be done only by one who is at odds with those around him.
60. Cf. Žába, pp. 155–56. It seems to me, however, that this is a reference to homosexuality. See now H. Goedicke, in *JARCE* 6 (1967): 97–102.
61. Omitted in Prisse but supplied from the Middle Kingdom manuscript in London.

who is near you; graciousness is a man's memorial in the years which follow the scepter.[62]

35. Know your neighbors while you have property and do not show ill-temper to your friends, it will be a river-bank which fills up; it is greater than its riches, for the property of one may belong to another, but the character of a man of rank will be beneficial to him,[63] and a good
15,5 reputation / will be a memorial.

36. Punish severely, teach thoroughly, for the suppression of wrongdoing leads to the establishing of a good character. As for a case not concerning wrongdoing, a complaint should be made through an opponent.[64]

37. If you take a wife who is . . . , who is frivolous and notorious to her fellow-citizens, and she is . . . be kind to her for a space, do not put her away, but let her eat. The frivolous woman . . .[65]

38. If you hear these things which I have said to you, all your counsels will be to the fore; if their truth remains, they mean wealth. The memory of them will move in the mouths of men because their maxims are good, every word will be used, and ⟨they⟩ will not perish in this land for-ever. It is done and well-expressed, and magistrates will
15,10 speak of it; it is to teach a man to speak to / him who shall come after that he may hear it, having become an expert who is heard, for it is good to speak to him who shall come after, and it is he who will hear it. If a good

62. I.e. after he has laid down his authority in death.
63. To know your neighbor is of greater importance than riches, for good repute will be of more use than wealth when misfortune befalls.
64. I.e. punish crime for the sake of your reputation, but leave civil actions to be started by the aggrieved party.
65. The three dots in this paragraph indicate that the phrases in all three cases are untranslatable.

deed comes to pass by the hand of one who is a chieftain, he will be well-famed forever, and all his wisdom will be everlasting. It is the learned man who helps his soul when establishing his good fortune on earth by means of it, and the learned man will be satisfied by what he has learned. Is the magistrate at his good deed? [66] His heart and his

16,1 tongue ⌜are in harmony⌝,[67] / his lips are accurate when he speaks, his eyes see, his ears are pleased at hearing what is good for his son, who does what is right and is devoid of falsehood.

39. Hearing is good for a son who hears, when hearing enters into the hearer, for he who hears will become a judge.[68] Hearing is good and speaking is good, but he who

16,5 hears is a possessor of benefits. / Hearing is good for the hearer, and better is hearing than anything, for fair love comes (thus) into being. How good it is that a son should accept what his father says! Old age comes about for him by means of it; he who hears is one whom God loves, but one who does not hear is one whom God detests. It is the heart which educates its owner in hearing or in not hearing, for the life, prosperity, and health of a man depend on [69] his heart; it is the hearer who hears what is said, and he who acts according to what is said is one who

16,10 loves hearing. How good it is that a son should obey / his father, and how joyful is he to whom this is said! A son is pleasing to a lord of hearing,[70] (even) one who hears whoever says it to him, that he may be efficient in his body,

66. I.e. carrying out his duties properly.
67. The text is corrupt; Žába has guessed the sense to be that the heart and the tongue match each other, are in equilibrium.
68. Lit. "hearer"; an attentive son will profit by what he is told. From here on the author makes much play on the stem *sḏm*, "hear."
69. Lit. "are."
70. One who expects to be heard.

one honored by his father, and he will be remembered in the mouths of the living who survive on earth or who are yet to be.

40. If a man of rank accepts what his father says, he will not upset any plan of his. Your teaching is in your 17,1 son, a hearer / who will be well-pleasing to the magistrates and who will guide his speech according to what is said to him. He who sees is one who hears, a son who will be well-pleasing and whose actions will be distinguished. Error has entered early into him who does not hear, but a wise man will establish himself, while the fool is hard hit.

17,5 41. As for the fool who will not hear, / there is no one who can do anything for him. He regards knowledge as ignorance and what is beneficial as something harmful; he does everything hateful, so that men are angry with him every day. He lives on that whereby men die, and to distort speech is his food. His character in this respect is in the knowledge of the magistrates, dying alive every day; men pass over his deeds because of the multitude of troubles on him every day.

17,10 42. / A son who hears is a follower of Horus, and it goes well with him when he has heard. He grows old and attains honor, and talks of the like to his children when renewing his father's teaching, for every man is taught like his begetter. He talks to ⟨his⟩ children so that they may speak ⟨to⟩ their children. Achieve a good character, 18,1 / do not give offence; maintain justice, that your children may live. If ⌜the eldest of them⌝ comes suffering wrong, men will say of what they have seen: "Indeed, that is like it!" [71] Say to those who will hear: "Indeed, that is

71. A very obscure passage; I translate the words without grasping their meaning.

18,5 like it / also!" All men will see them,[72] and the masses will be satisfied, for there is no profit in riches without them.

43. Do not take away a word, do not bring it away, do not set one thing in the place of another, beware of opening . . .[73] in yourself. Wait on the speech of a sage and
18,10 listen, for you desire / that you may be established in the mouths of the listeners when you speak. Enter into the condition of an expert and speak to perfection, and every plan of yours will be in order.

44. Suppress your desires, control your mouth; so will your counsel be (heard) among the magistrates. Be utterly exact to your master and act so that he may say: "That is
19,1 my son," / and so that those who shall hear it may say: "Favored is he who begot him for himself." Be patient when you speak, and you will say distinguished things; then will the magistrates who shall hear say: "How good is his utterance!"

45. Act until your master says of you: "How good was the teaching of his father from whom he issued, from out of whose body, who spoke to him while he was yet entirely in the womb, and what was done for him was greater
19,5 / than what was said to him." Behold, a good son is a gift of God, one who does more than was said to him by his master; he acts rightly, and his mind has achieved more than his actions; according as you reach me,[74] your body will be hale and the king will be pleased with all that happens. You will surpass (my) years of life, and what I have done on earth is not little. I have passed 110 years of life through what the king gave to me, favors over and above

72. I.e. justice and a good character.
73. An unidentified plant. Apparently we have here a metaphor warning against giving way to bad thoughts.
74. I.e. attain to the height of the author's wisdom and experience.

those who went before, because of acting rightly for the king until the blessed state.

It is finished from beginning to end, in accordance with what was found in writing.

The Teaching for the Vizier Kagemni

The last part of this text is preserved in the Papyrus Prisse, which also contains the main text of the Maxims of Ptahhotpe. The author was evidently the father of Kagemni, and it has been conjectured that he was the sage Kaires cited in the passage about the writers of the past in Papyrus Chester Beatty IV (see quotation at beginning of our introduction). The text has been translated and studied by A. H. Gardiner, in JEA 32 (1946): 71–74, to which additional comments were made by W. Federn, in JEA 36 (1950): 48–50. See also A. Scharff, in ZÄS 77 (1941–42): 13–21; G. Posener, in RdE 6 (1951): 32–33; J. Yoyotte, in BSFE 11 (1952): 67–72; A. H. Gardiner, in JEA 37 (1915): 109–10; and E. Edel, MIO 1 (1953): 210–26. Translated also in Erman, The Ancient Egyptians, pp. xxvi, 66–67, and in Battiscombe Gunn, The Instruction of Ptah-hotep and the Instruction for Ke'gemni: The Oldest Books in the World (London: J. Murray, 1918). The Instruction is similar to that of Ptahhotpe to the extent that it is preserved.

W. K. S.

I,1   . . . the submissive man prospers, the moderate man is praised, the tent is open for the silent man, and the place of the contented man is wide.[1]

Do not talk (freely), for the flint knives are sharp against the one who strays from the road; ⌜there is no hastening, except indeed against his misdeed⌝.[2]

1. Federn: the sense seems to be, "He is influential." Gardiner: untrammeled freedom of personal movement seems to be involved, not influence over others.
2. Federn: "Talk not! Ready are knives against the refractory,

177

If you sit with a crowd, abstain from the food you desire, for controlling your desire is (only for) a brief moment. Gluttony is despicable, / and one points one's finger at it. A cup of water quenches thirst, and a mouthful of ⌐leeks⌐ makes the heart strong. Take a (single) good thing instead of dainties, and a little bit instead of much. Base is one whose gut is greedy when the (meal)time has passed by. He should not be mindful of those who eat voraciously at home.

I,5

If you sit down with a glutton, eat when his satiety has passed. If you drink with a drunkard, accept (only) when his desire is satisfied.[3] Do not be quarrelsome about meat in the company of a greedy man. / Accept what he gives you; do not reject it. Then matters will be pleasant. No words can get the better of the man who is free from wrangling at meals, being ⌐meek⌐ to the degree of ⌐complaisance⌐. More pleasant to him than his (own) mother is one who argues.[4] All mankind are his servants.

I,10

So let your (good) name go forth, / while you are silent in your speech, and you will be summoned.[5] Yet do not be proud by virtue of (your) strength among your contemporaries. Take care not to be ⌐opprobrious⌐. One does not know what will happen nor what God does when He punishes.

II,1

Then the vizier had his children summoned, after he had comprehended the manner of mankind. And he ended

without proceeding, except for his fault"; i.e. they always lie in wait for him, but strike only when he commits himself.

3. Federn and others similarly: If you sit with a glutton, eat, and his surfeit will have passed. If you drink with a drunkard, accept, and he will feel satisfied.

4. Perhaps meaning that the silent man is overjoyed at the foolishness of his overtalkative opponent.

5. You will be called in order to be promoted or honored.

II,10 up by saying to them: As to all that is written in / this papyrus roll, heed it just as I have said it to you; do not go beyond what has been ordained. And they placed themselves on their bellies, and they read it out just as it was written. And it was more beautiful in their hearts than anything in this entire land. So they proceeded to live accordingly.

Then His Majesty the King of Upper and Lower Egypt, Huni, died and His Majesty the King of Upper and Lower Egypt, Snefru, was exalted as an excellent king in this entire land. Kagemni was then made overseer of the residence town and vizier.

It has come ⟨its beginning to its end, as it was found in writing⟩.

The Teaching for Merikare

*The principal source for this text is a papyrus in Leningrad which
dates from the New Kingdom, first studied by A. H. Gardiner in
JEA 1 (1914): 20–36. It is in rather poor condition, for of the first
twenty lines only isolated sentences or parts of sentences are preserved, so that no connected sense can be extracted from this part
of the text, and even later there are still numerous lacunae. Moreover,
the scribe Khamwese, who copied this work, was far from careful.
Some help is afforded, however, by other manuscripts which, though
even more fragmentary, do come to the rescue in places. The text
itself is interesting, both because it is a treatise on kingship addressed
by a king whose name is lost to his son and successor Merikare, and
because it sheds some light on an obscure period of Egyptian history
in what is known as the First Intermediate Period, when kings of
the Akhtoy family of Dynasty 9 / 10 ruled northern Egypt from
Heracleopolis and a rival dynasty of Inyotefs had their capital at
Thebes. Our text makes allusion to the intermittent war that raged
between them. As a matter of historical fact, the southern kingdom
ultimately overcame the northern to form Dynasty 11 over all Egypt,
but that still lay in the future so far as The Teaching is concerned.
Apart from the title of the work, the present translation begins in the
middle of line 21 of the Leningrad papyrus. For bibliography, consult Erman,* The Ancient Egyptians, *pp. xxviii, 75–84. The text is
also discussed by G. Posener in* Annuaire du College de France *62
(1962): 290–95; 63 (1963): 303–05; 64 (1964): 305–07; 65 (1965):
343–46; 66 (1966): 342–45. See also Donald Redford, in* JEA *51
(1965): 107–10, on the date of the accounts on the main papyrus; and
Jürgen von Beckerath, in* ZÄS *93 (1966): 20, in which the suggestion
is made that the king was Nebkure Akhtoy.*

R. O. F.

[Here begins the teaching which King . . . made] for his son Merikare [. . .].[1] ⌜As for⌝ [. . .] his kinsfolk [. . .] the citizens [. . .] him, and his partisans are many in sum [. . .] enter [. . .] he is pleasing in the sight of his serfs, being firmly established in [. . .]. A talker is a mischief-maker; suppress him, kill [him], erase his name, [destroy] his kinsfolk, suppress the remembrance of him and his partisans who love him.

25   / A violent man is a confuser of the citizens who always makes partisans of the younger generation. If now you find someone belonging to the citizenry [. . .] and his deeds have passed beyond you,[2] accuse him before the entourage and suppress [him], for he is a rebel indeed; a talker is a mischief-maker. Bend the multitude[3] and drive out hot temper from it; [. . .] will not rise [in] rebellion by means of the poor man when he is made to rebel.

[The mind] of the underling is confused; the army [. . .]; put an end to it by ⌜mixing⌝ [. . .]. Many are angry, for men are put in the labor establishment. Be
30   lenient [. . .] when you oppose; / when you fatten [herds, the people] are in joy. Justify yourself in the presence of God; then men will say [. . .] you [plan]. You shall contend against ⌜wrong⌝ [. . .] a good disposition is a man's heaven, but vilification by the ⌜ill-disposed⌝ man is dangerous.

Be skillful in speech, that you may be strong; [. . .] it is the strength of [. . .] the tongue, and words are braver than all fighting; none can circumvent the clever man [. . .] on the mat; a wise man is a [school] for the mag-

1. A gap of 20 broken lines.
2. I.e. have got beyond your control.
3. To your will.

nates, and those who are aware of his knowledge do not attack him. [Falsehood] does not exist near him, but truth comes to him in full essence,[4] after the manner of what the ancestors said.

35 / Copy your forefathers, for [work] is carried out through knowledge; see, their words endure in writing. Open, that you may read and copy knowledge; (even) the expert will become one who is instructed. Do not be evil, for patience is good; make your lasting monument in the love of you. Multiply [the people] whom the city has enfolded; then will God be praised because of rewards; ˹men will˺ watch over your [. . .] and give thanks for your goodness, and your health will be prayed for [. . .].

Respect the great; keep your people safe; consolidate your frontier and your ˹patrolled area˺,[5] for it is good to work for the future. Show respect [. . .] life for the clear-sighted, but the trusting man will suffer pain. Let 40 men be sent [. . .] / through your kindly disposition. Wretched is he who has bound the land to himself [. . .]; a fool is he who is greedy when others possess. [Life] on earth passes away, it is not long; he is fortunate who [has a good] remembrance in it. No man goes straight forward,[6] (even though) a million belong to the Lord of the Two Lands. [. . .] shall live forever; he who comes from the hand of Osiris shall depart, just as he who is self-indulgent shall be lost.

Make your magnates great, that they may execute your laws; one who is rich in his house will not be one-sided, for he who does not lack is an owner of property; a poor

4. Lit. "brewed."
5. Perhaps the debatable land beyond the frontier.
6. Meaning perhaps that out of the teeming population of the realm, no honest man can be found.

man does not speak truly, and one who says, "Would that I had," is not straightforward; he is one-sided toward the possessor of rewards.[7] Great is the great one whose
45 great ones are great;[8] / valiant is a king who owns an entourage; and august is he who is rich in magnates. Speak truth in your house, so that the magnates who are on earth may respect you, for a sovereign's renown (lies in) straightfowardness; it is the front room of a house that inspires the back room with respect.

Do justice, that you may live long upon earth. Calm the weeper, do not oppress the widow, do not oust a man from his father's property, do not degrade magnates from their seats. Beware of punishing wrongfully; do not kill, for it will not profit you, but punish with beatings and with imprisonment, for thus this land will be set in order, excepting only the rebel who has conspired,[9] for God
50 knows those who are disaffected, / and God will smite down his evil doing with blood. It is the lenient man who [. . .] lifetime; so do not kill a man of whose ability you are aware, and with whom you once recited writings,[10] but read in the ⌜account⌝ [. . .] because of God, and stride forward freely in a difficult place. The soul comes to the place which it knows, and it will not overstep the ways of the past; no magic can oppose it, and it will reach those who will give it water.[11]

As for the tribunal which judges the needy,[12] you know that they will not be lenient on that day of judging the poor; in the hour of exercising (their) function, wretched

7. I.e. toward him who has bribes to give.
8. A typically Egyptian jingle.
9. Lit. "who has found his plans."
10. I.e. an old schoolfellow.
11. I.e. keep it alive.
12. To hear their appeals for redress in the Hereafter.

is he who is accused as a wise man.[13] Do not put your
55   trust in length of years, / for they[14] regard a lifetime
as an hour; a man survives after death, and his deeds are
laid before him in a heap. Existence yonder is eternal, and
he who complains of it[15] is a fool, but as for him who
attains it, he will be like a god yonder, striding forward
like the lords of eternity.

Raise up your young troops, that the Residence may
love you. Multiply your partisans as neighbors; see, your
towns are full of newly settled folk. It is for twenty years
that the rising generation is happy in following its desire,
and neighbors come forth again;[16] he who is caused to
enter goes in for himself by means of children[17] [. . .].
60   Ancient times have fought for us, / and I raised (troops)
from them at my accession. Make your magnates great,
promote your [warriors], increase the rising generation
of your retainers, they being equipped with knowledge,
established with lands, and endowed with cattle.

Do not distinguish the son of a man of rank from a commoner, but take a man to yourself because of his actions,
so that every craft may be carried on [. . .] for the possessor of strength. Guard your frontier, marshal your
fortresses, for troops are profitable to their master. Con-
struct [fine] monuments to God, for it means the perpetu-
ation of the name of whoever does it, and a man should
do what is profitable to his soul, (namely) monthly service
as priest and the wearing of white sandals. Enrich the fane,

13. Because he has used his knowledge to oppress the poor.
14. The tribunal.
15. The tribunal again.
16. Meaning perhaps that the younger generation has reproduced
itself.
17. An obscure sentence of which I do not see the drift, except that
it seems in a way to refer to the advantage of having a family.

65   be discreet concerning the mysteries, enter / into the sanctuary, eat bread in the temple, richly provide the altars, increase the revenues, add to the daily offerings, for it is a profitable matter for whoever does it; maintain your monuments in proportion to your wealth, for a single day gives to eternity, an hour does good for the future, and God is aware of him who serves him. Dispatch your statues to a distant land [18] of which they [19] shall not render an inventory,[20] for he who destroys the goods of an enemy will suffer.[21]

    The enemy cannot be quiet (even) within Egypt,[22] but troops shall subdue troops, in accordance with the prophecy of the ancestors about it, and men fight against Egypt
70   (even) / in the necropolis.[23] Do not destroy ancient buildings with a destruction ⌜through action⌝; I acted thus and so it happened, just as he who had transgressed likewise did against God. Do not deal ill with the Southern Region,[24] for you know the prophecy of the Residence about it, and it has happened [even as] this shall happen; they shall not transgress as they said [. . .]. I turned back

18. To spread knowledge of you and your power.
19. The people in charge of transporting the statues.
20. I.e. shall not report on the resources of the land with an eye to future plunder.
21. Carrying on the thought behind the preceding clause and implying that it is inadvisable to exasperate even an enemy by destroying his goods. At this point the general admonitions as to good conduct come to an end, and we meet practical advice on maintaining the kingdom in the unhappy conditions of the time.
22. The scribe strangely marks the new section as beginning in the next sentence instead of here.
23. The old king goes on to describe with regret how in his reign this very thing happened, resulting in the destruction of ancient buildings.
24. Heracleopolitan monarch advises good relations with the southern kingdom, which at this time was ruled by the Inyotef family of Thebes.

⟨to⟩ Thinis [. . .] its southern boundary at Tawer, and
I captured it like a cloudburst,[25] though King Mer-
[. . .]re[26] did not do it. Be lenient about it[27] . . . [. . .]
75   ⌜renew contracts⌝. / There is no ⌜pure reason⌝ who is
caused to be hidden, and it is good to act on behalf of
posterity.

You stand well with the Southern Region, for the bear-
ers of loads come to you with produce; I did the same as
the ancestors, and there was none who had corn who gave
it.[28] Be kindly to those who are weak toward you, and
satisfy yourself with your own bread and beer. Granite
comes to you without hindrance, so do not destroy someone else's monument. Hew stone in Turah,[29] but do not
build your tomb of what has been thrown down, (or of)
what has been made for what is to be made. See, the king
80   is a possessor of joy; / you can be drowsy and you can
sleep through your strength of arm; follow your desire
through what I have done,[30] for there is no enemy within
your frontier.

I arose as ruler in my city,[31] but I[32] was anxious about
the Delta from He-shenu[33] to Sebak,[34] its southern bound-

25. An allusion to past fighting between Heracleopolis and Thebes.
26. Possibly King Meribre Akhtoy; at any rate, a predecessor of the
author.
27. The relations between North and South?
28. I.e. there was no need for charitable distribution.
29. The limestone quarries near Memphis.
30. The speaker is telling his son that it is the former's achievements
that will enable King Merikare to rule peacefully; possibly for
"your strength" we should read "my strength," since a confusion of
pronouns is a possibility at this point.
31. Heracleopolis.
32. M.S. "he" in accordance with common Egyptian usage; the
pronoun of the 3d person refers back to "ruler."
33. Possibly a locality near Heliopolis.
34. Situation unknown, but probably in the northern Delta.

ary being at the ⌜Canal of the Two Fishes⌝. I pacified the
west as far as ⌜the sand dunes⌝ of the Fayyum; it labors
and yields ⌜*meru*-wood⌝; men see *wan*-wood (once again)
and yield it to us. But the east is rich in foreigners, and
their taxes are [withheld]; the Middle Island is turned about,
(and also) everyone in it.[35] (Yet) the temples say of me:
85 O Great One, / men salute you.

See, [the land] which they [36] destroyed is made into districts and every great city [is restored]. The governance of
(each) one is in the hands of ten men, a magistrate is appointed ⌜who will levy⌝ [. . .] the amount of all the taxes.
The priest is provided with a farm, and men work for you
like a single gang. How is it that disaffection does not
occur? (Because) you will not suffer from a Nile which
fails to come, and the revenues of the Delta are in your
hand. See, the mooring post which I have made in the
east is driven in [37] from the limits of Hebnu to Road-of-
Horus,[38] settled with towns and full of people of the pick
90 of the entire land, to repel / enemies [39] from them. May I
see a brave man who will imitate it [40] and who will do
more than I have done [. . .] by the hand of a cowardly
heir.

Speak thus concerning the barbarian: [41] As for the

35. I.e. the eastern Delta is overrun with foreigners and the center
of the Delta (the Middle Island) is in chaos.
36. The foreigners who overran the Delta.
37. Figurative for "the stable conditions in the eastern Delta are of
my making."
38. Hebnu (Kom el-Ahmar) is north of Beni Hasan; Road-of-Horus
is a fortress on the northeastern frontier, on the main road to
Palestine. [Hebnu may be a Delta town————Ed.]
39. Lit. "babblers" in a foreign language.
40. I.e. what I have done.
41. Here begins a general characterization of the nomads of
Palestine.

wretched Asiatic, unpleasant is the place where he is, (with) trouble from water, difficulty from many trees, and the roads thereof awkward by reason of mountains. He does not dwell in one place, being driven hither and yon through want, going about [the desert] on foot. He has been fighting since the time of Horus; he never conquers, yet he is not conquered, and he does not announce a day of fighting,[42] like a thief whom a community has driven out.

95   But I lived, / and while I existed the barbarians were as though in the walls of a fortress; [my troops] broke open [. . .]. I caused the Delta to smite them, I carried off their people, I took away their cattle, ⌈until⌉ the detestation of the Asiatics was against Egypt. Do not worry about him, for the Asiatic is a crocodile on his riverbank; he snatches a lonely serf, but he will never rob in the vicinity of a populous town.

Dig a moat against [. . .] and flood the half of it at the Bitter Lakes, for see, it is the navel-string of the desert
100 dwellers;[43] / its walls and its soldiers are many and the partisans in it know how to take up arms, apart from the ⌈freemen⌉ of the camp; the region of Djed-esut[44] totals ten thousand men consisting of ⌈free⌉ untaxed commoners, and magnates have been in it since the time of the Residence.[45] ⟨Its⟩ boundary is established, its ⌈garrison⌉ is brave, and many northerners irrigate it to the limits of the Delta, they being taxed in corn like ⌈freemen⌉; it is . . .

42. I.e. he does not issue a formal challenge, as do civilized armies.
43. Apparently meaning: "it is the key to the frontier against the desert dwellers."
44. A name of a quarter of Memphis, here apparently used for the whole city. Memphis was the natural military base for the frontier defenses of the Delta.
45. I.e. since the kingship came into being.

the face of him who made it, and see, it is the door of
105 the Delta. They [46] made a moat for / Ninsu,[47] for a populous city is . . . . Beware of being surrounded by the
partisans of an enemy; watchfulness is what renews years.

When your frontier to the Southern Region is troubled,
it is the barbarians who have taken the ⌜belt⌝.[48] Build
castles in the Delta, for a man's name will not be diminished by what he has done, and a well-founded city cannot
be harmed. Build castles [. . .], for an enemy loves dis-
turbance, and his actions are mean.

110 The late King Akhtoy [49] ordained in a teaching: / "Be
inactive about the violent man who destroys altars, for God
will attack him who rebels against the temples." Men will
come about it [50] according as he [51] does it; [52] he [53] will be
satisfied with what is ordained for him,[54] (namely) a trap
for him; no one will use loyalty toward him on that day
of coming.[55] Protect the altars, worship God, and do not
say: "It is weakness of mind"; do not let your arms be
loose.[56] As for him who makes rebellion against you, it is
to destroy the sky.[57] Prosperity means a year of monuments; [58] even if an enemy knows, he will not destroy
them, through the desire that what he has done may be
embellished by another who comes after. There is no one

46. Earlier kings?
47. Egyptian name of Heracleopolis.
48. Apparently meaning: "have equipped themselves for war."
49. The family name of the Heracleopolitan line of kings.
50. The sacrilege in the temples.
51. God.
52. The punishment of the rebel.
53. The rebel.
54. Cf. colloquial English "He'll get what's coming to him."
55. I.e. when the disturber arrives, he will get no support from others.
56. I.e. do not be slack in well-doing.
57. An example of futile and fruitless effort.
58. I.e. the erection of many monuments.

115   devoid of / an enemy, but the ruler of the Two Banks[59] is a wise man, and a king who possesses an entourage cannot act stupidly.[60] He is wise from birth, and God will distinguish him above millions of men.

The kingship is a goodly office; it has no son and it has no brother who shall make its monuments endure,[61] yet it is the one person who ennobles the other;[62] a man works for his predecessor, through the desire that what he has done may be embellished by another who shall come after 120   him. A mean act was committed in my reign; / the territory of Thinis was devastated.[63] It indeed happened, but not through what I had done; I knew of it only after it was done. See, ⌐the consequences exceeded¬ what I had done, for what is damaged is spoiled, and there is no benefit for him who restores what he (himself) has ruined, who demolishes what he has built and embellishes what he has defaced; beware of it! A blow is repaid by the like of it, and all that is achieved is a hitting.

One generation of men passes to another, and God, who knows characters, has hidden Himself. There is none who will oppose the possessor of a hand,[64] and he is an attacker 125   of / what the eyes see,[65] so worship God upon his way.

59. Egypt.
60. Because he is advised by those about him.
61. I.e. it is self-perpetuating; the king will die, but the kingship goes on.
62. I.e. one generation passes on its achievements to the next.
63. Thinis was a city of especial sanctity, and its devastation would be a heinous crime. The author is referring here to an incident in the intermittent but long-drawn-out war between Heracleopolis and Thebes. A reference to the capture of Thinis has already occurred above.
64. I.e. one ready and willing to strike.
65. This state of affairs is presumably the result of God hiding himself.

Things are made of costly stone and fashioned in copper;
the mud flat is replaced with water; [66] there is no stream
that can be made to hide, for it means that the dike in
which it hid itself is destroyed. The soul goes to the place
it knows and does not stray on yesterday's road. Beautify
your mansion in the West,[67] embellish your place in the
necropolis with straightforwardness and just dealing, for
it is on that which their [68] hearts rely; more acceptable is
the character of the straightforward man than the ox of the
wrongdoer. Serve God, that He may do the like for you,
with offerings / for replenishing the altars and with carv-
ing; it is that which will show forth your name, and God is
aware of whoever serves Him. Provide for men, the cattle
of God, for He made heaven and earth at their desire. He
suppressed the greed of the waters, he gave the breath of
life to their noses, for they are likenesses of Him which
issued from His flesh. He shines in the sky for the benefit
of their hearts; He has made herbs, cattle, and fish to
nourish them. He has killed His enemies and destroyed
His own children,[69] because they had planned to make
rebellion; He makes daylight for the benefit of their hearts,
and He sails around in order to see them. He has raised
up / a shrine behind them, and when they weep, He hears.
He has made them rulers even from the egg, a lifter to lift
(the load) from the back of the weak man; He has made
for them magic to be weapons to ward off what may happen.

Be watchful over it [70] by night as by day. How has He

66. The results of worshiping God; affairs prosper.
67. Your tomb.
68. Your subjects.
69. An allusion to the myth of the destruction of mankind.
70. I.e. your conduct.

killed the disaffected? Even as a man strikes his son for his brother's sake, for God knows every name.

⌜Do not be distressed ⟨at⟩⌝[1] [71] my utterance even when it [72] gives laws concerning the king. ⌜Instruct yourself, that you may rise up⌝ as a man; then you will attain to my repute [73] without anyone who accuses you. Do not kill /anyone who approaches you, but favor him, for God knows him. He who flourishes on earth is one of them,[74] and they who serve the king are gods. Instill the love of you into all the world, for a good character is what is remembered. . . . is perished, and it is said of you: "He who will destroy the time of suffering by those who are at the back [75] in the House of Akhtoy, in praying for him who will come today.[76]

See, I have told you the best of my inmost thoughts,[77] which you should set steadfastly before your face.

(The Leningrad papyrus ends with a wordy colophon informing us that this particular copy was made by a scribe named Khamwese for his own use and that of his brother Mahu.)

71. Lit. "do not make a malady ⟨at⟩."
72. The "malady." The sense seems to be: "even if my rules for governance are hard, do not get unduly upset by them."
73. Lit. "reach me."
74. The gods?
75. The servants and underlings.
76. I.e. the new king who will set things right.
77. Lit. of my body.

The Teaching of King Ammenemes I
to His Son Sesostris

This text purports to be the posthumous advice of King Ammenemes I, who almost certainly was assassinated, to his son, heir, and co-regent, Sesostris I. The work must have been looked on as a classic in ancient times, as some seventy copies of parts of it are extant to-day. The principal and by far the best source for the text is a document known as the Millingen Papyrus, but the original is lost, and we are now dependent upon a hand copy made over a century ago by Peyron (see J. Lopez, in Revue d'Egyptologie *15 [1963]: 29–33). This papyrus was a good text in three pages of manuscript, but unfortunately the third page was destroyed except for the beginnings of the lines, so for the last part of the work we are dependent on the corrupt Papyrus Sallier II and some extracts on ostraca and on a writing board in the Brooklyn Museum. Though the "teaching" is put in the mouth of Ammenemes I, it was un-doubtedly composed under Sesostris I by a scribe named Akhtoy, and it takes a jaundiced, not to say a misanthropic, view of the relations of a king with his subordinates: "trust no brother, know no friend" is the keynote. Judging by the disillusioned, bitter expression on the faces of some of the statues of a later king of the dynasty, Sesostris III, it would seem that he shared this distrust of those about the person of the monarch. For bibliography and commentary, see Erman,* The Ancient Egyptians, *pp. xxvii, 72–74. A new edition has been prepared by W. Helck,* Der Text der "Lehre des Amenemhets I für seinen Sohn" *(Wiesbaden: 1969). There are also comments by Hans Goedicke in* JARCE *7 (1968): 15–21.*

R. O. F.

Here begins the teaching which the late King of Upper and Lower Egypt, Sehetepibre, the son of Re Ammenemes made when he spoke in imparting truth to his son the Lord of All. He said: O you who appear as a god, hear what I shall say to you, that you may be king of the land and rule the Banks,[1] and achieve abundance of good fortune. Be on your guard against all who are subordinate to you when there occurs something to whose terrors no thought has been given; do not approach them in your solitude, 1,5 trust no brother, know no friend, make / no intimates, for there is no profit in it. When you go to rest, guard your own heart, for no man has partisans on the day of trouble. I gave to the poor man, I cherished the orphan, I caused him who had nothing to attain (to wealth) like him who was wealthy, but it was he who ate my bread who raised levies; he to whom I had given my hands created terror thereby; those who wore my fine linen looked on me as a shadow; and they who smeared on my myrrh poured water under ⟨me⟩.[2]

O you living images of me, my heirs among men, make 1,10 for me a funeral oration[3] which has not / been heard (before), a great deed of battle which has not been seen,[4] for men fight in the arena and the past is forgotten; goodness cannot profit one who does not know him whom he should know. It was after supper, and night had fallen. I took an hour of recreation lying on my bed, for I was weary 2,1 and I began to doze,[5] / when weapons were brandished

---

1. Egypt.
2. The significance of this act is not clear, but in some way it showed gross ingratitude for favors received.
3. A clear indication that the supposed author of this work is in fact already dead.
4. A gladiatorial show or funeral games?
5. Lit. "my heart began to follow my sleep." Here we come upon an account of the assassination of the king. Although it is not stated in so many words, there can be no doubt that the attack

and men argued about me. I acted like the snake of the desert,⁶ for I awoke at the fighting and was by myself, and I found that it was a combat with the guard. If I had made haste with weapons in my hand, I would have made the cowards retreat ⌈in confusion⌉, but no one is brave at night, and no one can fight alone; no happy outcome 2,5 can result without a protector. / See, my injuries occurred while I was without you, before the entourage had heard that I was handing over to you, before I had sat down with you.⁷ Therefore I will give you good advice,⁸ because I neither fear them nor (even) think about them; ⌈I take no cognizance of⌉ the slackness of servants. Have women ever marshaled the ranks? Are brawlers nourished within a house? Are the waters opened up or the earthen banks destroyed?⁹ Are the citizens befooled because of what they have done?

Trouble has not come about me since I was born, and the like of my deeds through the exercise of my valor has 2,10 not come to pass.¹⁰ / I traveled to Elephantine, I turned back to the Delta; I have stood at the limits of the land and have seen its middle; I have attained the limits of my power by my strong arm and by my nature. It was I who made barley and loved grain; the Nile-god showed me respect in

---

achieved its aim and that the king was murdered; this is borne out by the haste with which Sesostris I, the co-king and heir, rushed home from his returning Libyan expedition, as recounted in the story of Sinuhe.

6. I.e. I lay low.

7. Since Ammenemes I had already had his son Sesostris I as coregent for ten years, this passage suggests that the old king had decided at last to abdicate in favor of his son, but that his murder took place before his intention had been made public.

8. Lit. "I will make your counsels."

9. I.e. Do men deliberately destroy the irrigation channels?

10. Ammenemes now goes on to recount his achievements.

3.1　　every open place,[11] and none went hungry in my years, none went thirsty in them.[12] / Men dwelt (in peace) through what I had done, talking of me, for everything that I commanded was in good order. I have curbed lions, I have carried off crocodiles, I have crushed the people of Wawat, I have carried off the Medjay, I have made the Asiatics slink like dogs. I have built for myself a house adorned

3,5　　with gold, its ceiling of lapis lazuli, its walls of silver, / the doors of copper and the door-bolts of bronze, it having been made for eternity and prepared for everlasting.[13] I know that the owner of it is the Lord of All.[14] Indeed, many children are in the streets; the wise man agrees and the fool says "no," inasmuch as he who does not know it is devoid of vision.[15] ⌜O my son⌝ [16] Sesostris, ⌜may⌝ your legs walk; you are my own heart, and my eyes watch ⌜you⌝. ⌜You were⌝ born in an hour of happiness in the presence of the sun-folk,[17] and they give you praise. See, I have made a beginning and you have arranged the

11. I.e. the inundation flooded all the available land.
12. At this point the Millingen papyrus fails us, only the beginnings of lines being preserved from here on, and we are largely dependent on corrupt later versions.
13. *Ḥr.s* at the end of this clause in P. Sallier II appears to be a later interpolation.
14. From here on the translation is open to doubt, owing to the corruption of the later sources. Perhaps what Ammenemes means is that his son and heir is now the sole owner of the house.
15. A garbled quotation from Admonitions, 6,12–14, without the help of which the interpretation of this passage would be impossible. Even now, its bearing on the context is not clear.
16. P. Sallier II has *n s* "to a man" and Deir el-Medineh ostracon no. 1103 has *s n* "a man of," in both instances followed by the cartouche of King Sesostris. Neither version makes sense, but the sound of the Egyptian would resemble that of the emendation "my son" closely enough to justify it, and it is further supported by the fact that the ostracon actually has "my son" after the cartouche.
17. Mythological beings associated with the sun-god.

3,10 end. I have moored . . . what is in your heart . . ./
⌐leaving¬ the White Crown for the seed of the god. The
fortification is in good order, ⌐beginning from¬ . . . vessels are in the bark of Re. The kingship came into being
⌐in my presence, and there are none who could achieve
my deeds of valor.¬ Erect monuments, embellish ⌐your
causeway¬,[18] fight for . . . because he does not desire it
in His Majesty's presence.

It has come happily to an end.

18. Of the pyramid.

The Loyalist Instruction from the Sehetepibre Stela

The composition which Georges Posener has designated The Loyalist Instruction is known, mainly through his efforts, from two papyri, a tablet, and over twenty ostraca with fragments of the text. These are Ramesside copies except for the tablet (early Dynasty 18), the Louvre papyrus (second half of Dynasty 18), and the stela of Sehetepibre (Dynasty 12). Posener has hazarded the guess that the sage Ptahemdjehuty, known from the list of authors in Papyrus Chester Beatty IV, was the author.

The text comprises two sections, the first admonishing the author's children to respect and obey the king, and the second outlining the nature of the people. An abridged version of the first part is represented in the stela of Sehetepibre, a high official of Sesostris III and Amenemhet III of Dynasty 12. This is the oldest copy of a part of the text, and it is translated here, following Kuentz and Posener, since it is the only consecutive text available. An edition of the instruction with the parallel texts and material not yet published remains to be done.

For the composition, consult Posener, Littérature et politique, *pp. 117–24, and* Annuaire du Collège de France *67e Année (1967–68): 349–54; 68e Année (1968–69): 407–10; 69e Année (1969–70): 379–82; 70e Année (1970–71): 369–98; C. Kuentz, "Deux versions d'un panégyrique royal,"* Studies Presented to F. Ll. Griffith *(London: Egypt Exploration Society, 1932), 97–110; Erman,* The Ancient Egyptians, *pp. xxviii, 84–85.*

W. K. S.

II,8   The beginning of the teaching which he made for his
children:

I have something important to say; I shall have you hear it, and I shall let you know it: the design for eternity, a II,10 way / of life as it should be and of passing a lifetime at peace.

Adore the king, Nymaatre,[1] living forever, in your innermost parts. Place His Majesty in friendly fashion in your thoughts.

He is Perception, which is in (all) hearts, and his eyes pierce through every being.

He is Re, by whose rays one sees, for he is one who illumines the Two Lands more than the sun disk.

He is one who makes (the land) green, even more than a high inundation: he has filled the Two Lands with victory and life.

Nostrils are cool when he starts to rage, but when he sets in peace, one can breathe the air (again).

He gives nourishment to those in his circle, and he feeds II,15 the one who sticks to / his path.

The king is Ka.[2]

His utterance is Abundance.

The one whom he brought up is one who will be somebody.

He is Khnum[3] for all limbs,

The Begetter of the begotten.

He is Bastet,[4] who protects the Two Lands.

The one who praises him will be protected by his arm.

He is Sakhmet[5] against those who disobey his orders,

1. The praenomen of Amenemhet III (1842–1797 B.C.), in whose reign the stela was erected. The original composition probably lacked the name of the king.
2. Erman, "Vital Force."
3. The creator god who fashioned mankind on a potter's wheel.
4. The goddess represented with a cat's head.
5. The fierce goddess of pestilence, with a lioness's head.

and the one with whom he disagrees will be laden with sorrows.

Fight on behalf of his name;[6] be obeisant to his life. Be free and clear of any instance of negligence.

The one whom the king loves shall be a well-provided spirit; there is no tomb for anyone who rebels against His Majesty, and his corpse shall be cast to the waters.

II,20   Do this, and your body will flourish, / and you will find it (excellent) for eternity.

6. Posener points out that this phrase, at the end of the first part of the instruction, corresponds with the phrase, "fight on behalf of the people," in the second part.

The Man Who Was Tired of Life

This remarkable Middle Kingdom text, contained in Papyrus Berlin 3024, consists of a dialogue between a disillusioned and despairing man and his soul on the topic of the use of going on living; the speaker sees death as the only escape from the miseries of the world as he sees it, and yet hesitates to take the plunge; the soul likewise vacillates between living and dying, but finally decides in favor of life. Unfortunately, the beginning of the manuscript is lost, and there are lacunae at the start of the existing text, but thereafter it is in good condition. The following translation is slightly adapted from that by the present writer in JEA 42 (1956): 21–40, by courtesy of the Egypt Exploration Society. On this text, see Erman, The Ancient Egyptians, *pp. xxix, 86–92. For a discussion of some of the problems, consult especially R. J. Williams, in JEA 48 (1962): 49–56. For recent monographs, see W. Barta, Das Gespräch eines Mannes mit seinem BA (Papyrus Berlin 3024) (Berlin: Bruno Hessling, 1969), and Hans Goedicke, The Report about the Dispute of a Man with His Ba (Papyrus Berlin 3024) (Baltimore: The Johns Hopkins Press, 1970).*

R. O. F.

[. . .] you in order to say [. . .] their [tongues] cannot ⌈question⌉, for it will be ⌈crookedness⌉ [. . .] payments, their tongues cannot ⌈question⌉.[1]

I opened my mouth to my soul, that I might answer
5   what it had said: / This is too much for me today, that my soul does not argue with me; it is too great for [exagger-

1. Obscure and broken sentences, rendered more difficult by the loss of what once preceded.

ation], it is as if one ignored me. Let my soul not depart, that it may attend to it for me [. . .] in my body like a
10 net of cord, / but it will not succeed in escaping the day of trouble. See, my soul misleads me, but I do not listen to it; draws me toward death ere ⟨I⟩ have come to it and
15 casts ⟨me⟩ on the fire to burn me [. . .] / it approaches me on the day of trouble and it stands on yonder side as does a . . .[2] Such is he who goes forth that he may bring himself for him.[3] O my soul, too stupid to ⌐ease⌐ misery in life and yet holding me back from death ere I come to it,[4] sweeten
20 / the West[5] for me. Is it (too much) trouble? Yet life is a transitory state, and even trees fall. Trample on wrong, for my misery endures. May Thoth[6] who pacifies the gods
25 judge me; may Khons[7] defend me, / even he who writes truly; may Re hear my plaint, even he who ⌐commands⌐ the solar bark; may Isdes[8] defend me in the Holy Chamber,[9] [because] ⌐the needy one is weighed down with⌐ [the burden] which he has lifted up from me; it is pleasant
30 that / the gods should ward off the secret (thoughts) of my body.[10]

2. Word of unknown meaning.
3. An obscure sentence with a characteristically Egyptian ambiguity of pronouns. Perhaps the sense is: "Such is the soul who goes forth that he may bring himself for the man's benefit," recalling the visits of the soul to the body after death, but even so, the passage remains well-nigh incomprehensible.
4. The man complains that the soul is unable to help him in life and yet restrains him from death, and is indeed quite ineffective.
5. I.e. make death easy.
6. The god of wisdom and learning who judged between the rivals Horus and Seth.
7. God of the moon.
8. A deity closely associated with or assimilated to Thoth.
9. The celestial Hall of Judgment.
10. The secret thoughts are evidently unpleasant, as one might expect in this context.

What my soul said to me: Are you not a man? Indeed you are alive, but what do you profit? Yet you yearn for life like a man of wealth.

I said: I have not gone, (even though) that is on the ground.[11] Indeed, you ⌐leap away¬, but you will / not be cared for.[12] Every prisoner says: "I will take you," but you are dead, though your name lives.[13] Yonder is a resting place ⌐attractive¬ to the heart; the West is a dwelling place, rowing [. . .] face. If my guiltless soul listens to me / and its heart is in accord with me, it will be fortunate, for I will cause it to attain the West, like one who is in his pyramid, to whose burial a survivor attended.[14] I will [. . . over] your corpse, so that you make another soul ⌐envious / in weariness¬. I will . . . ,[15] then you will not be cold, so that you ⌐make envious¬ another soul which is hot. I will drink water at the eddy, I will raise up ⌐shade¬, so that you ⌐make envious¬ another soul which is hungry. If / you hold me back from death in this manner, you will find nowhere you can rest in the West. Be so kind, my soul, my brother, as to become my heir who shall make offering and stand at the tomb on the day of burial, that he may ⌐prepare¬ a bier / for the necropolis.

My soul opened its mouth to me that it might answer what I had said: If you think of burial, it is a sad matter;

11. The sense of this is probably: "I have not died, though I have lost everything." The speaker is refuting the soul's accusation that he clings to life like a wealthy man.
12. The soul may run away, but it will reap no benefit by so doing.
13. These two passages seem to describe the abandoned state of the soul which does not accompany its owner; every prisoner would like to get hold of it, but it is as good as dead.
14. Here are recited the benefits accruing to a soul which does not desert its owner. "Yonder" and "the West" refer to the Beyond.
15. Word of unknown meaning.

it is a bringer of weeping through making a man miserable; it is taking a man from his house, he being cast on the high
60 ground; [16] never again will you go up that you may see / the sun. Those who built in granite and constructed ⌈halls⌉ in goodly pyramids with fine work, when the builders became gods their stelae were destroyed,[17] like the weary ones who died on the riverbank through lack of a survi-
65 vor,[18] / the flood having taken its toll and the sun likewise, to whom talk the fishes of the banks of the water. Listen to me; behold it is good for men to hear. Follow the happy day and forget care.

70 A peasant ploughed his plot [19] and loaded his harvest / aboard a ship, towing [20] it when his time of festival drew near. He saw the coming of the darkness of the norther, for he was vigilant in the boat when the sun set. He ⌈es-caped⌉ with his wife and children, but came to grief on a
75 lake infested by / night with crocodiles. At last he sat down and broke silence, saying: I weep not for yonder mother, who has no more going forth from the West for another (term) upon earth; I sorrow rather for her children broken in the egg, who have looked in the face of the crocodile-
80 god / ere they have lived.

16. I.e. will be interred on the desert plateau where the necropolis is situated.
17. A reference to the destruction which befell the royal pyramids after the fall of the Old Kingdom; a grand tomb is of no lasting benefit.
18. To attend to their last rites.
19. Here begins the first of two anecdotes related by the soul which at first sight seem to have little bearing on the topic under discussion; perhaps they were intended to convey to the would-be suicide that there were misfortunes worse than those of which he complains.
20. Presumably sailing was impracticable and the peasant could not afford to pay rowers.

A peasant asked for a meal,[21] and his wife said to him: There is ‹. . .›[22] for supper. He went out to . . .[23] for a moment and returned to his house (raging) as if he were ⌐an ape⌐.[24] His wife ⌐reasoned⌐ with him, but he would not listen to her; he . . .[25] and the bystanders were ⌐helpless⌐.

I opened my mouth to my soul that I might answer what it had said:

Behold, my name is detested,[26]
Behold, more than the smell of vultures
On a summer's day when the sky is hot.

Behold, my name is detested,
Behold, ‹more than the smell of› a catch of fish
90   / On a day of catching when the sky is hot.

Behold, my name is detested,
Behold, more than the smell of ducks,
More than a covert of reeds full of waterfowl.

Behold, my name is detested,
Behold, more than the smell of fishermen,
95   More than the creeks / of the marshes where they have
            fished.

Behold, my name is detested,
Behold, more than the smell of crocodiles,
More than sitting by ⌐sandbanks⌐ full of crocodiles.

21. The second anecdote.
22. A word or words omitted.
23. A verb of unknown meaning.
24. Following a suggestion by J. Gwyn Griffith in *JEA* 53 (1967): 157.
25. See n. 23, above.
26. In a series of poetic stanzas the man describes his miseries and the merits of death as he sees them.

Behold, my name is detested,
Behold, more than a woman
About whom lies are told to a man.

100   Behold, / my name is detested,
Behold, more than a sturdy child
Of whom it is said: "He belongs to his rival." [27]

Behold, my name is detested,
Behold, ⟨more than⟩ a town belonging to the monarch
Which mutters sedition when his back is turned.

To whom can I speak today?
Brothers are evil
And the friends of today unlovable.

105   To whom can I speak / today?
Hearts are rapacious
And everyone takes his neighbor's goods.

⟨To whom can I speak today?⟩ [28]
Gentleness has perished
And the violent man has come down on everyone.

To whom can I speak today?
Men are contented with evil
And goodness is neglected everywhere.

110   To whom can I speak / today?
He who should enrage a man by his ill deeds,
He makes everyone laugh ⟨by⟩ his wicked wrongdoing.

To whom can I speak today?
Men plunder
And every man robs his neighbor.

27. I.e. is the offspring of adultery.
28. A blank space left in the manuscript, suggesting that there was a lacuna in the scribe's copy; the restoration, however, is obvious.

To whom can I speak today?
The wrongdoer is an intimate friend

115 And the brother with whom one used to act is become /
      an enemy.

To whom can I speak today?
None remember the past,
And no one now helps him who used to do (good).

To whom can I speak today?
Brothers are evil,
And men have recourse to strangers for ⌜affection.⌝

To whom can I speak today?
Faces are averted,

120 And every man looks askance at / his brethren.

To whom can I speak today?
Hearts are rapacious
And there is no man's heart in which one can trust.

To whom can I speak today?
There are no just persons
And the land is left over to the doers of wrong.

To whom can I speak today?
There is lack of an intimate friend

125 And men have recourse to someone unknown / in order to
      complain to him.

To whom can I speak today?
There is no contented man,
And that person who once walked with him no longer
      exists.

To whom can I speak today?
I am heavy-laden with trouble
Through lack of an intimate friend.

To whom can I speak today?
The wrong which roams the earth,
130 / There is no end to it.

Death is in my sight today
⟨As when⟩ a sick man becomes well,
Like going out-of-doors after detention.

Death is in my sight today
Like the smell of myrrh,
Like sitting under an awning on a windy day.

Death is in my sight today
135 / Like the perfume of lotuses,
Like sitting on the shore of the Land of Drunkenness.

Death is in my sight today
Like a trodden way,
As when a man returns home from an expedition.

Death is in my sight today
Like the clearing of the sky,
140 Like a man who . . ./. . .[29] ⌜for⌝ something which he
does not know.

Death is in my sight today
As when a man desires to see home
When he has spent many years in captivity.

Verily, he who is yonder [30] will be a living god,
Averting the ill of him who does it.

Verily, he who is yonder will be one who stands in the
Bark of the Sun,
Causing choice things to be given / therefrom for the
temples.

29. Sense obscure.
30. I.e. in the realm of the dead.

Verily, he who is yonder will be a sage
Who will not be prevented from appealing to Re when he
    speaks.

What my soul said to me: Cast complaint upon ⌐the
peg⌐,[31] my comrade and brother; make offering on the
150 brazier / and cleave to life, according as ⌐I⌐ [32] have said.
Desire me here, thrust the West aside,[33] but desire that you
may attain the West when your body goes to earth,[34] that
I may alight after you are weary; then will we make an
abode together.[35]
155   It is finished / from its beginning to its end, just as it was
found in writing.

31. The soul seems to be urging the man to doff his misery as if
it were an unwanted garment, to be hung on a peg out of the way.
32. The original has the suffix of the second person, apparently in
error.
33. I.e. give up the idea of dying.
34. I.e. desire that death may come, when come it does, in the
natural course of events.
35. The last two sentences recall the representations of the soul as a
bird revisiting the body after death; if the man dies from natural
causes and is interred with the proper rites, the soul will return to
the body and dwell with it.

The Admonitions of an Egyptian Sage

This text, first edited in detail by Sir Alan Gardiner in 1909, refers to a period when Egypt was in a state of anarchy, most probably the First Intermediate Period, the time between the collapse of the Old Kingdom and the rise of the Middle Kingdom, although this dating is not universally accepted. The actual manuscript, written on the recto of the Leiden Papyrus No. 344 and probably of Nineteenth Dynasty date, is clearly a copy of a much earlier work written in Middle Egyptian, the original composition of which may well belong to the earlier part of Dynasty 12, when the calamity of the preceding revolution and civil wars would still have been fresh in the memory of the nation.

The papyrus in which the composition is preserved has lost both its beginning and its end, and is full of lacunae, while many textual corruptions and careless omissions have crept in. Nevertheless, the situation is clear: a wise man named Ipuwer is addressing an unnamed king whose identity may have been given in the lost beginning of the text. He describes the chaotic state into which the realm has fallen and blames the king for his failure to keep order; the sage urges the king to "destroy the enemies of the august Residence" and to attend to his religious duties so as to bring the gods to his aid; the attributes of the monarch should be authority, knowledge, and truth, yet the present incumbent has let the land fall into confusion.

The work as a whole is not likely to have been contemporary with the state of affairs it describes, but may have been written not long after the restoration of law and order. It may have been intended as a lesson in kingship by way of showing the monarch the consequences of misrule. On the other hand, it may have had a political purpose of supporting the reigning dynasty by contrasting its beneficent rule with the chaos which had gone before.

By a typically Egyptian literary device, the text falls largely into groups of paragraphs. Those of the first group all begin with the word indeed; *they are followed by a series in which* behold *is the first word; other keywords are* destroyed, destroy, remember, *and the phrase* it is good when. . . . *The translation below is reproduced with a few minor changes from the present author's article in* JEA *51 (1965): 53–62, following on a series of notes on the text published in* JEA *50 (1964): 24–36, by courtesy of the Egypt Exploration Society. For bibliography and notes, see* Erman, The Ancient Egyptians, *pp. xxix–xxx, 92–108.*

R. O. F.

       [. . .] The door[keepers] say: "Let us go and plunder." The confectioners [. . .]. The washerman refuses to carry his load [. . .] the bird[catchers] have drawn up in line of battle. [. . . the inhabitants] of the Delta carry shields.

1,5   The brewers / [. . .] sad. A man regards his son as his enemy. ⌈Confusion⌉ [. . .] another. Come and ⌈conquer⌉; ⌈judge⌉ [. . .] what was ordained for you in the time of Horus, in the age [of the Ennead . . .]. The virtuous man goes in mourning because of what has happened in the land [. . .] goes [. . .] ⌈the tribes of the desert⌉ have become Egyptians everywhere.

1,10   Indeed, the face is pale; / [. . .] what the ancestors foretold has arrived at [fruition . . .] the land is full of confederates, and a man goes out to plough with his shield.

       Indeed, the meek say: ["He who is . . . of] face is as a well-born man."

       Indeed, [the face] is pale; the bowman is ready, wrongdoing is everywhere, and there is no man of yesterday.[1]

       Indeed, the plunderer [. . .] everywhere, and the servant takes what he finds.

    1. I.e. no one of lineage to maintain order.

Indeed, the Nile overflows, yet none plough for it. Everyone says: "We do not know what will happen throughout the land."

Indeed, women are barren and none conceive. Khnum fashions (men) no more because of the condition of the land.

2,5 Indeed, poor men have become owners of wealth, and he who could not make / sandals for himself is now a possessor of riches.

Indeed, men's slaves, their hearts are sad, and magistrates do not fraternize with their ⌜people⌝ when they ⌜shout⌝.

Indeed, [hearts] are violent, pestilence is throughout the land, blood is everywhere, death is not lacking, and the mummy-cloth speaks even before one comes near it.

Indeed, many dead are buried in the river; the stream is a sepulcher and the place of embalmment has become a stream.

Indeed, noblemen are in distress, while the poor man is full of joy. Every town says: "Let us suppress the powerful among us."

Indeed, men are like ibises.[2] Squalor is throughout the land, and there are none indeed whose clothes are white in these times.

Indeed, the land turns round as does a potter's wheel; the robber is a possessor of riches and [the rich man is become] a plunderer.

Indeed, trusty servants are [. . .]; the poor man [complains]: "How terrible! What am I to do?"

2,10 / Indeed, the river is blood, yet men drink of it. Men ⌜shrink⌝ from human beings and thirst after water.

---

2. In what way men resemble ibises is not clear, but the context suggests that the quality they share is dirt.

Indeed, gates, columns and ⌐walls¬ are burnt up, while the ⌐hall¬ of the palace stands firm and endures.

Indeed, the ship of [the southerners] has broken up; towns are destroyed and Upper Egypt has become an empty waste.[3]

Indeed, crocodiles [are glutted] with the fish they have taken,[4] for men go to them of their own accord; it is destruction of the ⌐land¬. Men say: "Do not walk here; behold, it is a net." Behold, men tread [the water] like fishes, and the frightened man cannot distinguish it because of terror.[5]

Indeed men are few, and he who places his brother in the ground is everywhere. When the wise man speaks, [he flees without delay].[6]

Indeed, the well-born man [. . .] through lack of recognition, and the child of his lady has become the son of his maidservant.

3,1 / Indeed, the desert is throughout the land, the nomes are laid waste, and barbarians from abroad have come to Egypt.

Indeed, men arrive [. . .] and indeed, there are no Egyptians anywhere.

Indeed, gold and lapis lazuli, silver and turquoise, carnelian and amethyst, *Ibhet*-stone and [. . .] are strung on the necks of maidservants. Good things are throughout the land, (yet) housewives say: "Oh that we had something to eat!"

Indeed, [. . .] noblewomen. Their bodies are in sad

---

3. A collapse of all government in the south; note the metaphor of the ship of state.
4. A figure for the corpses the crocodiles have eaten.
5. I.e. in their misery and terror, men cannot tell land from water.
6. Apparently he dare not wait to see the effects of his words. The remaining traces suit the restoration.

plight by reason of (their) rags, and their hearts ⌐sink⌐ when greeting [one another].

3,5   Indeed, / chests of ebony are broken up, and precious *ssnḏm*-wood is cleft asunder in ⌐beds⌐ [. . .].

Indeed, the builders [of pyramids have become] cultivators, and those who were in the sacred bark are now yoked [to it]. None indeed sail northward to Byblos today; what shall we do for cedar trees for our mummies, with the produce of which priests are buried and with the oil of which [chiefs] are embalmed as far as Keftiu? [7] They come no more; gold is lacking [. . .] and ⌐materials⌐ for every kind of craft have come to an end. The <. . .> of the palace is despoiled. How often do the people of the oases come with their festival spices, ⌐mats, and

3,10   skins,⌐ with fresh *rdmt*-plants, / ⌐grease⌐ of birds . . . ?

Indeed, Elephantine and ⌐Thinis⌐ [are in the series] of Upper Egypt, (but) without paying taxes owing to civil strife. Lacking are ⌐grain⌐, charcoal, *irtyw*-fruit, *mꜣꜥw*-wood, *nwt*-wood, and brushwood. The work of craftsmen and [. . .] are the ⌐profit⌐ of the palace. To what purpose is a treasury without its revenues? Happy indeed is the heart of the king when truth comes to him! And every foreign land [comes]! *That* is our fate and *that* is our happiness! What can we do about it? All is ruin!

˅ Indeed, laughter has perished and is [no longer] made; it is groaning that is throughout the land, mingled with complaints.

Indeed, every dead person is as a well-born man.[8] Those

4,1   who were / Egyptians [have become] foreigners and are thrust aside.

˅   Indeed, hair [has fallen out] for everybody, and the

7. Probably Crete.
8. I.e. is fortunate to be dead.

man of rank can no longer be distinguished from him who is nobody.

Indeed, [. . .] because of noise; noise is not [. . .] in years of noise, and there is no end [of] noise.[9]

Indeed, great and small <say>: "I wish I might die." Little children say: "He should not have caused <me> to live."

Indeed, the children of princes are dashed against walls, and the children of the neck [10] are laid out on the high ground.[11]

Indeed, those who were in the place of embalmment are laid out on the high ground, and the secrets of the embalmers ⌈are thrown down because of it.⌉

4,5   Indeed, / that has perished which yesterday was seen, and the land is left over to its weakness like the cutting of flax.

Indeed, the Delta in its entirety will not be hidden, and Lower Egypt puts trust in trodden roads. What can one do? No [. . .] exist anywhere, and men say: "Perdition to the secret place!" Behold, it is ⌈in the hands⌉ of those who do not know it like those who know it. The desert dwellers are skilled in the crafts of the Delta.[12]

Indeed, citizens are put to the corn-rubbers, and those who used to don fine linen are beaten with . . . Those who used never to see the day have gone out ⌈unhin-
4,10   dered;⌉ those who were on their husbands' beds, / let them lie on rafts. I say: "It is too heavy for me," [13] concerning rafts bearing myrrh. Load them with vessels filled with

9. The play on the word "noise" is a regular literary device.
10. I.e. the equivalent of our "children in arms." The child is envisaged as sitting on his father's shoulder and clinging to his neck.
11. The desert plateau.
12. I.e. squeezing out the native craftsmen.
13. I.e. "I cannot bear to talk about it." The implication is that the rafts bearing myrrh no longer pass upon the river.

[. . . Let] them know the palanquin.[14] As for the butler, he is ruined. There are no remedies for it; noblewomen suffer like maidservants, minstrels are at the looms within the weaving-rooms, and what they sing to the Song-stress-goddess is mourning. ⌜Talkers⌝ [. . .] corn-rubbers.

Indeed, all female slaves are free with their tongues, and when their mistress speaks, it is irksome to the maidservants.

Indeed, trees are felled and branches are stripped off.

5,1 I have separated[15] him and his household slaves, / and men will say when they hear it: "Cakes are lacking for most children; there is no food [. . .]. What is the taste of it like today?"

Indeed, magnates are hungry and perishing, followers are followed [. . .] because of complaints.

⌐Indeed, the hot-tempered man says: "If I knew where God is, then would I serve Him."

Indeed, [Right] pervades the land in name, but what men do in trusting to it is Wrong.

5,5 Indeed, runners are fighting over the ⌜spoil⌝ [of] / the robber, and all his property is carried off.

Indeed, all animals, their hearts weep; cattle moan because of the state of the land.

Indeed, the children of princes are dashed against walls, and the children of the neck are laid out on the high ground. Khnum groans because of his weariness.

Indeed, terror kills;[16] the frightened man opposes what

14. "Them" in these two sentences refers to the gently-born ladies. Now they have to carry burdens and act as litter-bearers.
15. A sudden change of topic at this point suggests that the copyist may have omitted a portion of his text.
16. Apparently another textual omission here; the plural pronoun "your" in what follows has no antecedent.

is done against your enemies. Moreover, the few are pleased, while the ⌈rest⌉ are . . . Is it by following the ⌈crocodile⌉ and cleaving it asunder? Is it by slaying the lion roasted on the fire? [Is it] by sprinkling for Ptah and taking [. . .]? Why do you give to him? There is no reaching him. It is misery which you give to him.

5,10 Indeed, ⌈slaves⌉ . . ./throughout the land, and the strong man sends to everyone; a man strikes his maternal brother. What is it that has been done? ⌈I⌉ speak to a ruined man.

Indeed, the ways are [. . .], the roads are watched; men sit in the bushes until the benighted traveler comes in order to plunder his burden, and what is upon him is taken away. He is belabored with blows of a stick and murdered.[17]

Indeed, that has perished which yesterday was seen, and the land is left over to its weakness like the cutting of flax, commoners coming and going in dissolution [. . .]. Would that there were an end of men, without concep-
6,1 tion,/without birth! Then would the land be quiet from noise and tumult be no more.

Indeed, [men eat] herbage and wash ⟨it⟩ down with water; neither fruit nor herbage can be found ⟨for⟩ the birds, and [. . .] is taken away from the mouth of the pig. No face is bright which you have ⟨. . .⟩ [18] ⌈for⌉ me ⌈through⌉ hunger.

Indeed, everywhere barley has perished and men are stripped of clothes, ⌈spice⌉, and oil; everyone says: "There is none." The storehouse is empty and its keeper is
6,5 stretched on the ground; a happy state of affairs! . . ./

17. Lit. "killed in wrongness."
18. A verb omitted.

Would that I had raised my voice at that moment, that it might have saved me from the pain in which I am.

Indeed, the private council-chamber, its writings are taken away and the mysteries which were ⟨in it⟩ are laid bare.

Indeed, magic spells are divulged; ⌈*šmw*- and *šhnw*-spells are frustrated⌉ because they are remembered by men.

Indeed, public offices are opened and their inventories are taken away; the serf has become an owner of ⌈serfs⌉.

Indeed, [scribes] are killed and their writings are taken away. Woe is me because of the misery of this time!

Indeed, the writings of the scribes of the ⌈cadaster⌉ are destroyed, and the corn of Egypt is common property.

6,10   Indeed, the laws / of the council chamber are thrown out; indeed, men walk on them in the public places, and poor men break them up in the streets.

Indeed, the poor man has attained to the state of the Nine Gods, and the erstwhile procedure of the House of the Thirty [19] is divulged.

Indeed, the great council-chamber is a popular resort, and poor men come and go in the Great Mansions.[20]

Indeed, the children of magnates are ejected into the streets; the wise man agrees and the fool says "no," and it is pleasing in the sight of him who knows nothing about it.[21]

Indeed, those who were in the place of embalmment are laid out on the high ground, and the secrets of the embalmers are thrown down because of it.

19. The Supreme Court.
20. Probably the offices of the administration.
21. Apparently meaning that when wise men settle on a course of action, the fool opposes them, and the ignorant onlooker enjoys the argument.

7,1 / Behold, the fire has gone up on high, and its burning goes forth against the enemies of the land.

Behold, things have been done which have not happened for a long time past; the king has been deposed by the rabble.

Behold, he who was buried as a falcon [22] ⟨is devoid⟩ of biers, and what the pyramid concealed [23] has become empty.

Behold, it has befallen that the land has been deprived of the kingship by a few lawless men.

Behold, men have fallen into rebellion against the Uraeus,[24] the [. . .] of Re, even she who makes the Two Lands content.

Behold, the secret of the land whose limits were unknown is divulged, and the Residence is thrown down in a moment.

7,5 Behold, Egypt is fallen to / pouring of water, and he who poured water on the ground has carried off the strong man in misery.[25]

Behold, the Serpent [26] is taken from its hole, and the secrets of the Kings of Upper and Lower Egypt are divulged.

Behold, the Residence is afraid because of want, and [men go about] unopposed to stir up strife.

Behold, the land has knotted itself up with confederacies, and the coward takes the brave man's property.

Behold, the Serpent [. . .] the dead: he who could not make a sarcophagus for himself is now the possessor of a tomb.

22. The dead king.
23. The sarcophagus.
24. The cobra-symbol of royalty.
25. The meaning of this passage is obscure.
26. The tutelary spirit of the royal family.

Behold, the possessors of tombs are ejected on to the high ground, while he who could not make a coffin for himself is now ⟨the possessor⟩ of a treasury.

Behold, this has happened ⟨to⟩ men; he who could not build a room for himself is now a possessor of walls.

Behold, the magistrates of the land are driven out throughout the land: ⟨. . .⟩ are driven out from the / palaces.

7,10

Behold, noble ladies are now on rafts, and magnates are in the labor establishment, while he who could not sleep even on walls is now the possessor of a bed.

Behold, the possessor of wealth now spends the night thirsty, while he who once begged his dregs for himself is now the possessor of overflowing bowls.

Behold, the possessors of robes are now in rags, while he who could not weave for himself is now a possessor of fine linen.

Behold, he who could not build a boat for himself is now the possessor of a fleet; their erstwhile owner looks at them, but they are not his.

Behold, he who had no shade is now the possessor of shade, while the erstwhile possessors of shade are now in the ⌜full blast⌝ of the storm.

Behold, he who was ignorant of the lyre is now the possessor of a harp, while he who never sang for himself now vaunts the Songstress-goddess.

Behold, those who possessed vessel-stands of copper ⟨. . .⟩ not one of the jars thereof has been ⌜adorned.⌝

8,1

Behold, he who slept / wifeless through want [finds] riches, while he whom he never saw stands ⌜making dole⌝.

Behold, he who had no property is now a possessor of wealth, and the magnate praises him.

Behold, the poor of the land have become rich, and the ⟨erstwhile owner⟩ of property is one who has nothing.

Behold, serving-men have become masters of butlers, and he who once was a messenger now sends someone else.

Behold, he who had no loaf is now the owner of a barn, and his storehouse is provided with the goods of another.

Behold, he whose hair had fallen out and who had no oil has now become a possessor of jars of sweet myrrh.

8,5 ʳ/ Behold, she who had no box is now the owner of a coffer, and she who had to look at her face in the water is now the owner of a mirror.

Behold, ⟨. . .⟩.

Behold, a man is happy eating his food. Consume your goods in gladness and unhindered, for it is good for a man to eat his food; God commands it for him whom He has favored ⟨. . .⟩.[27]

⟨Behold, he who did not know⟩ his god now offers to him with incense of another [who is] not known [to him].

[Behold,] great ladies, once possessors of riches, now give their children for beds.

Behold, a man [to whom is given] a noble lady as wife, her father protects him, and he who has not ⟨. . .⟩ killing him.

8,10 Behold, the children of magistrates are [. . . the calves] / of cattle [are given over] to the plunderers.

Behold, ʳpriestsʳ transgress with the cattle of the poor [28] [. . .].

Behold, he who could not slaughter for himself now slaughters bulls, and he who did not know how to ʳcarveʳ now sees [. . .].

27. A considerable blank space, probably corresponding to a lacuna in the scribe's original.
28. I.e. take the offerings of livestock for their own use.

Behold, ⌜priests⌝ transgress with geese, which are given ⟨to⟩ the gods instead of oxen.

Behold, maidservants [. . .] offer ducks; noblewomen ⟨. . .⟩.[29]

Behold, noblewomen flee; the ⌜overseers⌝ of [. . .] and their [children] are cast down through fear of death.

⟨Behold,⟩ the chiefs of the land flee; there is no purpose for them because of want. The lord of [. . .].

9,1 [Behold,] / those who once owned beds are now on the ground, while he who once slept in squalor now lays out a skin-mat for himself.

Behold, noblewomen go hungry, while the ⌜priests⌝ are sated with what has been prepared for them.

Behold, no offices are in their right place,[30] like a herd running at random without a herdsman.

Behold, cattle stray and there is none to collect them, but everyone fetches for himself those that are branded with his name.

Behold, a man is slain beside his brother, ⌜who runs away and abandons him⌝ to save his own skin.

Behold, he who had no yoke of oxen is now the owner of a herd, and he who could find for himself no plough-oxen is now the owner of cattle.

9,5 Behold, he who had no grain is now the owner of granaries, / and he who had to fetch loan-corn for himself is now one who issues it.

Behold, he who had no dependents is now an owner of serfs, and he who was ⟨a magnate⟩ now performs his own errands.

Behold, the strong men of the land, the condition of the people is not reported ⟨to them⟩. All is ruin!

29. Another blank space.
30. I.e. are in disorder.

Behold, no craftsmen work, for the enemies of the land have impoverished its craftsmen.

[Behold, he who once recorded] the harvest now knows nothing about it, while he who never ploughed [for himself is now the owner of corn; the reaping] takes place but is not reported. The scribe [sits in his office], but his hands [are idle] in it.

Destroyed is [. . .] in that time, and a man looks [on his friend as] an ⌐adversary⌐. The infirm man brings cool-
9,10 ness [to what is hot . . .] fear [. . ./. . .]. Poor men [. . . the land] is not bright because of it.

Destroyed is [. . .] their food [is taken] from them [. . . through] fear of his terror. The commoner begs [. . .] messenger, but not [. . .] time. He is captured laden with his goods and [all his property] is taken away. [. . .] men pass by his door [. . .] ⌐the outside of the wall, a shed,⌐ and rooms containing falcons.[31] It is the
10,1 common man who will be vigilant, / the day having dawned on him without his dreading it. Men run because of ‹. . . for› the temple of the head, strained through a woven cloth within ⌐the house⌐. What they make are ⌐tents,⌐ just like the desert folk.

Destroyed is the doing of that for which men are sent by retainers in the service of their masters; they have no readiness. Behold, they are five men, and they say: "Go on the road you know, for we have arrived."

Lower Egypt weeps; the king's storehouse is the common property of everyone, and the entire palace is without its revenues. To it belong emmer and barley, fowl and fish; to it belong white cloth and fine linen, copper
10,5 and oil; / to it belong carpet and mat, [. . .] flowers and

31. Meaning probably images of the sacred falcon; the author may be referring to the outbuildings of a temple.

wheat-sheaf and all good revenues . . . If the . . .[32] it in the palace were delayed, men would be devoid [of . . .]

Destroy the enemies of the august Residence, splendid of magistrates [. . .] in it like [. . .]; indeed, the Governor of the City goes unescorted.

Destroy [the enemies of the august Residence,] splendid [. . .].

[Destroy the enemies of] that erstwhile august Residence, manifold of laws [. . .].

10,10 [Destroy the enemies of] / that erstwhile august [Residence . . .].

Destroy the enemies of that erstwhile august Residence [. . .] none can stand [. . .].

[Destroy the enemies of that] erstwhile august [Residence], manifold of offices; indeed [. . .].

Remember to immerse [. . .] him who is in pain ⌜when⌝ he is sick in his body; ⌜show respect⌝ [. . .] ⌜because of⌝ his god that he may guard ⌜the utterance⌝ [. . .] ⌜his⌝ children ⌜who are witnesses of⌝ the surging of the flood.

11,1 Remember to [. . ./ . . .]. . . ⌜shrine⌝, to fumigate with incense and to offer water in a jar in the early morning.[33]

Remember ⟨to bring⟩ fat r-geese, trp-geese, and ducks and to offer god's offerings to the gods.

Remember to chew natron[34] and to prepare white

32. Meaning doubtful here and at end of previous sentence.
33. A reference to the matutinal purification of the idol in the shrine. With the exception of the first, which seems to be concerned with healing the sick, all the paragraphs beginning with "Remember" appear to refer to the performance by the king of the ritual and offerings, acts essential to the well-being of the land.
34. To purify the mouth.

bread; a man ‹ ⌈should do it⌉ › on the day of wetting the head.

Remember to erect flagstaffs and to carve offering stones, the priest cleansing the chapels and the temple being plastered (white) like milk; to make pleasant the odor of the horizon[35] and to provide bread-offerings.

Remember to observe regulations, to fix dates correctly,[36] and to remove him who enters / on the priestly office in impurity of body, for that is doing it wrongfully, it is destruction of the heart[37] [. . .] the day ⌈which precedes⌉ eternity, the months [. . .] ⌈years are known⌉.

Remember to slaughter oxen [. . .]

Remember to go forth ⌈purged⌉ [. . .] who calls to you; to put r-geese on the fire [. . .] ⌈to open⌉ the jar [. . .] the shore of the waters [. . .] ⌈of women⌉ [. . .] clothing [. . ./. . .] to give ⌈praise⌉ . . . in order to appease ⌈you⌉.[38]

[. . .] lack of people; ⌈come⌉ [. . .] Re who ⌈commands⌉ [. . .] ⌈worshiping him⌉ [. . .] West until [. . .] ⌈are diminished⌉ [. . .].

Behold, why does he ⌈seek⌉ to fashion ‹men . . .›? The frightened man is not distinguished from the violent one. He[39] brings coolness upon heat; / men say: "He is the herdsman of mankind, and there is no evil in his heart." Though his herds are few, yet he spends a day to collect them, their hearts being ⌈on fire⌉. Would that he had perceived their nature in the first generation; then he would

---

35. The shrine of the god.
36. The dates of the regular religious festivals.
37. A mindless action? The heart as the seat of thought must surely be meant here.
38. The pronoun is plural.
39. The supreme god.

have imposed obstacles, he would have stretched out his arm against them, he would have destroyed their herds and their heritage. Men desire the giving of birth, but sadness supervenes, with needy people on all sides. So it is, and it will not pass away while the gods who are in the midst of it exist. Seed goes forth into mortal women, but none are found on the road.[40] Combat has gone forth, 12,5 / and he who should be a redresser of evils is one who commits them; neither do men act as pilot in their hour of duty. Where is he [41] today? Is he asleep? Behold, his power is not seen.

⌐If we had been fed, I would not have found you,¬ I would not have been summoned ⌐in vain¬;[42] "Aggression against it[43] means pain of heart" is a saying on the lips of everyone. Today ⌐he who is afraid¬ . . . a myriad of people; [. . .] ⌐did not see¬ [. . .] against the enemies of [. . .] at his outer chamber; ⌐who¬ enter the temple [. . .] ⌐weeping for him¬ [. . .] that one who confounds 12,10 what he has said . . . / The land has not fallen [. . .] the statues are burned and their tombs destroyed [. . .] he sees the day of [. . .]. He who could not make for himself ⟨. . .⟩ between sky and ground is afraid of everybody.

. . . ⌐if¬ he does it . . . what you dislike taking. Authority, knowledge, and truth are with you, yet confusion is what you set throughout the land, also the noise

40. Perhaps meaning that impregnation of women no longer produces offspring.
41. The supreme god again.
42. I.e. If affairs had not gone to rack and ruin, with people starving, I would not have sought this audience, only to speak to deaf ears; the person being addressed is the king whom the sage is admonishing. The proverb which follows is perhaps an equivalent of our saying, "It is no good kicking against the pricks."
43. The prevailing misery.

of tumult. Behold, one deals harm to another, for men conform to what you have commanded. If three men travel on the road, they are found to be only two, for the many kill the few. Does a herdsman desire death? Then 13,1 may you command reply to be made,[44] / because it means that what one loves another detests; it means that their ⸢existences⸣ are few everywhere; it means that you have acted so as to bring those things to pass. You have told lies, and the land is a weed which destroys men, and none can ⸢count on⸣ life. All these years are strife, and a man is murdered on his housetop even though he was vigilant in his gate lodge. Is he brave and saves himself? It means he will live.

When men send a ⸢servant⸣ for humble folk, he goes on the road ⸢until⸣ he sees the flood; the road is ⸢washed 13,5 out⸣ / and he stands ⸢worried⸣. What is on him is taken away, he is belabored with blows of a stick and wrongfully slain. Oh that you could taste a little of the misery of it! Then you would say [. . .] from someone else as a wall, over and above [. . .] hot . . . years . . . [. . .].

13,10 [It is indeed good] when ⸢ships⸣ fare upstream [. . ./ . . .] robbing them. It is indeed good [. . .].

[It is indeed] good when the net is drawn in and birds are tied up[. . .].

It is [indeed] good [. . .] ⸢dignities for⸣ them, and the roads are passable.

It is indeed good when the hands of men build pyramids, when ponds are dug and plantations of the trees of the gods are made.

It is indeed good when men are drunk; they drink *myt* and their hearts are happy.

It is indeed good when shouting is in men's mouths,

44. I.e. answer me back and reject my reproaches.

when the magnates of districts stand looking on at the
14,1 shouting / in ⌈their houses⌉, clad in a cloak, cleansed in
front and well-provided within.[45]

It is indeed good when beds are prepared and the head-
rests of magistrates are safely secured. Every man's need
is satisfied with a couch in the shade, and a door is now
shut on him who once slept in the bushes.

It is indeed good when fine linen is spread out on New
Year's Day [. . .] ⌈on⌉ the bank; when fine linen is spread
out and cloaks are on the ground. The overseer of [. . .]
14,10 the trees, the poor [. . ./. . .] in their midst like Asiatics
[. . .]. Men ⟨. . .⟩ the ⌈state⌉ thereof; they have come to
an end ⌈of themselves;⌉ none can be found to stand up
and protect ⌈themselves⌉ [. . .]. Everyone fights for his
sister and saves his own skin. Is it Nubians? Then will we
guard ourselves; warriors are made many in order to ward
off foreigners. Is it Libyans? Then we will turn away. The
Medjay [46] are pleased with Egypt. How comes it that
15,1 every man kills his brother? The troops / whom we
marshaled for ourselves have turned into foreigners and
have taken to ravaging. What has come to pass through it
is informing the Asiatics of the state of the land; all the
desert folk are possessed with the fear of it.[47] What the
plebs have tasted ⟨. . .⟩ without giving Egypt over ⟨to⟩
the sand. It is strong [. . .] speak about you after years
[. . .] devastate itself, ⌈it is the threshing floor which
nourishes their houses⌉ [. . .] to nourish his children
15,10 [. . .] said by the troops [. . ./. . .] fish [. . .] gum,
lotus leaves [. . .] excess of food.

45. Meaning perhaps: "well clad, well washed and well fed."
46. A Nubian tribe employed as soldiers and police.
47. I.e. awed by the collapse of a once great state.

What Ipuwer said when he answered the Majesty of the Lord of All: [48] [. . .] all herds. It means that ignorance of it is what is pleasing to the heart. You have done what was good in their hearts and you have nourished the people 16,1 with ⌈it⌉. They cover / their ⌈faces⌉ through fear of the morrow.

⌈That is how⌉ a man grows old before he dies, while his son is a lad without understanding; he begins [. . .] he does not open [his] mouth ⌈to speak⌉ to you, but you seize him in the doom of death [. . .] weep [. . .] go [. . .] after you, that the land may be [. . .] on every side. If men call to [. . .] weep [. . .] them, ⌈who⌉ break into the tombs and burn the statues [. . .] the corpses of 17,1 the nobles [. . ./ . . .] of directing work [. . .].

(The remainder of the text is lost)

48. The king's rejoinder to the preceding indictments is not given; this text is concerned only with Ipuwer's speeches.

The Lamentations of Khakheperre-sonbe

The author of our lamentations is included in the list of the authors of old, the great sages of the past, in Papyrus Chester Beatty IV. Our text recalls The Admonitions of Ipuwer, The Prophecies of Neferti, and The Man Who Was Tired of Life. In common with the first two, it describes the plight of a disorganized land in a time of troubles. Like the third, it has a discourse with the man's other self. If it were not that The Lamentations is a dialogue with the heart and The Man Tired of Life a dialogue with the soul (ba), one might suspect that The Lamentations represents a reworking of the lost beginning of the latter.

The text is written on both sides of a writing board of Dynasty 18 in the British Museum (No. 5645). It was probably composed in the Middle Kingdom or the Second Intermediate Period. The board is covered with a network of string over which stucco has been washed to form the writing surface, and it is pierced for suspension from a wall or hook. A transcription with translation and commentary is published in A. H. Gardiner, The Admonitions of an Egyptian Sage *(Leipzig: J. C. Hinrich, 1909). The text is analysed by S. Hermann,* Untersuchungen zur Überlieferungsgestalt mittelägyptischer Literaturwerke *(Berlin: Akademie Verlag, 1957), pp. 48–54. Bibliographical references and notes are provided in Erman,* The Ancient Egyptians, *pp. xxx, 108–10. A portion of the text also occurs on an ostracon in the Egyptian Museum in Cairo. This translation is dependent mainly on Gardiner's initial publication of the text, but I have profited from an excellent paper presented by Dr. Gerald Kadish at the annual meeting of the American Research Center in Egypt at Toronto in November 1970.*

The last line in the text is complete but lacks any indication that it represents the end of the composition. Perhaps the composition was continued on another tablet.

W. K. S.

Recto

1   The gathering together of sayings, the culling of phrases, the search for words by an inquisitive mind, which the *web*-priest of Heliopolis, Seny's son Khakheperre-sonbe, who is called Ankhu, wrote. /

2   He said: Would that I had unknown speeches, erudite phrases in new language which has not yet been used, free from the usual repetitions, not the phrases of past speech /

3   which (our) forefathers spoke. I shall drain myself for something in it in giving free rein to all I shall say. For indeed whatever has been said has been repeated, while what has been said has been said. There should be no pride

4   about the literature of the men of former times / or what their descendants discovered! /

5   What I say has not been said. One who will speak now speaks. What another has found will be said. Not a tale of telling after the fact: they did it before. Nor yet a story

6   for future telling. / Such is seeking disaster. It is falsehood. And there is no one who shall recall such a man's name to the people.

    I speak these things just as I have seen them, beginning

7   with the first generation down to / those who shall come afterward, when they (too) shall pass over into the past.

    Would that I might know what others do not know, even what has not yet been repeated, that I might speak

8   and my heart answer me, that I might explain to it my grief, and that I might thrust aside from it[1] the weight which is on my back, (and speak) thoughts about what

---

1. Or "thrust onto it."

afflicts me, that I might express to it what I suffer through

9   it, / that I might speak, Yea, about my feelings!

10   ˘ I am thinking about what has happened, the things that have come to pass throughout the land. Changes are taking place. It is not like last year; one year is more troublesome than the next. The turbulance of the land works to its destruction!

11   ✓ Justice has been cast out, and evil is inside the shrine. The designs of the gods are spoiled, and their perquisites are passed over. The land is in dire state. Mourning is

12   everywhere. / Towns and villages are in lamentation. All alike are grief-stricken. The back is turned on anything of worth; the tranquil are distressed. Troubles occur daily, and the face shrinks from what is about to happen.

13   I will say my say about it. / My limbs are heavy-laden. I am distressed in my heart, and it is painful to hide my thoughts about it. Although another heart would break, a stout heart in a difficult situation is the companion of its master.

14   O would that I had a heart / that knew how to suffer. Then I might let myself down on it, and I would load it with phrases of misery, and it might drive off from me my sorrow.

Verso

1   He said to his heart: Come now, my heart, that I may converse with you and you may answer my sayings, that you may interpret for me that which is throughout the land, for those who were radiant (in white garments) have been cast down.

I am thinking about what has taken place. Misery is

2   ushered in / today. By the morning the strangers have (still) not passed away. Everyone is silent about it. The entire land is in a serious plight, and there is nobody free from wrong: all people alike do it. Hearts are dejected.

3   The one who gives commands / is (now) one to whom commands are given, and the hearts of both are quieted.

One rises to these things daily, and hearts have not thrust them aside. Yesterday's state is like today's, because of the passing by of many things. The countenance is per-

4   plexed. There is no man wise enough to know it, / and there is no man angry enough to speak out. Every day one wakes to suffering.

Long and burdensome is my suffering. There is no champion for the wretched to rescue him from one stronger than him. Silence about what is heard is painful.

5   It is miserable to have to give an answer / to the ignorant. One who finds fault with a speech makes for disaffection. The heart does not accept truth. A reply to a speech is insufferable. All a man wants is his own talk. Everyone is lying in crookedness. Precision in speech is abandoned.

6   I speak to you, / my heart, that you may answer me. Yet a heart which is appealed to cannot speak. The needs of a servant are like those of a master. Plentiful (now) are the things which weigh upon you.[2]

2. The tablet ends here and perhaps the text as well.

The Prophecies of Neferti

Ammenemes I, the first king of Dynasty 12, gained his throne by usurpation from the ruling family of the Mentuhotpes, and to ensure his position used a certain amount of written propaganda, outstandingly represented by the present text, which has been studied by Gardiner in JEA *1 (1914): 100–06, by Axel Volten,* Zwei altägyptische politische Schriften: Die Lehre für König Merikarê (Pap. Carlsberg VI) und die Lehre des Königs Amenemhet, Analecta Aegyptiaca IV *(Copenhagen: Einar Munksgaard, 1945), and by Wolfgang Helck,* Die Prophezeihung des Nfr.tj *(Wiesbaden: Otto Harrassowitz, 1970). It opens with a situation which recalls that in* Cheops and the Magicians. *King Snefru of Dynasty 4 is represented as seeking entertainment, and his courtiers recommend to him a sage named Neferti. He is ushered in to the Presence and asked to speak about the future. Neferti thereupon foretells a whole series of calamities which will befall the land, but prophesies that order and prosperity will be restored by the advent of a King Ameny—that is, Ammenemes I; the text is indeed a blatant political pamphlet designed to support the new regime. The principal source of the text is a papyrus in Leningrad which is a copy of New Kingdom date. It is not a perfect copy either in preservation or in accuracy, but there are numerous minor sources on writing tablets and ostraca which provide some help. I am indebted for some valuable suggestions to Georges Posener's notes on this text in his* Littérature et politique, *pp. 145–57. See also Erman,* The Ancient Egyptians, *pp. xxx, 110–15; Lefebvre,* Romans et contes, *pp. 91–105; Wilson, in* ANET, *pp. 444–46. See now W. Barta in* MDIK *21 (1971): 35–45.*

R. O. F.

Now it so happened that when the late King Snefru was potent king in this entire land, one of these days it hap-

pened that the Council of the Residence entered into the Great House to give greeting,[1] and when they had given greeting, they went out in accordance with their daily custom. Then said His Majesty to the seal-bearer who was at his side: Go and fetch for me the Council of the Residence which has gone out from here after having given
5   greeting today. They were ushered in to him / immediately, and again they prostrated themselves before His Majesty. And His Majesty said to them: Comrades, see, I have caused you to be summoned in order that you may seek out for me a son of yours who is wise, a brother of yours who is trustworthy, or a friend of yours who has achieved some noble deed, someone who shall say some fine words to me, choice phrases at the hearing of which My Majesty will be entertained. They prostrated themselves again before His Majesty: There is a Great Lector
10 of Bastet,[2] O Sovereign our lord, / whose name is Neferti; he is a commoner valiant with his arm, he is a scribe skilled with his fingers, and he is a wealthy man who has more possessions than any of his equals. Let him be [permitted] to see Your Majesty. His Majesty said: Go and fetch him to me. And he was ushered in to him immediately.

He prostrated himself before His Majesty, and His Majesty said: Come, Neferti my friend, say some fine words to me, choice phrases at hearing which My Majesty will be entertained. The Lector Neferti said: Of what has happened or of what shall happen, O Sovereign, [my]
15 lord? / His Majesty said: Of what shall happen; today has come into being and one has passed it by. Thereupon he[3] stretched out his hand to a box of writing materials

1. To the king.
2. A cat-goddess.
3. The king.

and took out a papyrus-roll and a palette, and he put into writing what the Lector Neferti said; he was a sage of the East [4] who belonged to Bastet when she rises and he was a native of the Heliopolitan nome.

He brooded over what should happen in the land and considered the condition of the east, when the Asiatics raid [5] and terrorize those at the harvest, taking away their teams engaged in ploughing. / He said: stir yourself, my heart, weep for this land in which you began, for he who is silent is a wrongdoer. See, that (now) exists which was spoken of as something dreadful. See, the great one is overthrown in the land in which you began. Do not become weary; see, they [6] are before your eyes; rise up against what is before you. See, there are great men in the governance of the land, yet what has been done is as though it had never been done. Re must begin by refounding the land, which is utterly ruined, and nothing remains; not even did a fingernail profit from what had been ordained. This land is destroyed and there are none who care for it; there are none who speak and there are none who act. Weeper, how fares this land? The sun is veiled, / and will not shine when the people would see; none will live when ⟨the sun⟩ is veiled ⟨by⟩ cloud, and everyone is dulled by the lack of it.

I will speak of what is before my eyes, I will never foretell what is not to come. The river of Egypt is dry and men cross the water on foot; men will seek water for ships in order to navigate it, [7] for their course has become the riverbank, and the bank (serves) for water; the place of

4. I.e. the eastern Delta.
5. Lit. "travel in their power."
6. The facts of the case.
7. The river.

water ⌜has become⌝ a riverbank, the south wind will oppose the north wind, and the sky will not be with one
single wind. A strange bird [8] will be born in the marshes
of the Delta, and a nest shall be made for it on account of
30 the ⌜neighbors,⌝ / for men have caused it to approach
through want. Perished are those erstwhile good things,
⌜the fish ponds⌝ of those who carry slit fish, teeming with
fish and fowl. All good things have passed away, the land
being cast away through trouble by means of that food of
the Asiatics who pervade the land. Enemies have come
into being in the east; Asiatics have come down into
Egypt, for a fortress lacks another beside it,[9] and no guard
will hear. Men will hold back and ⌜look out⌝ by night,[10]
the fortress will be entered, and sleep will be ⌜banished⌝
35 from my eyes, / so that I spend the night wakeful. Wild
game will drink from the river of Egypt, taking their ease
on their riverbanks through lack of anyone ⌜to fear⌝. This
land is in commotion, and no one knows what the result
may be, for it is hidden from speech, sight, and hearing
because of dullness, silence being to the fore.

I show you the land in calamity, for what had never
happened has now happened. Men will take weapons of
40 war and the land will live in / confusion. Men will make
arrows of bronze, men will beg for the bread of blood,
men will laugh aloud [11] at pain; none will weep at death,
none will lie down hungry at death,[12] and a man's heart
will think of himself alone. None will dress hair today;

8. A bird of ill-omen.
9. To support it so as to keep the barbarians out.
10. I.e. will not venture out, but stare apprehensively into the
darkness.
11. Lit. "laugh with a laughing."
12. Meaning that men will not fast after a death.

hearts are entirely ⌜astray⌝ because of it, and a man sits quiet, turning his back, while one man kills another.

I show you a son as an enemy, a brother as a foe, a
45   man / killing his father. Every mouth is full of "Love me"; all good things have passed away; a law is decreed for the ruin of the land. Men wreak destruction on what has been made and make a desolation of what has been found; what has been made is as though it had never been made; a man's possessions are taken from him and are given to an outsider.

I show you the owner of (but) a little, while the outsider is content. He who did not fill for himself now goes empty;[13] men give (something) unwillingly, so as to silence a talking mouth. A sentence is answered and a hand goes out with a stick; [men say]: "Do not kill him,"
50   but the discourse of speech is like fire to the heart, / and none can endure utterance. The land is diminished, though its controllers are many; he who was rich in servants is despoiled and corn is trifling, even though the corn-measure is great and it is measured to overflowing.[14] Re separates himself from men; he shines, that the hour may be told,[15] but no one knows when noon occurs,[16] for no one can discern his shadow, no one is dazzled when [he] is seen; there are none whose eyes stream with water, for he is like the moon in the sky, (though) his accustomed times do [not] go astray, and his rays are in (men's) sight as on former occasions.[17]

I show you the land in calamity; the weak-armed now

13. The result of improvidence.
14. I.e. those who should issue the corn keep it in store.
15. Lit. "that the hour may exist," referring to dawn.
16. The sun is too weak to cast the necessary shadow.
17. The sun performs its normal motions but sheds no more light than the moon.

55 possesses an arm, and men / salute one who used to do the
saluting. I show you [the lowermost] uppermost, ⌜men
pursuing him who flees away;⌝ [18] men are living in the
necropolis. The poor man will achieve wealth, while the
great lady will [beg] to exist; it is the poor who will eat
bread, while servants are . . . ; there will be no Heliopolitan nome to be the birth-land of every god.

A king of the South will come, Ameny by name,[19] the
son of a woman of Zety-land,[20] a child of Khenkhen.[21] He
will assume the White Crown, he will wear the Red
60 Crown, / he will join together the Double Crown, he will
propitiate the Two Lords[22] with what they desire; the
land will be enclosed in ⟨his⟩ grasp, the oars swinging;[23]
the people of his reign will rejoice, the well-born man will
make his name forever and ever. Those who have fallen
into evil and have planned rebellion have stultified[24] their
utterances through fear of him; the Asiatics will fall at the
dread of him; the Libyans will fall at his flaming, the rebels
65 at his wrath, the disaffected at / the awe of him, while the
uraeus[25] which is on his forehead will pacify the disaffected. Men will build "Walls of the Ruler,"[26] and there

18. Lit. "men turn round after him who turns his body round" in
order to run away.
19. Here the real purpose of this work begins to show; it is propaganda in favor of Ammenemes I, the savior who will set right the
miseries of the preceding period of chaos. Ameny is a shortened
form of his name.
20. This geographical term embraced the territory both north and
south of the First Cataract; here the northern portion, the first
nome of Upper Egypt, is probably what is intended.
21. A name for Upper Egypt.
22. Horus and Seth.
23. When he is rowed on his royal progresses through the land.
24. Lit. "have caused to fall."
25. The royal cobra.
26. The frontier fortifications in the Wadi Tumilat, built by
Ammenemes I.

will be no letting the Asiatics go down into Egypt that they may beg water after their accustomed fashion to let their herds drink. Right will come to its place (again) and Wrong will be thrust outside; joyful will be [he] who will see (it) and he who will serve the king. The learned man shall pour [a libation to me when he sees that what I have said] has come to pass.

It has come happily to an end.

The Instruction of Amenemope

This major text was first made available for study in 1923 through the publication of a magnificent, virtually complete manuscript in the British Museum (B.M. 10474). The text is written in short lines like poetry, and the sections are consecutively numbered from chapter 1 to 30. Portions of the text are also known from writing boards in the Turin Museum, the Pushkin Museum in Moscow, and the Louvre, an ostracon in Cairo, and a fragmentary papyrus in Stockholm. A still unpublished thesis on the text by J. Ruffle was presented at Liverpool University in 1964, and a study by Irene Grumach is due to be published presently. Bibliographical information about this important text can be followed through the articles by B. J. Peterson in JEA 52 (1966): 120–28, and R. J. Williams in JEA 47 (1961): 100–06, the latter a convincing refutation of the suggestion that the text is a translation of a Semitic original. There are indeed close parallels between verses in Amenemope and the Book of Proverbs, especially Proverbs 22:17, 24:22. For the most part, however, the concepts presented in Amenemope are present in earlier Egyptian instruction literature and must be viewed in that context. The contrast between the intemperate, hot-headed man and the tranquil, truly silent man is one of the main themes of the text. The present consensus places the date of composition in the New Kingdom, although the manuscripts in the main do not predate Dynasty 21. The author of The Instruction was a resident of Akhmim in the Panopolite nome north of Abydos. This was the area from which the family of Queen Teye came, and one might suggest as a date for the composition the years just before the Amarna period, perhaps the reign of Amenhotpe III.

A new and reasonably authoritative translation should be based on a thorough restudy of the text with full reference to the most recent literature. The present version cannot hope to achieve this goal. I hope that it will prove serviceable if not free from errors of inter-

pretation. It is a relatively free translation indebted in the main to the version presented by F.Ll. Griffith in JEA 12 (1926): 191–231.

W. K. S.

(*Introduction*)

1,1 The beginning of the instruction about life,
   The guide [1] for well-being,
 All the principles of official procedure,
   The duties of the courtiers;
 To know how to refute the accusation [2] of one who made
   it,
   And to send back a reply to the one who wrote; [3]
 To set one straight on the paths of life,
   And make him prosper on earth;
 To let his heart settle down in its chapel, [4]
1,10   And steer clear of evil; [5]
 To save him from the talk of others,
   As one who is respected in the speech of men.

 Written by the superintendent of the land, experienced in
   his office, [6]
   The offspring of a scribe of the Beloved Land,
 The superintendent of produce, who fixes the grain mea-
   sure,
   Who sets the grain tax amount for his lord,

1. Lit. "testimony."
2. Perhaps only, "to return an answer."
3. Or, "to the one who sent him."
4. Griffith notes that the heart is shown in a kind of shrine or chapel in amulets of the New Kingdom; perhaps the idea of self-composure is intended.
5. The metaphors of sailing and rowing are frequent in the text.
6. Here begins an extended description of the offices and duties of Amenemope.

Who registers the islands which appear as new land
>over the cartouche of His Majesty,[7]
>And sets up the land mark at the boundary of the
>arable land,

2,1 Who protects the king by his writings,
>And makes the Register of the Black Land.[8]

The scribe who places the divine offerings for all the gods,
>The donor of land grants to the people,

The superintendent of grain who administers the food
offerings,
>Who supplies the storerooms with grain.

A truly silent man in Tjeni in the Ta-wer nome,
>One whose verdict is "acquitted" in Ipu,

The owner of a pyramid tomb on the west of Senut,

2,10 As well as the owner of a memorial chapel in Aby-
>dos,

Amenemope, the son of Kanakht,
>Whose verdict is "acquitted" in the Ta-wer nome.[9]

For his son, the youngest of his children,[10]
>The least of his family,

Initiate of the mysteries of Min-Kamutef,
>Libation pourer of Wennofre;[11]

---

7. When the annual inundation of the lands subsided, the newly formed islands in the Nile were immediately designated as royal property.

8. The usual name for Egypt.

9. Tjeni in the Ta-wer nome (Abydos) was the great temple and cult site of the god Osiris, where many royal and private memorial buildings were dedicated. Ipu and Senut are in the Panopolite nome to the north of Abydos, the area of modern Akhmim, of which the patron god was Min-Kamutef.

10. As in other instructions, the addressee is the man's son, in this case Hor-em-maa-kheru, whose name means "Horus is vindicated," the son of Amenemope and Tawosret.

11. Min-Bull-of-his-Mother, the god of Akhmim; Wennofre is an epithet of Osiris.

Who introduces Horus upon the throne of his father,
> His stolist in his august chapel,

. . . .

3,1   The seer of the Mother of God,
The inspector of the black cattle of the terrace of Min,
> Who protects Min in his chapel,

Horemmaakheru is his true name,
> A child of an official of Ipu,

The son of the sistrum player of Shu and Tefnut,
> The chief singer of Horus, the lady Tawosret.

He Says: Chapter 1

Give your ears and hear what is said,
3,10   Give your mind over to their interpretation:
It is profitable to put them in your heart,[12]
> But woe to him that neglects them!

Let them rest in the shrine of your insides
> That they may act as a lock in your heart;

Now when there comes a storm of words,
> They will be a mooring post for your tongue.

If you spend a lifetime with these things in your heart,
> You will find it good fortune;

4,1 You will discover my words to be a treasure house of life,
> And your body will flourish upon earth.

Chapter 2

Beware of stealing from a miserable man
> And of raging against the cripple.

12. Possibly, "profitable is he who places it in your heart."

Do not stretch out your hand to touch an old man,
> Nor snip at the words of an elder.

Don't let yourself be involved in a fraudulent business,
> Not desire the carrying out of it; [13]

4,10 Do not get tired because of being interfered with, [14]
> Nor return an answer on your own account. [15]

The evildoer, throw him ⟨in⟩ the canal, [16]
> And ⌜he will bring back its slime⌝.

The north wind comes down and ends his appointed hour,
> It is joined to the tempest;

The thunder is high, the crocodiles are nasty,
> O hot-headed man, what are you like?

He cries out, and his voice (reaches) heaven.
> O Moon, make his crime manifest!

5,1 Row that we may ferry the evil man away,
> For we will not act according to his evil nature; [17]

Lift him up, give him your hand,
> And leave him ⟨in⟩ the hands of God; [18]

Fill his gut with your own food
> That he may be sated and ashamed.

Something else of value in the heart of God
> Is to stop and think before speaking.

Chapter 3

5,10 Do not get into a quarrel with the argumentative man
> Nor incite him with words;

13. Or, "nor desire (the company of) the one who does it."
14. Or, "do not revile someone you have hurt," or "do not act the part of a tired one (be downcast) toward the one you deceive."
15. Do not plead your own case in person?
16. Or, "the shore abandons him."
17. Not act like one of his kind.
18. Or, "the hands of God will abandon him."

Proceed cautiously before an opponent,
  And give way to an adversary;
Sleep on it before speaking,
  For a storm comes forth like fire in hay.
The hot-headed man in his appointed time:
  May you be restrained before him;
Leave him to himself,
  And God will know how to answer him.

If you spend your life with these things in your heart,
  Your children shall behold them.

5,20 *Chapter 4*

6,1 The hot-headed man in the temple
  Is like a tree grown outdoors;
Suddenly it loses its ⌜branches⌝,
  And it reaches its end in the carpentry shop;
It is floated away far from its place,
  Or fire is its funeral pyre.

The truly temperate man sets himself apart,
  He is like a tree grown in sandy soil,
But it flourishes, it doubles its yield,
6,10 It stands before its owner;
Its fruit is something sweet, its shade is pleasant,
  And it reaches its end in a garden.[19]

Chapter 5

Do not take by violence the shares of the temple,

19. The parable of the two trees has been frequently discussed. See, for example, Etienne Drioton, in *Drevnii Mir* (Moscow, 1962), pp. 76–80 (Struve Festschrift).

> Do not be grasping, and you will find overabun-
>   dance;
> Do not take away a temple servant
>   In order to do a favor for someone else.
> Do not say today is the same as tomorrow,
>   Or how will matters come to pass?

7,1 When tomorrow comes and today is past,
>   The deep waters sink from the canal bank,[20]
> Crocodiles are uncovered, the hippopotamuses are on dry
>   land,
>   And the fishes gasping for air;
> The wolves are fat, the wild fowl in festival,
>   And the nets are ⌈drained⌉.

> Every temperate man in the temple says,
>   "Great is the benevolence of Re."
> So hold fast to the temperate man, you will find life,

7,10 And your body shall flourish upon earth.

Chapter 6

> Do not displace the surveyor's marker on the boundaries
>   of the arable land,
>   Nor alter the position of the measuring line;
> Do not be greedy for a plot of land,
>   Nor overturn the boundaries of a widow.

> As for the road in the field worn down by time,
>   He who takes it violently for fields,
> If he traps by deceptive attestations,
>   Will be lassoed by the might of the Moon.[21]

20. Possibly meaning that the time for action is now past.
21. Or, "if he is caught. . . ."

8,1   To one who has done this on earth, pay attention,
>For he is a tormentor to the weak;

He is an enemy overturning [all] within you,
>Taking life away is in his eye;

His household is hostile to the community,
>His storerooms are toppled over,

His property taken from his children,
>And to someone else his possessions given.

8,10 Take care not to topple over the boundary marks of the arable land,
>Not fearing that you will be brought to court; [22]

Man propitiates God by the might of the Lord
>When he sets straight the boundaries of the arable land.

Desire, then, to make yourself prosper,
>And take care for the Lord of All; [23]

Do not trample on the furrow of someone else,
>Their good order will be profitable for you.[24]

So plough the fields, and you will find whatever you need,
>And receive the bread from your own threshing floor:

Better is the bushel which God gives you

8,20   Than five thousand deceitfully gotten;

9,1   They do not spend a day in the storehouse or warehouse,
>They are ⌈no use for dough for beer⌉;

Their stay in the granary is short-lived,
>When morning comes they will be swept away.

---

22. Or, "lest fear carry you off."
23. Osiris? See Goedicke, in *JARCE* 7 (1968): 16–17.
24. Griffith: "It is good for thee to be sound concerning them."

Better, then, is poverty in the hand of God
> Than riches in the storehouse;
Better is bread when the mind is at ease
> Than riches with anxiety.

Chapter 7

9,10 Do not set your heart upon seeking riches,
> For there is no one who can ignore Destiny and
> Fortune; [25]
Do not set your thoughts on external matters:
> For every man there is his appointed time.

Do not exert yourself to seek out excess
> So that your wealth will prosper for you; [26]
If riches come to you by theft
> They will not spend the night with you;
As soon as day breaks they will not be in your household;
> Although their places can be seen, they are not
> there.

9,20 When the earth opens up its mouth, it reckons him and
> swallows him up,
10,1 > And it drowns them in the deep;
They have made for themselves a great slit in their mea-
> sure,
> And they have sunk themselves in the tomb; [27]
Or they have made themselves wings like geese,
> And they fly up to the sky.
Do not be pleased with yourself (because of) riches ac-
> quired through robbery,

25. Shay and Ernutet: deities of Destiny and Fortune.
26. Or, "your own property is good enough for you."
27. John Ruffle, in *JEA* 50 (1964): 177–78.

Neither complain about poverty.
If an officer commands one who goes in front of him,
    His company leaves him;
10,10 The boat of the covetous is abandoned ⟨in⟩ the mud,
        While the skiff of the truly temperate man ⌜sails on⌝.
When he rises you shall offer to the Aten,
        Saying, "Grant me prosperity and health."
And he will give you your necessities for life,
        And you will be safe from fear.

Chapter 8

Set your good deeds throughout the world
        That every man may greet you;
They make rejoicing for the Uraeus,
10,20   And spit against the Apophis.
Keep your tongue safe from words of detraction,
11,1   And you will be the loved one of the people,[28]
Then you will find your place within the temple
            And your offerings among the bread deliveries of
            your lord;
You will be revered, and you will be concealed ⟨in⟩ your
            grave,
            And be safe from the might of God.

Do not accuse a man,[29]
        But suppress the news of an escape.
If you hear something good or bad,
        Say it outside, where it is not heard;
11,10 Set a good report on your tongue,
            While the bad thing is covered up inside you.

28. Or, "that you may do what people love."
29. "Summon up a crime."

Chapter 9

Do not fraternize with the hot-tempered man,
    Nor approach him to converse.
Safeguard your tongue from answering your superior,
    And take care not to speak against him.
Do not allow him to stop talking only to entrap you,[30]
    And be not too free [31] in your replies;
With a man of your own station discuss the reply;
11,20   And take care of ⌐speaking thoughtlessly¬;
12,1 When the heart is upset, words travel faster
    Than wind before water.

He ruins and creates with his tongue,[32]
    And he speaks slander;
He makes an answer deserving of a beating,
    For its work is evil;
He sails among all the world,[33]
    But his cargo is false words; [34]
He acts the ferryman in knitting words:
12,10   He goes forth and comes back arguing.

But whenever he eats or whenever he drinks inside,
    His accusation (waits for him) without.
The day when his evil deed is brought to court
    Is a disaster for his children.
Even Khnum will straightway come, even Khnum will
    straightway come,[35]

30. Lit. "lasso."
31. *ntfi*, a word used of unharnessing horses and untying captives.
32. He makes and breaks reputations.
33. The Stockholm fragment begins here. See Peterson, in *JEA* 52 (1966): 120–28.
34. Lit. "he is laden <with> false words."
35. Peterson, in *JEA* 50 (1966): 125.

> The creator of the ill-tempered man
> Whom he molds and fires ⌜. . .⌝;
>> He is like a wolf cub in the farmyard,
> And he turns one eye to the other (squinting),

13,1
>> For he sets families to argue.
> He goes before all the winds like clouds,
>> He diminishes his character in the sun;
> He crocks his tail like a baby crocodile,
>> He curls himself up as if injured;
> His lips are sweet, but his tongue is bitter,
>> And flame burns inside him.

> Do not fly up to join that man
>> Not fearing you will be brought to account.

10,13 *Chapter 10*

> Do not address your intemperate friend in your unright-
>> eousness,[36]
>> Nor destroy your own mind;
> Do not say to him, "May you be praised," not meaning it
>> When there is fear within you.
> Do not converse with false men,
>> For it is the abomination of God.
> Do not separate your mind from your tongue,[37]
>> All your plans will succeed.[38]
> You will be important before others,[39]

14,1
>> While you will be secure in the hand of God.

36. Or, "in forcing yourself."
37. Say what you really mean (Lange).
38. Or, "all your good plans will come to pass."
39. Lit. "It will happen that you will be weighty in the presence of other men."

God hates the falsification of words,
>His great abomination is duplicity.

Chapter 11

Do not covet the property of the poor [40]
>Nor hunger for his bread;
The property of a poor man is moisture for (his) throat,
>It is spittle for the gullet.[41]
If he has engendered it by false oaths,
10,14   His heart slips back inside him.
It is through the ⌐disaffected⌐ that ⌐success⌐ is ⌐lost⌐,[42]
>Bad and good elude.

If you are ⌐at a loss⌐ before your superior,
>And are confused in your speeches,
Your requests are turned back with curses,
>And your humble actions by beatings.
Whoever fills the mouth with too much bread swallows it
>   and spits up,
>So he is emptied of his good.[43]

To the examination of a poor man give thought
15,1   While the sticks touch him,
And while all his people are fettered with manacles:
>Who is to have the execution? [44]

40. Here ends the fragmentary duplicate text in Stockholm.
41. Perhaps meaning that the limited property of a poor man is barely enough to keep him alive, like moisture in his throat. The connection with the next verses is unclear to me.
42. Or perhaps, "do not let disaffection wear away success."
43. Lit. "O filler of the mouth with a large bite of bread, you swallow it, you vomit it, you are emptied. . . ."
44. Griffith: "and where(?) is the executioner?"

When you are too free [45] before your superior,
> Then you are in bad favor with your subordinates.
So steer away from the poor man on the road,
> That you may see him and keep clear of his property.

Chapter 12

Do not covet the property of an official,
10,15 And do not fill (your) mouth with too much food
> extravagantly;
If he sets you to manage his property,
> Respect his, and yours will prosper.

Do not deal with the intemperate man,
> Nor associate yourself to a disloyal party.

If you are sent to transport straw,
> Respect its account;
If a man is detected in a dishonest transaction,
> Never again will he be employed.

Chapter 13

15,20 Do not lead a man astray ⟨with⟩ reed pen or papyrus
> document:
> It is the abomination of God.
16,1 Do not witness a false statement,
> Nor remove a man (from the list) by your order;
Do not enroll someone who has nothing,
> Nor make your pen be false.
If you find a large debt [46] against a poor man,

45. See n. 31, above.
46. Arrears, default, debit balance.

Make it into three parts;
Release two of them and let one remain:
You will find it a path of life;
16,   You will pass the night in sound sleep; in the morning
9–10   You will find it like good news.

Better is the praise that comes through the love of men
Than wealth in the storehouse;
Better is bread when the mind is at ease
Than riches with troubles.

Chapter 14

Do not pay attention to a person,
Nor exert yourself to seek out his hand,
If he says to you, "take a bribe,"
It is not an insignificant matter to heed him;
16,20 Do not avert your glance from him, nor bend down your head,
Nor turn aside your gaze.
Address him with your words and say to him greetings;
17,1   When he stops, your chance will come;
Do not repel him at his ⌐first approach⌐,
Another time he will be brought (to judgment).

Chapter 15

Do well, and you will reach ⌐the state I am in⌐;
Do not dip (your) reed against the one who sins.
The beak of the Ibis is the finger of the scribe;[47]
Take care not to disturb it;
The Ape (Thot) rests (in) the temple of Khmun,[48]

47. The Ibis here is Thot, patron god of the scribe.
48. Hermopolis, the town of Thot.

17,10   While his eye travels around the Two Lands;
      If he sees one who sins with his finger (that is, a false
          scribe),
          He takes away his provisions by the flood.
      As for a scribe who sins with his finger,
          His son shall not be enrolled.

      If you spend your life with these things in your heart,
          Your children shall see them.

Chapter 16

      Do not unbalance the scale nor make the weights false,
          Nor diminish the fractions of the grain measures;
17,20 Do not wish for the grain measures of the fields
          And then cast aside those of the treasury.[49]
      The Ape sits by the balance,
18,1   While his heart is the plummet.
      Where is a god as great as Thot,
          The one who discovered these things,[50] to create
          them?

      Do not get for yourself short weights;
          They are plentiful, yea, an army by the might of
          God.
      If you see someone backsliding,
          At a distance you must pass him by.
      Do not be avaricious for copper,
          And abjure fine clothes;
18,10 What good is a cloak of fine linen woven as *mek*,[51]

49. Do not use different measures to your own benefit?
50. Hieroglyphs?
51. Černý, *Hieratic Inscriptions from the Tomb of Tut'ankhamūn*, p. 8.

When he backslides before God.
⌐Faience⌐ sheathed [52] with gold leaf
    At daybreak turns to lead.

Chapter 17

Beware of ⌐doing violence⌐ [53] to the grain measure
        To falsify its fractions;
Do not act wrongfully ⌐when the Great Constellation ap-
            pears⌐,[54]
        Although it is empty inside;
May you have it measure exactly as to its size,
18,20   Your hand stretching out with precision.

Make not for yourself a measure of two capacities,[55]
        For then it is toward the depths that you will go.
The measure is the eye of Re,
19,1   Its abomination is the one who takes.
As for a grain measurer who multiplies the faults,
        His eye will seal up against him.

Do not receive the harvest tax of a cultivator,
        Nor bind up a papyrus against him when he is led
            astray.
Do not enter into collusion with the grain measurer,
        Nor play ⌐"arranging the interior,"⌐
Mightier is the threshing floor for barley
        Than swearing by the Great Throne.

52. Same word as "violence(?)" in the next note.
53. Same word as sheathed(?)" in preceding note. Perhaps "coating"
or the like suits both cases, or else the words merely sound alike.
54. Interpreted variously, and possibly a corrupt text.
55. So Griffith. A measure which can be read two ways?

19,10 *Chapter 18*

Do not go to bed fearing tomorrow,
      For when day breaks what is tomorrow like?
Man knows not how tomorrow will be!
God is success,
      Man is failure.
The words which men say pass on one side,
      The things which God does pass on another side.

Do not say, "⌜I am⌝ without fault,"
      Nor try to seek out trouble.
19,20 Fault is the business of God,
      It is locked up with his ⌜seal⌝.
There is no success in the hand of God,
      Nor is there failure before Him;
20,1 If He turns Himself about to seek out success,
      In a moment He destroys it.

Be strong in your heart, make your mind firm,
      Do not steer with your tongue;
The tongue of a man is the steering oar of a boat,
      And the Lord of All is its pilot.

Chapter 19

Do not enter the council chamber in the presence of a
      magistrate
And then falsify your speech.
20,10 Do not go up and down with your accusation
      When your witnesses stand readied.
Do not ⌜overstate⌝ ⟨through⟩ oaths in the name of your
      lord,
      ⟨Through⟩ pleas ⟨in⟩ the place of questioning.

Tell the truth before the magistrate,
>Lest he gain power over your body;
If you come before him the next day,
>He will concur with all you say;
He will present your case [56] ⟨in⟩ court before the Council
>of the Thirty,
>And it will be ⌜lenient⌝ another time as well.

20,20 *Chapter 20*

Do not corrupt the people of the law court,
>Nor move the just man.
21,1 Do not agree because of garments of white,
>Nor accept one in rags.
Take not the gift of the strong man,
>Nor repress the weak for him.
Justice is a wonderful gift of God,
>And He will render it to whomever He wishes.
The strength of one like him
>Saves a poor wretch from his beatings.

Do not make false ⌜enrollment⌝ lists,
21,10 >For they are a serious affair deserving death;
They are serious oaths of the kind promising not to misuse
>an office,
>And they are for inquiry by an informer.

Do not falsify the oracles [57] on a papyrus
>And (thereby) alter the designs of God.
Do not arrogate to yourself the might of God
>Without (the authority of) Destiny and Fortune.[58]

56. Lit. "he will say your speech."
57. G. Posener, in *ZÄS* 90 (1963): 99.
58. See n. 25, above.

Hand property over to its (rightful) owners,
    And seek out life for yourself;
Let not your heart build in their house,[59]
21,20   For then your neck will be on the execution block.

Chapter 21

22,1 Do not say, find me [60] a potent protector
    For a man in your town has injured me; [61]
Do not say, find me [62] a ransomer,
    For a man who hates has injured me.[63]

Indeed, you cannot know the plans of God;
    You cannot perceive tomorrow.
Sit yourself at the hands of God;
    Your tranquility will annihilate them.

As for a crocodile deprived of ⌐his tongue¬,
22,10   The fear of him is negligible.[64]
Empty not your soul to everybody
    And do not diminish thereby your importance;
Do not circulate your words to others,
    Nor fraternize with ⌐one who is too candid¬.

Better is a man whose knowledge is inside him
    Than one who talks to disadvantage.
One cannot run to attain perfection;
    One cannot create (only) to destroy it.

59. Meaning: "do not build within another's property"?
60. Or, "I have found."
61. Or, "I have transgressed against a man in your town."
62. See n. 60, above.
63. Or, "I have transgressed against a hostile person."
64. G. Posener, in *Festschrift für Siegfried Schott zu seinem 70. Geburtstag,* ed. W. Helck (Wiesbaden: Otto Harrassowitz, 1968), pp. 106–11.

Chapter 22

22,20 Do not castigate your companion in a dispute,
And do not ⟨let⟩ him say his innermost thoughts;
Do not fly up to greet him
23,1 When you do not see ⌐how he acts⌐.
May you first comprehend his accusation
And cool down ⌐your opponent⌐.

Leave it to him and he will empty his soul;
⌐Sleep knows how to find him out⌐;[65]
Take his feet,[66] do not bother him;
Fear him, do not underestimate him.
Indeed, you cannot know the plans of God,
You cannot perceive tomorrow.
23,10 Sit yourself at the hands of God;
Your tranquility will annihilate them.

Chapter 23

Do not eat a meal in the presence of a magistrate,
Nor set to eating first.
If you are satisfied with meals fraudulently gained,
Enjoy yourself with your spittle.

Look at the cup in front of you,
And let it suffice your need.
Even as a noble is important in his office,
23,20 He is like the abundance of a well when it is
drawn.[67]

65. Griffith: "Know how to sleep and he will be comprehended."
66. Meaning?
67. "He is abundant like a well from which one draws water."

Chapter 24

Do not listen to the accusation of an official indoors,
24,1   And then repeat it to another outside.[68]
Do not allow your discussions to be brought outside
      So that your heart will not be grieved.

The heart of a man is the beak of the God,
      So take care not to slight it;
A man who stands ⟨at⟩ the side of an official
      Should not have his name known (in the street).

Chapter 25

Do not jeer at a blind man nor tease a dwarf,
24,10   Neither interfere with the condition of a cripple;
Do not taunt a man who is in the hand of God,
      Nor scowl at him if he errs.

Man is clay and straw,
      And God is his potter;
He overthrows and He builds daily,[69]
      He impoverishes a thousand if He wishes.
He makes a thousand into examiners,
      When He is in His hour of life.
How fortunate is he who reaches the West,
24,20   When he is safe in the hand of God.

68. The Turin text supplies a duplicate from here to the end of the second paragraph of chap. 26 (line 25,9).
69. The creative and destructive powers of God are also stressed in chap. 18. See also n. 32, above, for the association of ideas.

Chapter 26

Do not stay in the tavern
25,1   And join someone greater than you,
Whether he be high or low in his station,
        An old man or a youth;
But take as a friend for yourself someone compatible:
        Re is helpful though he is far away.

When you see someone greater than you outside,
        And attendants following him, respect (him).
And give a hand to an old man filled with beer:
        Respect him as his children would.[70]

25,10 The strong arm is not ⌜hurt⌝ when it is uncovered,
        The back is not broken when it is bent;
Poverty will not befall a man who speaks well
        Any more than riches when his speech is dry.

A pilot who sees into the distance
        Will not let his ship capsize.

Chapter 27

Do not reproach someone older than you,
        For he has seen the Sun before you;
Do not let yourself be reported to the Aten when he rises,
25,20   Saying, "Another young man has reproached an
        elder."
Very sick in the sight of Re
26,1   Is a young man who reproaches an elder.

70. The Turin text duplicate ends here.

Let him beat you with your hands folded,
>Let him reproach you while you keep quiet.
Then when you come before him the next day
>He will give you bread freely.
The food of a hound is (the business) of his master:
>He barks to the one who gives it.

Chapter 28

Do not expose a widow if you have caught her in the
>fields,
26,10>Nor fail to give way if she is accused.
Do not turn a stranger away ⟨from⟩ your oil jar
>That it may be made double for your family.
God desires the good treatment of the poor
>More than respect for the noble.

Chapter 29

Do not turn people away from crossing the river
>When you have room in your ferryboat;
If a steering oar is given you in the midst of the deep
>waters,
>You will bend back your hands ⟨to⟩ take it up.
26,20 It is not an abomination in the hand of God
27,1>If a boatman does not consent.

Do not acquire a ferryboat on the river,
>And then attempt to seek out its fares;
Take the fare from the man of means,
>But (also) accept the destitute (without charge).

Chapter 30

Mark for your self these thirty chapters:
> They please, they instruct,
They are the foremost of all books;
27,10 > They teach the ignorant.
If they are read to an ignorant man,
> He will be purified through them.
Seize them; put them in your mind
>> And have men interpret them, explaining as a
>> teacher.
As to a scribe who is experienced in his position,
> He will find himself worthy of being a courtier.

[Colophon]

It is finished.
28,1 By the writing of Senu, son of the god's father Pamiu.

PART 4

Songs, Poetry, and Hymns

Poetry from the Oldest Religious Literature

This series of poems comes from the oldest collection of religious texts surviving from Ancient Egypt, known as the Pyramid Texts because they are found in royal pyramids of Dynasties 5 and 6. In the first poem, The Dead King Hunts and Eats the Gods (sometimes known as the Cannibal Hymn), the dead king, newly arrived in heaven to the accompaniment of a cosmic cataclysm, hunts, cooks, and eats the gods in order to absorb their powers into himself, thus becoming Omnipotence. The hieroglyphic texts of this and the poems which follow will be found in Kurt Sethe, Die altaegyptischen Pyramidentexte, *vols. 1 and 2 (Leipzig, 1908–10): the translations are taken from R. O. Faulkner,* The Ancient Egyptian Pyramid Texts *(Oxford: The Clarendon Press, 1969), by courtesy of the Oxford University Press.*

R. O. F.

The Dead King Hunts and Eats the Gods [1]

393 The sky is overcast,
    The stars are darkened,
    The celestial expanses quiver,
    The bones of the earth-gods tremble,
    The ⌐planets¬ are stilled,
394 For they have seen the King appearing in power
    As a god who lives on his fathers
    And feeds on his mothers;
    The King is a master of wisdom

1. Pyramid utterances 273–74.

Whose mother knows not his name.

395   The glory of the King is in the sky,
His power is in the horizon
Like his father Atum [2] who begot him.
He begot the King,
And the King is mightier than he.

396   The King's powers are about him,
His ⌐qualities⌐ [3] are under his feet,
His gods [4] are upon him,
His uraei [5] are on the crown of his head,
The King's guiding serpent is on his brow,
Even that which sees the soul,
Efficient ⌐for burning;⌐ [6]
The King's neck is on his trunk. [7]

397   The King is the Bull of the sky,
Who ⌐conquers⌐ at will,
Who lives on the being of every god,
Who eats their ⌐entrails⌐,
Even of those who come with their bodies full of magic
From the Island of Fire. [8]

398   The King is one equipped,
Who assembles his spirits;

2. The primeval sun-god of Heliopolis.
3. *Ḥmwst*, a word which has no exact equivalent in English.
4. I.e. the sacred royal insignia, which would have amuletic protective power.
5. I.e. images of cobras about to strike.
6. A difficult passage; "efficient for burning," if that be the correct translation, refers to the royal serpent's efficiency in spitting fire at hostile beings.
7. I.e. in its proper place and not detached from the body.
8. A mythical locality where apparently the dead foregather before passing on to their respective destinies. In later religious texts it plays a more prominent part than in the pyramids, where it is mentioned only twice, here and in §265.

The King has appeared as this Great One,
A possessor of helpers;
He sits with his back to Geb,[9]

399 For it is the King who will give judgment
In company with Him whose name is hidden
On that day of slaying the Oldest Ones.
The King is a possessor of offerings who knots the cord [10]
And who himself prepares his meal;

400 The King is one who eats men and lives on the gods,
A possessor of porters who despatches messages;

401 It is Grasper-of-topknots who ⌈is⌉ Kehau [11]
Who lassoes them for the King;
It is the Serpent with raised head
Who guards them for him
And restrains them for him;
It is He who is over the ⌈blood-offering⌉ [12]
Who binds them for him;

402 It is Khons [13] who slew the lords
Who strangles them for the King
And extracts for him what is in their bodies,
For he is the messenger whom the King sends to restrain.

403 It is Shezmu [14] who cuts them up for the King
And who cooks for him a portion of them
On his evening hearthstones.
It is the King who eats their magic
And gulps down their spirits;

404 Their big ones are for his morning meal,

9. I.e. in front of him; Geb is the earth-god.
10. To bind the sacrificial victim.
11. Or possibly "who is in Kehau."
12. The shedding of the victim's blood?
13. The moon-god.
14. The wine-press god.

Their middle-sized ones are for his evening meal,
Their little ones are for his night meal,
Their old men and their old women are for his incense-
burning.

405 It is the Great Ones in the north of the sky [15]
Who set the fire for him
To the cauldrons containing them
With the thighs of their oldest ones.

406 Those who are in the sky serve the King,
And the hearthstones are wiped over for him
With the feet of their women.
He has traveled around the whole of the two skies,[16]
He has circumambulated the Two Banks,[17]

407 For the King is a great Power
Who has power over the Powers;
The King is a sacred image,
The most sacred of the sacred images of the Great One,[18]
And whomsoever he finds in his way,
Him he devours ⌐piecemeal¬.
The King's place is at the head
Of all the august ones who are in the horizon,

408 For the King is a god, older than the oldest.
Thousands serve him,
Hundreds offer to him,
There is given to him a warrant as Great Power
By Orion, father of the gods.

409 The King has appeared again in the sky,
He is crowned as Lord of the horizon;
He has broken the backbones
And has taken the hearts of the gods;

15. The circumpolar stars.
16. I.e. of the upper world and the netherworld.
17. Of the Nile, i.e. Egypt.
18. Plays on the words for "power" and "sacred image" respectively.

410   He has eaten the Red Crown,
       He has swallowed the Green One.[19]
       The King feeds on the lungs of the Wise Ones,
       And is satisfied with living on hearts and their magic;
411   The King revolts against licking the . . .[20]
       Which are in the Red Crown.
       He enjoys himself when their [21] magic is in his belly;
       The King's dignities shall not be taken away from him,
       For he has swallowed the intelligence of every god.
412   The King's lifetime is eternity,
       His limit is everlastingness
       In this his dignity of:
       "If he wishes, he does;
       If he dislikes, he does not,"
       Even he who is at the limits of the horizon forever and
              ever.
413   See, their souls are in the King's belly,
       Their spirits are in the King's possession
       As the surplus of his meal ⌜out of⌝ the gods
       Which is cooked for the King out of their bones.[22]
       See, their souls are in the King's possession,
       Their shades are (removed) from their owners,
414   While the King is this one who ever appears and endures,
       And the doers of (ill) deeds have no power to destroy
       The favorite place [23] of the King among those who live in
              this land
       Forever and ever.

19. An allusion to the conquest of the north at the beginning of
history. The Red Crown was worn by the King of Lower Egypt,
and the Green One, the goddess Wadjet, was his guardian deity.
20. *Sbšw*, a plural word of unknown meaning, but apparently referring to something of evil taste.
21. Referring to the "hearts" previously mentioned.
22. I.e. the bones of the gods are boiled for soup.
23. The royal pyramid.

The King, Newly Dead, Appeals to the Gods Not to Forget Him [24]

327   Be not unaware of me, O God;
      If you know me, I will know you.
      Be not unaware of me, O God;
      Of me it is said: "He who has perished."

328   Be not unaware of me, O Re;
      If you know me, I will know you.
      Be not unaware of me, O Re;
      Of me it is said: "Greatest of all who have been completely destroyed."

329   Be not unaware of me, O Thoth;
      If you know me, I will know you.
      Be not unaware of me, O Thoth;
      Of me it is said: "He who rests alone."

330   Be not unaware of me, O Har-Sopd;
      If you know me, I will know you.
      Be not unaware of me, O Har-Sopd;
      Of me it is said: "Miserable One."

331   Be not unaware of me, O Dweller in the Netherworld;
      If you know me, I will know you.
      Be not unaware of me, O Dweller in the Netherworld;
      Of me it is said: "He who wakes healthy." [25]

332   Be not unaware of me, O Bull of the sky;
      If you know me, I will know you.
      Be not unaware of me, O Bull of the sky;
      Of me it is said: "This star of the Lower Sky."

24. From Pyramid Utterance 262. The text, which is not altogether devoid of corruption, was certainly couched originally in the first person and has been translated accordingly. The repeated refrains are typical of much Egyptian poetry.
25. An epithet of the dead Osiris, here applied to the king.

The Dead King Ferries across the Sky to Join the Sun-God.[26]

342   The reed-floats [27] of the sky are set down for Horus,
That he may cross on them to the horizon, to Harakhti.
The reed-floats of the sky are set down for me,
That I may cross on them to the horizon, to Harakhti.
The reed-floats of the sky are set down for Shezemti,[28]
That he may cross on them to the horizon, to Harakhti.
The reed-floats of the sky are set down for me,
That I may cross on them to the horizon, to Harakhti.

343   The Nurse-canal [29] is opened,
The Winding Waterway [30] is flooded,
The Fields of Rushes [31] are filled with water,
And I am ferried over
To yonder eastern side of the sky,

344   To the place where the gods fashioned me,
Wherein I was born, new and young.

A Censing Prayer [32]

346   The fire is laid, the fire shines;
The incense is laid on the fire, the incense shines.
Your perfume comes to me, O Incense;

26. From Pyramid Utterance 264. Again the first person is certainly original.
27. Floats made of bundles of reeds, used even into modern times in remote districts for crossing the Nile or a canal.
28. A god of the east.
29. Part of the Milky Way?
30. Designation of the Milky Way, here used loosely to denote a waterway the king must cross to reach the eastern region.
31. Part of the celestial landscape.
32. From Pyramid Utterance 269. Here again the first person is original.

May my perfume come to you, O Incense.

347 Your perfume comes to me, you gods;
May my perfume come to you, you gods.
May I be with you, you gods;
May you be with me, you gods.
May I live with you, you gods;
May you live with me, you gods.

348 I love you, you gods;
May you love me, you gods.[33]

The Gods are Warned Not to Curse or Hinder the Dead King on His Way to Heaven.[34]

492 If I be cursed, then will Atum be cursed;
If I be reviled, then will Atum be reviled;
If I be smitten, then will Atum be smitten;
If I be hindered on this road, then will Atum be hindered,

493 For I am Horus,
I have come following my father,
I have come following Osiris.

Another Text Threatening the Sun-God[35]

1435 The birth of "Limitless"[36] in the horizon will be prevented
If you prevent me from coming to the place where you are.

33. A good example of Egyptian poetic form; note here the arrangement in couplets, each with a slightly different theme.
34. From Pyramid Utterance 310. A good example of the Egyptian way of threatening their gods if they do not act as the speaker wishes.
35. From Pyramid Utterance 569.
36. I.e. the sun-god himself.

The birth of Selket [37] will be prevented

If you prevent me from coming to the place where you
are.

1436 The Two Banks [38] will be held back from Horus

If you prevent me from coming to the place where you
are.

The birth of Orion will be prevented

If you prevent me from coming to the place where you
are.

1437 The birth of Sothis will be prevented [39]

If you prevent me from coming to the place where you
are.

The Two Apes of Re,[40] his beloved sons, will be held off

If you prevent me from coming to the place where you
are.

1438 The birth of Wepwawet in the *Pr-nw* [41] will be prevented

If you prevent me from coming to the place where you
are.

Men will be held back from the King,[42] the son of the god,

If you prevent me from coming to the place where you
are.

1439 Your crew of the Imperishable Stars will be prevented
from rowing,

37. The scorpion-goddess.
38. Egypt.
39. Sothis is Sirius, the Dog Star. The heliacal rising of Sothis
marked the start of the annual rise of the Nile and the beginning
of the agricultural year, so that the prevention of her birth meant
the starvation of all Egypt.
40. The baboons who salute the rising sun.
41. Wepwawet, "Opener of the Ways," is a jackal-god who acts as
guide to the dead. The *Pr-nw* is an important shrine in Dep, one of
the twin cities which constituted the ancient Delta capital of Buto.
42. This is the newly reigning king, who whom his subjects will be
denied access. "The god" here is the speaker, the dead king.

If you prevent them from allowing me to go aboard this
    bark of yours.
Men will be prevented from dying [43]
If you prevent me from going aboard this bark of yours.
1440 Men will be held back from food
If you prevent me from going aboard this bark of yours.

The Dead King Flies Up to the Sky [44]

1484 Someone flies up from you, O men, as do ducks,
He wrests his hands from you as does a falcon, [45]
He has removed himself from you as does a kite,
The King is saved from him who was obstructive on earth,
The King is loosed from him who attacked him.

43. The threat lies in the subversion of the natural order.
44. From Pyramid Utterance 573.
45. The allusion is to the Egyptian habit of carrying live birds by
their wings; the king is envisaged as a bird escaping from the hand
of the fowler.

Cycle of Songs in Honor of Sesostris III

*This series of six songs, of which only the first four are well pre-
served, is part of the archive of papyri from Illahun. They were
first published by F. Ll. Griffith,* Hieratic Papyri from Kahun and
Gurob *(London: B. Quaritch, 1898), text, pp. 1–3; pls. 1–3. The
hieratic of the first four songs is reproduced in G. Möller,* Hieratische
Lesestücke *(Leipzig: J. C. Hinrichs, 1909), 1, pls. 4–5, and the
hieroglyphic in K. Sethe,* Ägyptische Lesestücke *(Leipzig: J. C.
Hinrichs, 1924), pp. 65–67. There is an analytical study and translation by Hermann Grapow: "Der Liederkranz zu Ehren Königs
Sesostris des Dritten aus Kahun,"* MIO *1 (1953): 189–209. More
recently there is Hans Goedicke's valuable study with translations,
"Remarks on the Hymns to Sesostris III,"* JARCE *7 (1968): 23–26.
In the second, third, and fourth songs the lines after the first are
indented, so that the first words are to be repeated at the beginning
of the following verses. The first four are closely allied in subject
matter and expression. Erman suggests that they were composed for
the arrival of the king at a town south of Memphis. A related
composition is* The Loyalist Instruction *studied by Georges Posener
in his* Littérature et politique, *where these songs are also considered
(pp. 127–30). Although they belong to religious (as opposed to
secular) literature, the dividing line between the categories is not
sharp. The songs embody ideas about the nature of the kingship in
the Middle Kingdom, and as examples of poetry they are of particular significance.*

W. K. S.

I.

I,1   The Horus Godlike of Transformations, the Two Ladies
     Godlike of Births, the Horus of Gold Kheper, the King of

Upper and Lower Egypt Khakaure, the Son of Re Sen-
wosret takes possession of the Two Lands as one who is
vindicated: [1]

2   Salutations to you Khakaure, our Horus Godlike of
               Transformations,[2]

    Protecting the land, extending your borders,[3]

3   Overwhelming the foreign lands with your crown,

    Enclosing the Two Lands with the deeds of your hands,

4   [Encompassing] the foreign lands with the strength of
               your arms,

5   Slaying the bowmen,[4] / without striking a blow,

    Shooting an arrow, without drawing a bow.

    Terror of you strikes the cave dwellers [5] in their land,

6   Fear of you slays the nine bows.[6]

    Your slaughtering causes thousands to die among the bar-
               barians,

    [And the enemies] who approach your borders.

7   When shooting an arrow as Sekhmet does,[7]

    You fell thousands who know you not.

8   The tongue of Your Majesty / restrains Nubia,

    And your words rout the Asiatics.

    1. The full five-part titulary of Senwosret III.

    2. "Our" Horus is elsewhere unattested; the idea of "our king" is
unusual but perhaps suits the context of a hymn addressed to the
ruler by his people. Neteri-kheperu means "divine in respect to
(his) transformations."

    3. The song is set in the third person, lit. "one who protects the
land, one who extends his borders." In the translation of this song I
have substituted "you" for "he" and "your" for "his" throughout,
in accordance with English usage.

    4. Foreigners from the north.

    5. Probably Nubians in the south.

    6. The traditional subjects or foes of the king, represented in
statuary as bows beneath his feet. See E. Uphill, "The Nine Bows,"
JEOL 19(1967): 393–420.

    7. Sekhmet is the goddess of plague and warfare.

9   Unique divine being, youthful one, / [fighting] on your
         border,
     Not allowing your people to grow weary,
10   Letting men sleep until daybreak;
     Your young men can sleep
     Since your heart protects them.
11   Your decrees create your borders,
     Your speech draws together the two banks of the river.

2.

II,1 How joyful are [your gods],
         For you have reestablished their offerings.
2   How joyful are your [people],
         For you have fixed their boundaries.
3   How joyful are your fathers who came before,
         For you have increased their shares.
4   How joyful are the Egyptians because of your might,
         For you have protected [their] traditions.
5   How joyful are men with your counsel,
         For your might has taken possession of [their] /
         increase.
6   How joyful are the two banks of the river in awe of you,
         For you have extended their portions.
7   How joyful are the recruits,
         For you have brought them to manhood.
8   How joyful are your honored old folk,
         For you have made [them] young.
9   How joyful are the Two Lands because of your vigor,
         For you have protected their ramparts.

10   Its ⌜burden:⌝ Horus, protecting your border, may you re-
         peat eternity!

3.

11   How great is the Lord for his City!
        He is Re, and other rulers of men are insignificant.[8]

12   How great is the Lord for his City!
            Yea, he is a dam which holds back the river against
            its floodwaters.

13   How great is the Lord for his City!
            Yea, he is a cool place which lets every man sleep
            to daybreak.

14   How great is the Lord for his City!
        Yea, he is a rampart of walls of copper from Goshen.[9]

15   How great is the Lord for his City!
        Yea, he is a refuge ⌜whose bolt does not waver.⌝

16   How great is the Lord for his City!
            Yea, he is a resting place which protects the fearful
            man from his enemy.

17   How great is the Lord for his City!
            Yea, he is a shade ⌜in⌝ the Inundation season, a cool
            place in Summer.

18   How great is the Lord for his City!
            Yea, he is a warm, dry corner in time of Winter.

19   How great is the Lord for his City!
            Yea, he is a mountain which wards off the storm
            at the time of tempest.

20   How great is the Lord for his City!
            Yea, he is Sekhmet against the enemies who tread
            upon [his] border.

8. This new reading is owed to Goedicke; for "rulers," perhaps
read "fathers."

9. The geographical term Shesem is used of the Sinai peninsula,
a source for copper and turquoise. Through a later misreading the
term comes to be represented in the Old Testament as Goshen, and
I have therefore used it thus here.

4.

III,1 He has come to us that he might take possession of the
      Southland,[10]
   And the Double Crown be set upon his head.

2   He has come, he has tied together the Two Lands,
   And has joined the Sedge to the Bee.[11]

3   He has come, he has ruled the Egyptians,[12]
   And he has placed the desert under his control.

4   He has come, he has protected the Two Lands,
   And he has pacified the two banks of the river.

5   He has come, he has nourished the Egyptians,
   And he has dispelled its poverty.

6   He has come, he has nourished the people,
   And he has given breath to the throat of the popu-
       lace.

7   He has come, he has trampled upon the foreign lands,
   And he has beaten off the cave dwellers who know
       not the fear of him.

8   He has come, he has [fought upon] his border,
   And he has rescued one robbed [of his possessions].

9   He has come, his arms have [received] the honor
   Which his valor has brought us.

10   He has come, [he has seen to it that we have raised] our
       children,
   And we have buried our elders. . . .

10. This verse suggested to Erman that the songs were recited upon
the triumphal entry of the king to a city south of Memphis.
11. The sedge is the heraldic plant of the south, the bee emblematic
of the north—hence, "to join Upper to Lower Egypt."
12. The people of Egypt, a term based on Kemet, used only here.

5.

1 . . . .
2 May you love Khakaure,[13] who lives forever and ever . . .
3 He gives you nourishment, and rescues . . .
4 Our shepherd who knows how to give breath . . .
5 May you repay him with life and dominion forever . . .

6.

1 The praise of Khakaure, living forever and [ever] . . .
2 I raise sail on . . . . . .
3 Overlaid with gold to . . . . . .
4 . . . the two banks of the river
5 They have [lost] the way . . .

13. Or "may Khakaure love you," in which case the song is not addressed to the king. Indeed, the last two songs are probably not part of the cycle represented by the first four.

The Victorious King

King Tuthmosis III of Dynasty 18 reigned from 1490 to 1436 B.C. He was the greatest soldier that ever ruled in Egypt, carrying his arms in the north across the Euphrates at Carchemish and ruling the valley of the Upper Nile well into the Sudan. After his wars were over, a stela was set up in the temple of Amun-Re at Karnak to celebrate his victories. The inscription represents the god as welcoming the king into his presence as his son, and after a dozen lines of introduction recounting what he had done for the king and what the latter has achieved, the god breaks into a poem of ten verses, finally giving his beloved son his blessing. The poetic portion of the inscription represents the god as granting to the king victory over all nations, and even in translation it is possible to catch an echo of the tramp of armies. A convenient edition of the hieroglyphic text is in A. de Buck, Egyptian Readingbook *(Leiden: Nederlandsch Archaeologisch-Philologisch Instituut voor het Nabije Oosten, 1948), pp. 53 ff.*

R. O. F.

13　I have come that I may cause you to trample on the great
　　　　　ones of Djahi,[1]
　　That I may spread them out under your feet throughout
　　　　　their lands;
　　That I may cause them to see Your Majesty as lord of sun-
　　　　　rays
　　When you shine in their faces in the likeness of me.

14　I have come that I may cause you to trample on the
　　　　　dwellers in Asia

　　1. Palestine and part of Phoenicia.

And to smite the heads of the Amu of Retjnu; [2]

That I may cause them to see Your Majesty equipped in
    your panoply

When you take weapons of warfare in the chariot.

15   I have come that I may cause you to trample on the
        eastern land

And to tread down those who are in the regions of To-
    nuter; [3]

That I may cause them to see Your Majesty as a lightning-
    flash,

Strewing its levin-flame and giving its flood of water.

16   I have come that I may cause you to trample on the
        western land,

Crete and Cyprus being possessed with the awe of you;

That I may cause them to see Your Majesty as a young
    bull,

Firm of heart and sharp of horn, whom none can tackle.

17   I have come that I may cause you to trample on the
        ⌈Islanders⌉,[4]

The lands of Mitanni [5] trembling through fear of you;

That I may cause them to see Your Majesty as a crocodile,

Lord of fear in the waters, who cannot be approached.

18   I have come that I may cause you to trample on the
        Islanders

2. The people of northern Phoenicia and Syria.

3. A name usually given to the land of Punt, possibly in Somali-
land, but here apparently applied to a region in or adjoining Syria;
perhaps Transjordan is meant.

4. Translation not quite certain; at any rate, a people distinct from
the islanders mentioned in the next verse.

5. A people whose western border was on the Euphrates.

In the midst of the sea, who are possessed with your war
shout;
That I may cause them to see Your Majesty as the Protector
Who appears on the back of his wild bull.[6]

19 I have come that I may cause you to trample on Libya
And the isles of Utjena[7] through the power of your
might;
That I may cause them to see Your Majesty as a fierce
lion
When you make them into corpses throughout their
valleys.

20 I have come that I may cause you to trample on the utter-
most parts of the earth,
What the Ocean encircles being held in your grasp;
That I may cause them to see Your Majesty as lord of the
falcon-wings
Who takes what he sees at will.

21 I have come that I may cause you to trample on those
who are in the Southland
And to bind the Sand-dwellers as captives;
That I may cause them to see Your Majesty as a jackal of
Upper Egypt,
The lord of speed, the runner who courses through the
Two Lands.

6. The "Protector" is Horus, the protector of his father Osiris,
who is imagined as standing on the back of, i.e. subduing, a wild
bull typifying Seth, the enemy of Osiris. Compare *Pyr.* §1977[b],
where the slayer of Osiris is likened to a wild bull.
7. An unknown locality.

I have come that I may cause you to trample on the
      Nubians,
As far as Shat [8] being in your grasp;
That I may cause them to see Your Majesty as your Two
      Brothers,[9]
For I have joined together their hands for you in victory.

8. Unidentified locality in Nubia.
9. I.e. Horus and Seth, the two national gods embodied in the
royal person. This is a totally different aspect of Seth from that
mentioned in n. 6, above.

The Hymn to the Aten

In the reign of Amun-hotpe IV-Akhenaten of Dynasty 18 the royal family espoused the worship of the sun disk, the Aten, and neglected the older state and local gods, particularly Amun-Re. The king changed his name from Amun-hotpe (Amun is pleased) to Akhenaten (the effective spirit of the Aten), and he constructed a new residence city at Amarna called Akhet-Aten, the Horizon of the Aten, marked out by royal boundary stelae and filled with temples, palaces, villas for the nobles, workshops for the artisans, and housing for the laborers. Throughout Egypt the names of the old gods were systematicaly hacked out whenever they appeared in public inscriptions on temple walls and elsewhere. The movement was viewed as a reformation, a return to the royal sun-cult of the pyramid builders. It was later regarded as a heresy and did not survive the king's reign. Akhenaten emphasized the international supremacy of the sun disk and his relation to it as a son. In effect, he interposed himself between the Aten and the people, with his worship directed to the Aten and the people's attention focused upon him as the son and interpreter of the Aten. Whether the system can be considered monotheism is debatable. The broad outlook represented in these texts is a development of earlier Egyptian thought with new elements. Noteworthy is the almost anthropological view of the races of mankind differentiated in color and language. There are close parallels in wording, thought, and sequence of ideas to the verses of Psalm 104. The text is presented in hieroglyphic in N. de G. Davies, The Rock Tombs of el Amarna *(London: Archaeological Survey of Egypt, 1908), Pt. 6, pl. 27; this version derives from the tomb of Eye. For a lucid and interpretive account of the king's reign and times, consult Cyril Aldred,* Akhenaten, Pharaoh of Egypt, a New Study *(London: Thames and Hudson, 1968).*

W. K. S.

1 Worship (Re-Horakhty who Rejoices in the Horizon)|
(In his Name as the Shu who is in the Aten)| living for-
ever and ever, the Living Aten, the Great One who is in
Jubilee, Master of all that the Aten encircles, Master of
Heaven, Master of the Earth, Master of the Per-Aten in
Akhet-Aten; [1] and the King of Upper and Lower Egypt,
the one Living on Maat, Master of Regalia (Akhenaten)|,
the long lived; and the Foremost Wife of the King, whom
he loves, the Mistress of Two Lands (Nefer-nefru-Aten
Nefertiti)|, living, well, and young forever and ever.

2 He says:

You rise in perfection on the horizon of the sky,
living Aten, who started life.
Whenever you are risen upon the eastern horizon
you fill every land with your perfection.
You are appealing, great, sparkling, high over every land;
your rays hold together the lands as far as everything you
            have made.

3 Since you are Re, you reach as far as they do,
and you curb them for your beloved son.
Although you are far away, your rays are upon the land;
you are in their faces, yet your departure is not observed.

Whenever you set on the western horizon,
the land is in darkness in the manner of death.
They sleep in a bedroom with heads under the covers,
and one eye does not see another.

1. Just as the king's name is inscribed in a pair of cartouches, so
too the Aten is regarded as a king with cartouches for his names
and is considered to celebrate the royal jubilee festivals. Re-
Horakhty is the sun god Re united with Horus of the Horizon.
Shu is the ancient god of air and light. The Per-Aten is the house
(temple) of Aten in Akhet-Aten.

If all their possessions which are under their heads were
     stolen,
they would not know it.

4   Every lion who comes out of his cave and all the serpents
     bite,
for darkness is a blanket.
The land is silent now, because he who made them
is at rest on his horizon.

But when day breaks you are risen upon the horizon,
and you shine as the Aten in the daytime.
When you dispel darkness and you give forth your rays
the two lands are in festival,
alert and standing on their feet,
now that you have raised them up.

5   Their bodies are clean, / and their clothes have been put
     on;
their arms are ⟨lifted⟩ in praise at your rising.

The entire land performs its work:
all the cattle are content with their fodder,
trees and plants grow,
birds fly up to their nests,
their wings ⟨extended⟩ in praise for your Ka.
All the kine prance on their feet;
everything which flies up and alights,
6   they live when you have risen for them.
The barges sail upstream and downstream too,
for every way is open at your rising.
The fishes in the river leap before your face
when your rays are in the sea.

You who have placed seed in woman
and have made sperm into man,

who feeds the son in the womb of his mother,
who quiets him with something to stop his crying;
7   you are the nurse in the womb,
giving breath to nourish all that has been begotten.
When he comes down from the womb to breathe
on the day he is born,
you open up his mouth ⌜completely⌝, and supply his
        needs.
When the fledgling in the egg speaks in the shell,
you give him air inside it to sustain him.
When you grant him his allotted time to break out from the
        egg,
he comes out from the egg to cry out at his fulfillment,
and he goes upon his legs when he has come forth from it.

How plentiful it is, what you have made,
although they are hidden from view,
8   sole god, without another beside you;
you created the earth as you wished,
when you were by yourself, ⟨before⟩
mankind, all cattle and kine,
all beings on land, who fare upon their feet,
and all beings in the air, who fly with their wings.

The lands of Khor and Kush [2]
and the land of Egypt:
you have set every man in his place,
you have allotted their needs,
every one of them according to his diet,
and his lifetime is counted out.
Tongues are separate in speech,

2. Khor is Syro-Palestine in the northeast, and Kush is the Nubian
region in the Sudan to the south.

9   and their characters / as well;
     their skins are different,
     for you have differentiated the foreigners.
     In the underworld you have made a Nile
     that you may bring it forth as you wish
     to feed the populace,
     since you made them for yourself, their utter master,
     growing weary on their account, lord of every land.
     For them the Aten of the daytime arises,
     great in awesomeness.

     All distant lands,
     you have made them live,
     for you have set a Nile in the sky
     that it may descend for them
10   and make waves upon the mountains like the sea
     to irrigate the fields in their towns.
     How efficient are your designs,
     Lord of eternity:
     a Nile in the sky for the foreigners
     and all creatures that go upon their feet,
     a Nile coming back from the underworld for Egypt.[3]

     Your rays give suck to every field:
     when you rise they live,
     and they grow for you.
     You have made the seasons
     to bring into being all you have made:
11   the Winter to cool them,
     the Heat that you may be felt.

3. Egypt is essentially rainless and watered only by the Nile. Hence the rains of other lands are here regarded as a Nile in the sky.

You have made a far-off heaven
in which to rise
in order to observe everything you have made.
Yet you are alone,
rising in your manifestations as the Living Aten:
appearing, glistening, being afar, coming close;
you make millions of transformations of yourself.
Towns, harbors, fields, roadways, waterways:
every eye beholds you upon them,
for you are the Aten of the daytime on the face of the
earth.
12 When you go forth
every eye [is upon you].
You have created their sight
but not to see (only) the body . . .
which you have made.

You are my desire,
and there is no other who knows you
except for your son (Nefer-kheperu-Re Wa-en-Re),[4]
for you have apprised him of your designs and your
power.
The earth came forth into existence by your hand,
and you made it.
When you rise, they live;
when you set, they die.
You are a lifespan in yourself;
one lives by you.
13 Eyes are / upon your perfection until you set:
all work is put down when you rest in the west.

4. The king's praenomen. His exclusive relation to the Aten is
stressed.

When (you) rise, (everything) grows
for the King and (for) everyone who hastens on foot,
because you have founded the land
and you have raised them for your son
who has come forth from your body,
the King of Upper and Lower Egypt, the one Living on
        Maat,
Lord of the Two Lands (Nefer-kheperu-Re Wa-en-Re),
son of Re, the one Living on Maat, Master of Regalia,
(Akhenaten), the long lived,
and the Foremost Wife of the King, whom he loves,
the Mistress of the Two Lands,
(Nefer-nefru-Aten Nefertiti),
living and young, forever and ever.

The Love Songs and The Song of the Harper

The love songs of the New Kingdom were arranged in most cases in groups corresponding to cycles. Alfred Hermann has provided a particularly perceptive and sympathetic treatment of them in Altägyptische Liebesdichtung. *He lists fifty-five songs and four additional fragments from Gardiner and Černý,* Hieratic Ostraca I. *Our numbering follows Hermann's list, although the last few (nos. 48–55 and the additional fragments) have been omitted as too miscellaneous and fragmentary. For an excellent translation with notes, commentary, and related material, see Siegfried Schott,* Altägyptische Liebeslieder mit Märchen und Liebesgeschichten *(Zurich: Artemis-Verlag, 1950), or the French edition translated by Paule Kriéger under the title,* Les Chants d'amour de l'Egypte ancienne, *in the series* L'Orient ancien illustré *(Paris: A. Maisonneuve, 1956). There is also Pierre Gilbert,* La Poésie égyptienne *(Brussels: Fondation Egyptologique Reine Elisabeth, 1949). The reader unable to use sources in German and French is urged to read the delightful and informative discussion and translations in A. H. Gardiner,* The Library of A. Chester Beatty, Description of a Hieratic Papyrus . . . The Chester Beatty Papyri, No. 1 *(London: Oxford University Press, 1931). This last is a magnificently printed folio with the first edition of several sets of poems. A free modern rendering of some of the songs is provided in* Love Poems of Ancient Egypt, *translated by Ezra Pound and Noel Stock (Norfolk, Conn.: New Directions, 1962). There are perceptive and fine translations of a few selections in T. Säve-Söderbergh,* Pharaohs and Mortals *(London: Robert Hale, 1963). For bibliographical notes, consult the works of Hermann and Schott cited above. Some of the manuscripts are particularly difficult. The following translations are thus appreciably less reliable than many of the other translations in this volume, and in cases I have intentionally adopted rather personal, idiosyncratic renderings. Although in each case I have used the hieroglyphic* transcriptions of the poems in working with the songs, I am particularly indebted to and dependent upon the translations by Möller, Schott, Gardiner, and others. The language is Late Egyptian, and the translations are intended to convey a colloquial flavor. The Egyptian word for sister is used to designate the lady, and the word for brother, her lover. Frequently I have rendered the former as lady, lady love, or girl, and the latter as love or boy.

In the manuscript of Papyrus Harris 500 The Song of the Harper occurs between the second and third groups of love poems (between nos. 16 and 17). Although the song is represented in a different version in tombs, it is this version, thus placed among the love poems, which we translate here. It has been studied by M. Lichtheim in JNES 4 (1945): 178–212, and E. F. Wente in JNES 21 (1962): 118–28; see also H. Brunner in JNES 25 (1966): 130–31. If it seems incongruous to include it among the love poems, the incongruity has an ancient precedent.

The footnotes to this section are kept to a minimum. There are doubtful or alternative readings for many lines, and a thorough set of notes would easily exceed by several times in bulk the length of the text itself.

W. K. S.

[SONGS OF THE CITY OF MEMPHIS]

The Songs of Papyrus Harris 500 [1]

I.

. . . .

If I am [not] with you, where will you set your heart?
If you do [not] embrace [me], [where will you go?]

1. There are three groups. The first has several references to the Memphite region (nos. 1–8). The first song(s) and the title are missing. For the second (nos. 9–16) and third (nos. 7–19) groups the title is preserved. Between the second and third groups is The Song of the Harper with its title (see introduction to this section).

If good fortune comes your way, [you still cannot find] happi-
      ness.
But if you try to touch my thighs and breasts,
[Then you'll be satisfied.]

Because you remember you are hungry
      would you then leave?
Are you a man
      thinking only of his stomach?
Would you [walk off from me
      concerned with] your stylish clothes
and leave me the sheet?

Because of hunger
      would you then leave me?
      [or because you are thirsty?]
Take then my breast:
      for you its gift overflows.
Better indeed is one day in your arms . . .
      than a hundred thousand [anywhere] on earth.

2.

My love for you is mixed throughout my body
like [salt] dipped in water,
like a medicine to which gum is added,
like milk shot through [water] . . .

So hurry to see your lady,
like a stallion on the track,
or like a falcon [swooping down] to its papyrus marsh.

Heaven sends down the love of her
as a flame falls in the ⌜hay⌝ . . .

. . . .

3.

Distracting is the ⌜foliage⌝ of my ⌜pasture⌝:
[the mouth] of my girl is a lotus bud,
her breasts are mandrake apples,
her arms are [vines],
[her eyes] are fixed like berries,
her brow a snare of willow,
and I the wild goose!
My [beak] snips [her hair] for bait,
as worms for bait in the trap.

4.

My heart is not yet happy with your love,
my wolf cub, so be lascivious unto drunkenness.

Yet I will not leave it unless sticks beat me off
to dally in the Delta marshes
or ⟨driven⟩ to the land of Khor with cudgels and maces
to the land of Kush [2] with palm switches
to the highground with staves
to the lowland with rushes.

So I'll not heed their arguments
to leave off needing you.

5.

I sail downstream in the ferry by ⌜the pull of the current⌝,
my bundle of reeds in my arms.
I'll be at Ankh-towy,[3]

2. Khor is the region of Syria and Palestine; Kush is Nubia, the
southern area south of the First Cataract at Aswan.
3. "Life of the Two Lands," a designation for Memphis or a part
of it.

and say to Ptah,[4] the lord of truth,
give me my girl tonight.

The sea is wine,
Ptah its reeds,
Sekhmet its ⌈kelp⌉,
the Dew Goddess its buds,
Nefertum its lotus flower.[5]

[The Golden Goddess] rejoices
and the land grows bright at her beauty.
For Memphis is a flask of mandrake wine
placed before the good-looking god.[6]

6.

Now I'll lie down inside
and act as if I'm sick.
My neighbors will come in to visit,
and with them my girl.
She'll put the doctors out,
for she's the one to know my hurt.[7]

7.

Back at the farmstead of my girl:
the doorway in the center of the house,
her door left ajar,

4. The creator and artificer god of Memphis.
5. Sekhmet, a lion-headed goddess, and Nefertum, the god on the lotus, are also Memphite deities.
6. The Golden Goddess is Hathor; in many ways she is the patron goddess of women. The phrase, "good-looking god," lit. "beautiful of countenance," applies to Ptah.
7. For the theme, see no. 37.

her door bolt sprung;
my girl is furious!

If I were made the doorkeeper
I could make her mad at me;
then at least I'd hear her voice when she is angry,
and I'd play the child afraid of her.

8.

I'm sailing downstream on the Canal of the Prince
and entering into the Canal of Pre,[8]
for I must go to prepare the booths
on the hill overlooking the locks.

As I raise sail and hasten, without a stop,
my heart remembers Pre;
I'll watch my lover's arrival
as he is headed for the ⌜park⌝.

I'll wait with you at the entrance of the locks
that you may take my heart to Heliopolis of Re.
I'll retire with you to the trees
which belong to the ⌜park⌝.

I'll cut from the trees of the ⌜park⌝
a handful for my fan,
and I'll watch how it is fashioned,
my face set toward the shed.

My arms are full of Persea branches,
my tresses laden with salves.
Whenever I am there, I am the Mistress of the Two Lands,[9]
I am [the happiest of all].

8. Named after the sun-god Pre or Re.
9. A title of the queen.

THE BEGINNING OF THE SONGS OF EXCELLENT ENJOYMENT,
FOR YOUR SISTER, BELOVED IN YOUR HEART,
WHEN SHE RETURNS FROM THE FIELDS

9.[10]

My brother, my loved one,
my heart chases after your love
and all that has been fashioned for you.
So I'll relate to you a vision of what happens.

When I return from birdcatching,
my bird traps are in my hand
and in my other hand a bird cage
and my ⌐boomerang⌐.

All the birds of Punt [11]
alight in the land of Egypt, anointed with myrrh;
the first to come
takes my lure.

His perfume comes from Punt,
and his talons are filled with gums.
Since my heart is inclined toward you,
let us let him go and have time to be alone together.

I let you hear my voice lamenting
for my myrrh-anointed beauty,
and you were with me there
when I prepared the trap again.

For one who is loved
how pleasant to go to the fields.

10. Nos. 9–16 are spoken by the lady.
11. Probably a spice land on the African coast of the Red Sea,
although there are other suggestions for its location.

10.

The voice of the wild goose,
caught by the bait, cries out.
Love of you holds me back,
and I can't loosen it at all.

I shall set aside my nets.
But what can I tell my mother
to whom I return every day
when I am laden with catch?

I did not set my traps today;
love of you has thus entrapped me.

11.

The wild goose soars and alights
and dives into the fowl-yard pool;
many birds are circling now,
and I must give orders to myself.

But I turn around toward love of you
when I am by myself again;
my heart is balanced with your heart:
I cannot be far from all this beauty.

12.

Now must I depart from the brother,

. . . .

and [as I long] for your love,
my heart stands still inside me.

If I see sugar cakes,
[they are to me like] salt;

sweet pomegranate wine in my mouth
is bitter as the gall of birds.

But your embraces
alone give life to my heart;
may Amun give me what I have found
for all eternity.

13.

Most beautiful youth who ever happened,
I want to take your house as housekeeper;
we are arm in arm,
and love of you goes round and round.

I say to my heart within me in prayer:
if far away from me is my lover tonight,
then I am like someone already in the grave.
Are you not indeed well-being and life?

Joy has come to me through your well-being,
my heart seeks you out.

14.

The voice of the turtledove speaks out. It says:
day breaks, which way are you going?
Lay off, little bird,
must you so scold me?

I found my lover on his bed,
and my heart was sweet to excess.

We said:

I shall never be far away [from] you
while my hand is in your hand,

and I shall stroll with you
in every favorite place.

He set me as first of the girls
and he does not break my heart.

15.

When toward the outer door I set my mind,
lo, the brother comes to me,
my eyes upon the road, my ears listening,
that I may ambush Pa-mehy.[12]

As my sole concern I have set the love of my brother;
for him my heart will not keep silent.

It sent me a messenger,
hurrying on foot,
coming and going,
to tell me he has wronged me.

[In] other words: you have found another,
and she is dazzling in your sight.
But shall the intrigues of another woman
serve to pack me off?

16.

My heart remembers well your love,
one half of my temple was combed,
I came rushing to see you,
and I forgot my hair.

12. Mehy or Pa-Mehy is mentioned in several of the songs and
fragments. Was he a real prince, a real lover who inspired the songs,
or a fictional set character? Perhaps the name conceals the identity
of a real prince or noble.

[But if you let me go],
my tresses will be dressed,
I'll be ready straightaway.

[THE SONG OF THE HARPER] [13]

THE SONG WHICH IS IN THE CHAPEL OF KING INYOTEF,
THE VINDICATED, AND IS IN FRONT OF THE SINGER
AT THE HARP.

Flourishing is he, this prince,
For destiny is good, and destruction is complete.
Bodies pass on while others endure,
Since the time of those who came before,
The Gods and those who came into being before me,
And who rest in their pyramid tombs.

The nobles and spirits too,
Being entombed in their pyramids,
They built chapels, but their cult stations are no more.
What became of them?

Now I have heard the sayings
Of Iyemhotep and Hardedef,
Which are quoted
In the proverbs so much.

What are their cult places?
Their walls are dismantled,

13. The Song of the Harper, as indicated in the introduction, exists
in several versions. Iyemhotep, the sage and architect of the Step
Pyramid in the time of Djoser in Dynasty 3, and Hardedef, the
son of Cheops who appears in the story of King Cheops and the
Magicians, both wrote books of sayings. Of the latter a portion is
preserved. The singer reflects that the tomb chapels of these famous
men no longer exist. Cones of fat with myrrh were placed on the
heads of men and women at banquets, and they then melted gradually to provide an aroma and face lotion.

And their cult places exist no more,
As if they had never been.

There is no one who can return from there,
To describe their nature, to describe their dissolution,
That he may still our desires,
Until we reach the place where they have gone.

So may your desire be fulfilled:
Allow the heart to forget
The performance of services for you.
Follow your desire while you live.

Place myrrh upon your head,
Clothe yourself in fine linen,
Anointed with real wonders
Of the god's own stores.

Increase your beauty,
And let not your mind tire.
Follow your desire and what is good:
Acquire your possessions on earth.

Do not control your passion
Until that day of mourning comes for you.
The Weary-Hearted [14] does not hear their sobbing,
[Their] sobbing cannot save the heart of a man from the tomb.

⌈Chorus⌉: Make holiday,
But tire yourself not with it.
Remember: it is not given to man to take his goods with him.
No one goes away and then comes back.

14. An aspect of Osiris in the underworld.

BEGINNING OF THE SONGS OF ENTERTAINMENT [15]

17.

Mekhmekh-flowers,
my heart inclines toward you,
I shall do for you what it seeks,
when I am in your arms.

I wish to paint my eyes,
so if I see you, my eyes will glisten.
When I approach you and see your love,
you are the richest in my heart.

How pleasant is this hour,
may it extend for me to eternity;
since I have lain with you
you have lifted high my heart.

In mourning or in rejoicing
be not far from me.

18.

A dense growth is in it,
in the midst of which we become ennobled.

I am your best girl:
I belong to you like an acre of land
which I have planted
with flowers and every sweet-smelling grass.

15. Nos. 17–19, a group of three recited by the lady, follow The
Song of the Harper. Each begins with a play of like sounding
words: *mekhmekh*-flowers and incline, dense growth and ennoble,
and *tjet*-flowers and pluck. The manuscript breaks off in the middle
of no. 19, although parts of words can be made out.

Pleasant is the channel through it
which your hand dug out
for refreshing ourselves with the breeze,
a happy place for walking
with your hand in my hand.

My body is excited, my heart joyful,
at our traveling together.

Hearing your voice is pomegranate wine,
for I live to hear it,
and every glance which rests on me
means more to me than eating and drinking.

19.

Tjet-flowers are in it,
and I'll pluck wreathes for you.

If you return intoxicated
and lie upon your bed,
I'll rub your feet,
and the children in your [gardens]
[shall hide behind the gate] . . .

The Cairo Love Songs [16]

20.

My god, my [lover . . .],
it is pleasant to go to the [canal]

. . . .

and to bathe in your presence.

16. The first song is recited by the lady and the following seven by
her lover.

I shall let [you see . . .] my perfection
in a garment of royal linen, wet [and clinging].

Then I'll go into the water at your bidding,
and I'll come out to you with a red fish
who will be happy in my fingers . . .
So come and look me over.

21.

The love of my sister lies on yonder side,
and the river is between [us];
a crocodile waits on the sandbank.

Yet I'll go down to the water,
I'll head into the waves;
my heart is brave on the water,
and the waves like land to my legs.

22.

It is love of her which strengthens me,
as if for me she made a water spell.

I'll watch the lady love return.
My heart rejoices and my arms spread out to clasp her,
my heart is giddy in its seat,
as if this were [not] fated forever.

Do not keep away, but come to me, my lady.

23.

I embrace her,
and her arms open wide,
I am like a man in Punt,
like someone overwhelmed with drugs.

I kiss her,
her lips open,
and I am drunk
without a beer.

24.

What is the last thing for preparing her bed?
I tell you, boy,
set fine linen between her limbs,
draw not the covers with royal sheets,
but care [for her] with simple white stuffs,
sprinkled with fine scented oils.

25.

I wish I were her Negro maid
who follows at her feet;
then the skin of all her limbs
would be [revealed] to me.

26.

I wish I were her washerman,
if only for a single month,
then I would be [entranced],
washing out the Moringa oils
in her diaphanous garments . . .

27.

I wish I were the seal ring,
the guardian of her [fingers],
then [. . .]

Turin Love Songs: Songs of the Orchard [17]

28.

[The pomegranate] says:
Like her teeth my seeds,
Like her breasts my fruit,
[foremost am I] of the orchard
since in every season I'm around.

The sister and brother make [holiday],
[swaying beneath] my [branches];
high on grape wine and pomegranate wine are they,
and rubbed with Moringa and pine oils. . . .

All, all pass away,
except for me, from the fields.
Twelve months I spend
[within the park] waiting.

Where drops a flower,
another bud within me springs.
[Of the orchard] foremost am I, . . .
but only as a second you regard me.

If they try to do it again,
I'll not keep silence for them;
[I'll no longer hide] her,
and they will see the lie.

Then will the loved one be taught
so that she will not [spread]
her ⌜pollen⌝ of white and blue lotus,
[flowers] and buds . . . ointments . . .

17. In each of the three songs the speaker is a different kind of
garden tree.

[For now he is sated]
with ale of every kind.
You can spend today gloriously,
a hideaway of reeds in a guarded place. . . .

See, she is come out right,
come, let us cajole her;
let her pass the day long
[in the shade of the tree] which hides him.

29.

The sycamore fig gives out his say,
his leaves spread out to speak.
[How pleasant] to be cultivated!
For my mistress I'll come forth.

She is a noble like myself,
and if there are no maidservants
I will be the slave
[brought from the land of] Syria
as booty for my lady love.

She had them place me in her garden,
but she did not give me [drink]
[on the] day of festivity,
nor did she fill my trunk with water
from the waterskins.

They find me laughable indeed
because of my not drinking.
As my soul lives, O lady love,
you will be brought to court.

30.

The little sycamore,
which she planted with her hand,
sends forth its words to speak.

The flowers [of its stalks]
[are like] an inundation of honey;
beautiful it is, and its branches shine
more verdant [than the grass].

It is laden with the ripeness of notched figs,
redder than carnelian,
like turquoise its leaves,
like glass its bark.

Its wood is like the color of green feldspar,
its sap like the *besbes* opiate;
it brings near whoever is not under it,
for its shade cools the breeze.

It sends a message by the hand of a girl,
the gardener's daughter;
it makes her hurry to the lady love:
come, spend a minute among the maidens.

The country celebrates its day.
Below me is an arbor and a hideaway;
my gardeners are joyful
like children at the sight of you.

Send your servants ahead of you
supplied with their cooking gear;
I am heady when hastening to you
without having a drink.

These servants of yours
come with their stuffs,
bringing beer of every sort,
all kinds of kneaded dough for beer,
heady wine of yesterday and today,
all kinds of fruit for enjoyment.

Come spend the day happily,
tomorrow and the day after tomorrow, for three days,
seated in my shade,

Her friend is on her right.
She gets him drunk
while doing what he says;
and the wine cellar is disordered in drunkenness,
as she stays with her lover.

She has ample room beneath me,
the lady love as she paces;
I am discreet
and will not say that I have seen their discourse.

The Chester Beatty Love Songs [18]

THE BEGINNING OF THE SONGS OF EXTREME HAPPINESS

31.

[First Stanza]

One, the lady love without a duplicate,
more perfect than the world,

18. The Chester Beatty Cycle of Seven Songs (nos. 31–37) has its
own title. With the exception of the first, each song has a chapter
heading, "Second Stanza," "Third Stanza," etc. The first and last
word in each stanza is the respective numeral or a play of words

see, she is like the star rising
at the start of an auspicious year.

She whose excellence shines, whose body glistens,
glorious her eyes when she stares,
sweet her lips when she converses,
she says not a word too much.

High her neck and glistening her nipples,
of true lapis her hair,
her arms finer than gold,
her fingers like lotus flowers unfolding.

Her buttocks droop when her waist is girt,
her legs reveal her perfection;
her steps are pleasing when she walks the earth,
she takes my heart in her embrace.

She turns the head of every man,
all captivated at the sight of her;
everyone who embraces her rejoices,
for he has become the most successful of lovers.

When she comes forth, anyone can see
that there is none like that One.

32.

Second Stanza

Lover excites my desire with his voice,
he gets a sickness to seize me,

---

on the number. For example, in the fifth stanza the words "to
praise" sound like the word for "five." The speaker alternates
regularly between the lover and his lady, with the odd-numbered
stanzas recited by the lover and the even-numbered stanzas by his
lady. This cycle was translated from earlier translations by Ezra
Pound with considerable success.

for though he is a neighbor to my mother's house,
I know not how to go to him.
Is my mother good to restrict me so?
Leave off seeing her!

My heart is troubled whenever he is thought of:
his love possesses me.
See, he is mindless,
yet I am like him.

He does not know my lust to embrace him,
or that he could write my mother.
Lover, I am given over to you
by the Golden Goddess of womankind.

Come to me that I can see your perfection;
my father and my mother will be glad.
All men with one accord rejoice for you,
rejoice they for you, Lover.

33.

Third Stanza

My heart proposed to see her beauty,
while I was sitting in her house.

I found Mehy in his chariot on the road
with his burly gang.

I do not know how to take myself from his presence:
Shall I pass by him at a walk?

See, the river is a roadway,
for I know not a place for my feet.

How foolish you are, my heart,
why would you stroll by Mehy?

If I pass beside him
I'll have to tell him my troubles.

See, I am yours, I'll say to him,
and he'll shout out my name.

But he'd pass me on to the harem
of the first man of his troop.

34.

Fourth Stanza

Forth goes my heart in haste
since first I brought my love for you to mind.

It does not let me walk like other humans,
but springs up from its place;
it does not let me don a robe
nor cover myself with a fan.

My eyes I cannot paint,
nor oil myself at all.
Don't wait, go home,
so says my heart, each time he is remembered.

My heart, don't play so dumb!
Why must you act the fool?
Sit tight, the lover comes to you,
my eye is ⌐blinded so¬.

Don't let the women talk against me:
there's a girl dragged down by love.
Be firm each time you think on him,
my heart, and leap not Forth.

35.

Fifth Stanza

I praise the Golden Goddess,
I exalt Her Majesty.
I raise high the Lady of Heaven,
I make praise for Hathor,
and chants for my Mistress.

I tell Her all, that She may hear my plaints;
so may my Lady give her to me;
she has come back to see me,
something heavy is happening to me.

I shout for joy, I'm happy, I'm great,
ever since they said: see, she's here.

See, she came back, and the youngsters bent down
through the charisma of her love.

So I'll make a vow to my Goddess,
and She'll give me the lady love as a present in return.

Three days have passed since I petitioned in Her Name:
may she come forth on the Fifth.

36.

Sixth Stanza

I passed by the precinct of his house,
I found his door ajar,
the lover standing by his mother,
with him his brothers and sisters.

Love of him captures the heart
of all who walk the road.

Handsome guy, no one like him,
a lover of perfect taste.

He stares me out when I walk by,
and all alone I cry for joy;
how happy in my delight
with the lover in my sight.

If only mother knew my wish,
she would have gone inside by now.
O, Golden Goddess, place him in her heart too,
then I'll rush off to the lover.

I'll kiss him in front of his crowd,
I'll not be ashamed because of the women.
But I'll be happy at their finding out
that you know me this well.

I'll make festivals for my Goddess,
my heart trembles to come forth,
and to let me look over the lover tonight.
How happy, how happy is this passing by.

37·

Seventh Stanza

Seven days have passed, and I've not seen my lady love;
a sickness has shot through me.
I have become sluggish,
I have forgotten my own body.

If the best surgeons come to me,
my heart will not be comforted with their remedies.
And the prescription sellers, there's no help through them;
my sickness will not be cut out.

Telling me "she's come" is what will bring me back to life.
It's only her name which will raise me up.
It's the coming and going of her letters
which will bring my heart to life.

To me the lady love is more remedial than any potion;
she's better than the whole Compendium.
My only salvation is her coming inside.
Seeing her, then I'm well.

When she opens her eyes my body is young,
when she speaks I'll grow strong,
when I embrace her she drives off evil from me.
But by now the days of her absence amount to Seven.

THE CHESTER BEATTY CYCLE OF THREE SONGS [19]

38.

Please come quick to the lady love
like a king's agent
whose master is impatient
for his letters
and desires to hear them

all the stables are made ready for him
horses are harnessed at the stopping places
chariots are fitted out at their stations
there's no relaxation on the road for him

and when he reaches the house of the lady
his heart is overwhelmed with joy.

19. In this cycle the lady compares her desired lover to a king's
messenger, the king's champion steed, and a hunted gazelle.

39.

Please come quick ‹to the lady love›
like the king's steed,
the pick of a thousand from all the herds,
the foremost of the stables.

It is set apart from the others in its feed
and its master knows its gaits.
As soon as it hears the crack of a whip
it knows no holding back.

There's not a captain in the chariotry
who can pull ahead of it,
but well the lady love knows
he cannot go far from her.

40.

Please come quick to the lady love
like a gazelle
running in the desert
its feet are wounded
its limbs are exhausted
fear penetrates its body

the hunters are after it
the hounds are with them
they cannot see
because of the dust

its sees its rest place like a ⌜mirage⌝
it takes a canal as its road.

Before you have kissed your hand four times,
you shall have reached her hideaway
as you chase the lady love.

For it is the Golden Goddess
who has set her aside for you, friend.

THE NAKHT-SOBEK CYCLE OF PAPYRUS CHESTER BEATTY I [20]

Beginning of the pleasant sayings discovered while carrying a
scroll written by Nakht-Sobek, the scribe of the cemetery.

41.

If you bring them to the house of the lady love
and ⌜blow⌝ ⟨them⟩ into her ⌜hideaway⌝,
it will seem like a ⌜slaughterhouse⌝,
for the mistress of the house will kill her.

Supply her with song and dance,
wine and ale are her desire,
confuse her ⌜cunning⌝,
and gain her this night.

She'll tell you:
put me in your arms;
when day breaks
⌜let's start again⌝.

42.

If you bring them to the window of the lady love,
alone without another,
you can accomplish your desire with her ⌜lattice⌝.

⌜The shutters will clatter⌝,
and the heavens will pour down with a storm
which they cannot hold up.

20. Nos. 41–47. In nos. 41 and 42 the phrase, "if you bring them,"
probably refers to the poems written by the lover to his lady. For
a free version of the first six of these poems, see John L. Foster, in
The Beloit Poetry Journal 21, no. 2 (winter 1970–71): 6–15.

They will bring you their aroma,
the scent of inundation which intoxicates
those who are present.

So will the Golden One give her to you as a gift
to let you fulfill your time.

43.

How well the lady knows to cast the noose
yet still escape the cattle tax.

With her hair she throws lassoes at me,
with her eyes she catches me,
with her necklace entangles me
and with her seal ring brands me.

44.

Why need you hold converse with your heart?
To embrace her is all my desire.
As Amun lives, I come to you,
my loin cloth on my shoulder.

45.

I found the lover at the ford,
his feet set in the water;
he builds a table there for feasts
and sets it out with beer.

He brings a blush to my skin,
for he is tall and lean.

46.

See what the lady has done to me!
Faugh! Shall I keep silent for her sake?

She made me stand at the door of her house
while she went inside.
She didn't say to me, come in, young man,
but deaf to me remained tonight.

47.

I passed by her house in the dark,
I knocked and no one opened.
What a beautiful night for our doorkeeper!

Open, door bolts!
Door leaves you are my fate, you are my genie.
Our ox will be slaughtered for you inside.
Door leaves do not use your strength.

A long-horned bull will be slaughtered to the bolt,
a short-horned bull to the door pin,
a wild fowl to the threshold,
and its fat to the key.

But all the best parts of our ox
shall go to the carpenter's boy,
so he'll make us a door of grass
and a door bolt of reeds.

And any time when the lover comes
he'll find her house open,
he'll find beds made with linen sheets
and in them a lovely girl.

And the girl will say to me:
this place belongs to the captain's boy!

Selected Reading

The aim of this volume has been to provide the reader with a straightforward translation of the selections without extensive textual annotation or bibliography. References to general studies of Egyptian literature are included in the footnotes to the introduction. For specific studies of individual texts references to sources which include bibliographies are mentioned in the headnotes to each text. Recent articles and monographs on specific texts, however, are cited either in the headnotes to the text or in the footnotes, since they will not be available in the earlier bibliographies. For an introduction to ancient Egypt the following texts in English have been selected for their diversity of subject and range of approach.

Aldred, Cyril. *Akhenaten, Pharaoh of Egypt: A New Study*. London: Thames and Hudson, 1968.

de Cénival, Jean-Louis. *Living Architecture: Egyptian*. New York: Grosset and Dunlap, 1964.

Desroches-Noblecourt, Christiane. *Tutankhamen: Life and Death of a Pharaoh*. New York: New York Graphic Society, 1963.

Edwards, I. E. S., James, T. G. H., and Shore, A. F. *A General Introductory Guide to the Egyptian Collections in the British Museum*. London: British Museum, 1964.

Frankfort, H., Frankfort, H. A., Wilson, J. A., and Jacobson, T. *Before Philosophy*. Baltimore: Pelican Books, 1954.

Frankfort, Henri. *Kingship and the Gods*. Chicago: University of Chicago Press, 1948.

Gardiner, Sir Alan. *Egypt of the Pharaohs*. Oxford: Oxford University Press, 1961.

Glanville, S. R. K., ed. *The Legacy of Egypt*. Oxford: Oxford University Press, 1942.

Hallo, William W., and Simpson, William Kelly. *The Ancient Near East: A History*. New York: Harcourt Brace Jovanovich, 1971.

Kees, Hermann. *Ancient Egypt: A Cultural Topography*. Edited by T. G. H. James. Chicago: University of Chicago Press, 1961.

Smith, W. Stevenson. *The Art and Architecture of Ancient Egypt*. Baltimore: Penguin Books, 1958.

Wilson, John A. *The Culture of Ancient Egypt*. Chicago: University of Chicago Press, 1951.

1. *Papyrus Chester Beatty I before unrolling.*

2. *Prince Khuenre, eldest son of King Mycerinus, as a scribe. Giza, Dynasty 4.*

snnw.i ʿnḫw psš.i m rmṯ, irw n.i ḳmdt n sḏm.tw.f
bw ʿꜣ n [ʿḥꜣ] n mꜣn.tw.f, ist ʿḥꜣ tw ḥr mtwn, smḫ sf, nn
km n bw nfr n ḫm rḫ.f; r-sꜣ msyt pw, ḫꜣw ḫpr

sꜣḳ.tw r smdt rf tmt ḫpr, tmmt rdi ib m-sꜣ ḥr(y)t.s m tk[n]
im.sn [m] wʿw.k, m mḫ ib.k m sn, m rḫ ḫnms, m sḫpr n.k ʿḳ[w]

*O you living images of me, my heirs among men, make for me a funeral oration
which has not been heard (before), a great deed of [battle] which has not been
seen, for men fight in the arena and the past is forgotten; goodness cannot profit
one who does not know him whom he should know. It was after supper and night
had fallen . . . (Corresponding to Pap. Millingen I, 9–11)*

*Be on your guard against all who are subordinate to you when there occurs
something to whose terrors no thought has been given; do not approach them [in]
your solitude, trust no brother, know no friend, make no intimates. (Corresponding
to Pap. Millingen I, 3–5)*

3. Reverse of a writing board with part of The Teaching of King Ammenemes I, transcription into hieroglyphic, transliteration, and translation.

4. Detail of scribe from chapel of Nofer at Giza, Dynasty 4.

5. Scribe's palette with reeds, inkwell, ink, and notations.

6. *Relief from a tomb wall at Sakkara, with figures of famous men of the past. These include the sages Iyemhotep, Kaires, Khety, and Khakheperre-sonbe. Dynasty 19.*